iPhoto™ 2

FOR

DUMMIES®

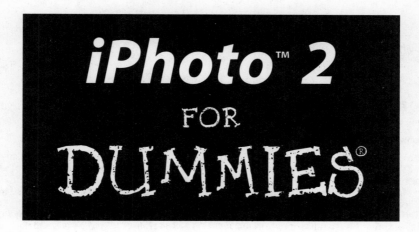

iPhoto™ 2

FOR DUMMIES®

by Curt Simmons

WILEY

Wiley Publishing, Inc.

iPhoto™ 2 For Dummies®

Published by
Wiley Publishing, Inc.
909 Third Avenue
New York, NY 10022

www.wiley.com

Copyright © 2003 by Wiley Publishing, Inc., Indianapolis, Indiana

Published by Wiley Publishing, Inc., Indianapolis, Indiana

Published simultaneously in Canada

For general information on our other products and services or to obtain technical support, please contact our Customer Care Department within the U.S. at 800-762-2974, outside the U.S. at 317-572-3993, or fax 317-572-4002.

Wiley also publishes its books in a variety of electronic formats. Some content that appears in print may not be available in electronic books.

Library of Congress Control Number: 2003101848

ISBN: 0-7645-3937-X

Manufactured in the United States of America

10 9 8 7 6 5 4 3 2 1

1B/RX/QU/QT/IN

About the Author

Curt Simmons is a freelance technology author and trainer. The author of more than 30 computing books on Apple and Microsoft operating systems, Internet technologies, networking, and other fun gadgets, Curt is also the instructor of several online photography courses. When he is not writing or taking photos, he spends his time with his wife and daughters. Visit Curt on the Internet at www.curtsimmons.com.

Dedication

For Hannah and Mattie, the sources of my best photos.

Author's Acknowledgments

Thanks to Bob Woerner and all the gang at Wiley for the opportunity to write this book — it was great fun. Thanks to Linda Morris, my project editor at Wiley, for the eagle eye and the great suggestions. Also thanks to Greg Willmore for a fine technical review and to Becky Huehls for catching all the details during copyedit. Finally, thanks to Margot Hutchison, my literary agent, for always working on my behalf, and to my family, for their constant support.

Publisher's Acknowledgments

We're proud of this book; please send us your comments through our online registration form located at `www.dummies.com/register`.

Some of the people who helped bring this book to market include the following:

Acquisitions, Editorial, and Media Development

Project Editor: Linda D. Morris

Acquisitions Editor: Bob Woerner

Copy Editor: Rebecca Huehls

Technical Editor: Greg Willmore

Editorial Manager: Kevin Kirschner

Media Development Manager: Laura VanWinkle

Media Development Supervisor: Richard Graves

Editorial Assistant: Amanda Foxworth

Cartoons: Rich Tennant, `www.the5thwave.com`

Production

Project Coordinator: Dale White

Layout and Graphics: Beth Brooks, Jennifer Click, Seth Conley, Carrie Foster, LeAndra Johnson, Stephanie D. Jumper, Michael Kruzil, Jeremey Unger

Proofreaders: John Greenough, Susan Moritz, Carl William Pierce, TECHBOOKS Production Services

Indexer: TECHBOOKS Production Services

Publishing and Editorial for Technology Dummies

Richard Swadley, Vice President and Executive Group Publisher

Andy Cummings, Vice President and Publisher

Mary C. Corder, Editorial Director

Publishing for Consumer Dummies

Diane Graves Steele, Vice President and Publisher

Joyce Pepple, Acquisitions Director

Composition Services

Gerry Fahey, Vice President of Production Services

Debbie Stailey, Director of Composition Services

Contents at a Glance

Table of Contents

Introduction

••

*O*nly a few short years ago, the digital camera was a novelty in the technology world — something cool to use with your computer, but not a real camera and certainly nothing that would ever be used by a real photographer. Have times changed quickly! Today, more digital cameras than film cameras are sold, and digital cameras are equipped with most all the features and photographic quality you would expect from a standard 35 mm camera. The digital camera is certainly here to stay, and rightly so. After all, with a digital camera, you have more control over the pictures you keep, the ability to edit and store them on your computer, and no film and developing expense.

As digital cameras have become more popular, software developers have rushed to keep up. Now that the average person like you and I uses a digital camera, we needed a great software program to manage our pictures, to create electronic albums and slide shows, and to help us share our pictures on the Internet with family and friends.

Enter iPhoto, the friendly digital photo-management tool that comes free with Mac OS X. Since its debut, iPhoto has become very popular among Mac users. And why not? iPhoto is fun and easy, and it works great!

About This Book

I wrote this book to help you make the most of iPhoto. Sure, iPhoto is rather easy and intuitive, but there are plenty of hidden functions and secrets that you probably won't take advantage of on your own, so that's why this book is here. In this book, you find practically everything about iPhoto that you need to know. You'll see how to import photos, organize and manage them, edit photos, and produce products: In fact, I'll even show you how to use your photos with iMovie and iDVD as well!

Maybe you are just starting out with iPhoto and need a friendly guide to help along the way, or maybe you have been using iPhoto, but really want to take your iPhoto skills to the next level. Perhaps you've used earlier versions of iPhoto, but are new to iPhoto 2. No matter your iPhoto needs, this book is just for you. It's written in an easy-to-read, nontechnical way, so that you can get the information you need quickly and easily without having to wade around in technical language and jargon.

Foolish Assumptions

As I wrote this book, I thought a lot about you. After all, this book is written for you, so as I wrote it, I made the following assumptions about you, the reader:

- ✔ You have Mac OS X. You know how to use the computer, but you may not be a Mac genius either. As I wrote the book, I assumed that you know the basics of how to use your Mac.

- ✔ You have probably toyed with iPhoto and decided you need some extra help, or you perhaps you use iPhoto a lot, but want a book to make sure you know how to use iPhoto to the fullest.

- ✔ You love your pictures. Whether you are using a digital camera or have scanned hundreds of old film pictures, you love the idea of working with pictures on your computer.

- ✔ You like to do things with your pictures. You like to create slide shows, or e-mail pictures to people. Maybe you even have your own Web site where you show off your photos.

- ✔ You are naturally curious and want the best from your digital photography experience using iPhoto.

- ✔ You want to spend your time working with your photos, not fumbling with your computer and software. You want to this book to make things quick and easy for you.

- ✔ You are an intelligent, attractive person with exceptionally high standards in all facets of your life. After all, you bought this book!

How to Use This Book

This book is designed to give you information in a fast and easy manner. You don't need to have a bachelor's degree in digital photography or computers to use this book. In fact, you don't need to know much of anything at all. As I wrote this book, I realized that you didn't want to wade through hundreds of pages of background information or dwell on lofty technology ideas that don't impact your life. I do know that you want to make the best use of iPhoto and you want this book to help you reach that goal.

Like all *For Dummies* books, this book is a reference. That means it is designed to give you information quickly. It's not a novel — you don't have to read it in any particular order, and I wrote it in such a way that it will make sense wherever you start reading. If you are just getting started with iPhoto, you may decide to start with Chapter 1 and read to the end. That's fine. You may thumb to a particular chapter and start reading there. That's fine, too. In fact, you can jump around all over this book and read it in just about anyway you want.

How This Book Is Organized

To make the information in this book as accessible as possible, I've organized the book into six parts. Each part explores some specifics of using iPhoto or related applications.

Here's a brief overview of what you'll find in each part.

Part 1: Getting Started with iPhoto

So, you're new to iPhoto. Maybe you have opened iPhoto and taken a look, or maybe you are still figuring out how to use your digital camera and haven't even tried to use iPhoto yet. That's no problem. In Chapter 1, you get an overview of iPhoto and the world of digital photography. You can explore some common themes and ideas and see how digital photography fits into your life and your photography goals. In Chapter 2, you get to know iPhoto by exploring the iPhoto interface and getting your feet wet with this powerful digital photography management tool. In Chapter 3, you take your first steps and find out how to import photos into iPhoto.

Part II: Organizing with iPhoto

iPhoto is a great tool to organize and manage your photos. In Chapter 4, you find out how to work with the Photo Library and how to create and mange albums. You discover some fundamental skills and techniques for keeping your photos organized, safe, and sound. iPhoto also gives you several tools to label your photos, find them using keyword searches, as well as some other important functions to keep you organized. You can find out about these features in Chapter 5.

Part III: Editing Photos

iPhoto is photo-management software. It is not photo-editing software, like a number of other products on the market. However, iPhoto does give you some limited editing capabilities so you can fix the most common problems that occur when you take digital pictures. In Chapter 6, you find out how to use these editing features, such as adjusting a picture's size, fixing brightness and contrast problems, and fixing that vampire effect known as *red-eye*. After you master these skills, you may be hungry for more editing power. To show you what else is available, Chapter 7 explores editing beyond iPhoto, with applications such as Adobe's Photoshop Elements. You can discover what you can do beyond iPhoto and how you can get creative with your digital photo editing.

Part IV: Sharing with iPhoto

What fun are digital photos if you can't share them? Not much fun at all, and the good news is iPhoto gives you a full palette of sharing features you can use. In Chapter 8, you can explore printing your photos from within iPhoto, and I show you how to get those great prints you've been wanting. In Chapter 9, you find out how to use digital photos electronically, such as e-mailing them, posting them to Web sites, and how to use the Web as your own photo album.

Part V: Fun iPhoto Projects

In this part of the book, I explain how to do a number of fun iPhoto projects. Using iPhoto, you can assemble your photos into a book, create captions and lay it out the way you like, send it to Apple, and have a hardbound version shipped to you. In Chapter 10, you find out how. In Chapter 11, I show you how to use iPhoto to create your own slide show, manage the slides, add your own music, and even save it as a QuickTime movie so that you can share it with others. In Chapter 12, you find out how to extend your slide show skills by using your photos in iMovie. You discover how to mix video clips and photos, how to use transitions and titles, and how to assemble a really attractive, professional movie in no time. In Chapter 13, you see how to use OS X's iDVD software so that you can burn your slide shows and movies on a DVD and watch them on your TV. It's fast, fun, and looks great! Finally, in Chapter 14, you find out about some final fun output that you can create. For example, did you know you use iPhoto to create your own desktop picture or screen saver? You can — and Chapter 14 shows you how.

Part VI: The Part of Tens

Ah, the Part of Tens, that great "extra" information place that you find in all *For Dummies* books. This part unveils ten tips for taking great photos, ten common iPhoto problems and solutions, ten of the best overall tips for working in iPhoto, and ten output tips you can use time and time again.

Conventions Used in This Book

This book is designed to help you get the information you need quickly and painlessly. In order to get that information to you, I employ a number of features that you will find helpful:

✔ Tables are used to compare information. They are used judiciously so that they only give you information that is important. Be sure to pay special attention to any tables you see as you read.

✔ Bullet lists give you a quick snapshot of information. They are often used to list features or even potential problems, so always skim through a bullet list when you see it. The bullet lists often give you just the information you are looking for.

✔ I use a monotype font to point to the addresses of Web sites where you can find more information, such as www.apple.com.

✔ This book contains a number of step-by-step processes that show you how to use iPhoto. You can follow those step lists exactly on your Mac.

✔ This book contains a few sidebars, shaded in gray, here and there. Sidebars aren't critical, but they give you extra information that you might find interesting or might come in handy as you work with iPhoto.

✔ If you need to access a series of menus, I format them with arrows. For example, iPhoto⇨Preferences indicates that you should click iPhoto and then click Preferences from the menu that appears.

Icons Used in This Book

Icons are used in this book to point out specific information that you should pay special attention to. These icons make it easy to locate specific kinds of information, and I use them only when there is something important to draw your attention to. Here are the icons used in this book:

A Tip is a piece of friendly advice that gives you a little additional information. The Tip may save you time, or may give you one of those "Ah-ha" moments.

The Remember icon points out some really important piece of information that you should not forget.

The Warning icon alerts to some potential problem or pitfall. Be sure to check these out!

_____

Where to Go from Here

Are you ready? iPhoto is waiting for you, and it's all there for the taking. So, dive into this book, get the information you need, and start enjoying all iPhoto has to offer. Let's go!

Part I

Getting Started with iPhoto

THE GLACIER MOVEMENT PROJECT UPDATE THEIR WEBSITE

Camera ready? Wait a minute, hold it. Ready? Wait for the action... steady...steady... not yet...eeeasy. Hold it. Okay, stay focused. Ready? Not yet...steeeady...eeeasy...

In this part . . .

So you want to explore the world of iPhoto? You've come to the right place! In this part, you get to know iPhoto and explore what you can do with this cool software from Apple. In Chapter 1, you take a quick look at iPhoto and find some great tips for taking photos with your digital camera. In Chapter 2, you get to know iPhoto by discovering the interface and finding your way around. In Chapter 3, you begin importing photos from your camera and other sources to iPhoto.

Chapter 1

Welcome to iPhoto and Digital Photography

Welcome to iPhoto and the world of digital photography. Only a few years ago, digital photography was barely a hobby. After all, any *real* photographer would use a film camera. But times have changed since then, and today, millions of digital cameras have been sold. These cameras support virtually the same features and functions as film cameras — without the hassle of film. Just check out your local electronics store, and you'll see as many digital cameras as film cameras for sale.

Of course, I probably don't need to tell you that. You likely already have a digital camera and are loving it, and now, you want to use Apple's very cool iPhoto application to help you manage and edit your digital photos. You've come to the right place!

In this book, you can explore all that iPhoto has to offer. You can find out how to quickly and easily use this application to manage your photos. In this chapter, I get you started by taking a quick look at iPhoto and what it offers, and then we'll spend a little time exploring the world of digital photography.

Welcome to iPhoto

Before you start using any software, taking a global look at it first is always a good idea. This simply means that you should know the overall approach of the software and the purpose of using the software. Sounds simple, sure, but many photo packages are so complicated that you may not even be sure if you need them.

Not so with iPhoto. iPhoto is a great software package designed to work with you and your digital photos. So, what does iPhoto do? A lot, actually, but its overriding goal is simply to help you manage and use your digital photos.

The great thing about digital photos is that they are electronic — no film to buy and no developing charges to worry about. This gives you the freedom to take as many photos as your memory cards or disks can hold. But with more photos come the tasks of storing, organizing, and using them. For example, say you took 200 photos on your vacation and return home with your memory cards and disks. Now what do you do? Traditional photo-editing software doesn't help you manage your photos, so you end up putting the photos in different folders, hoping you can find the photos you need when you need them.

Enter iPhoto. iPhoto is photo-management software. You can import photos directly from your digital camera into iPhoto, and then iPhoto automatically organizes them for you in its Photo Library, a place where your photos are kept safe and where you can easily find them. iPhoto can manage thousands and thousands of photos (as many as your Mac's hard drive can hold), and it even allows you to create albums to further organize your pictures in a way that works for you. All this power is wrapped into a simple-to-use, easy interface, shown in Figure 1-1.

After you import your photos into iPhoto, the fun is just getting started. Although Chapter 2 goes into more detail about the things you can do, for now, check out some of the fun stuff you can do with iPhoto:

- Import photos from your digital camera or your hard drive.
- Manage photos by creating albums. You can create albums of photos within iPhoto so you can organize your pictures in a way that makes sense to you.
- Create titles and labels for your photos to help you find them more easily.
- Export photos in a standard photo file format that is suitable for sending over the Internet.
- Crop your photos to remove unwanted portions and to assure that your photo adheres to a standard print size, such as 5 x 7 inches.

- ✔ Fix the brightness and contrast of the photo.

- ✔ Easily remove annoying red-eye from your photos of people.

- ✔ Change a photo to black and white with one click.

- ✔ Create slide shows, complete with music that you choose, which you can share via the Internet.

- ✔ Create and order over the Internet a high-quality, hardbound book of your favorite photos.

- ✔ Print photos and photo pages directly from within iPhoto.

- ✔ Directly e-mail pictures from within iPhoto.

- ✔ Order prints of your photos from Kodak from within iPhoto.

- ✔ Use iPhoto and Mac.com to create your own home page on the Web, even if you don't know a thing about creating Web pages.

- ✔ Create your own desktop picture and screen effects.

- ✔ . . . and much more!

As you can see, iPhoto is a well-rounded software application that helps you import, manage, and use your photos. Throughout the rest of this book, I explain how to use these features and how iPhoto is really the software-management program of choice for Mac users. I even explain how to use iPhoto with iMovie and iDVD to extend the capabilities of your digital pictures!

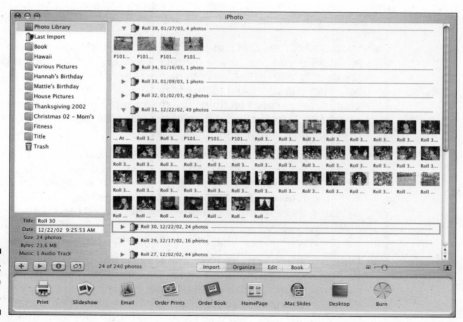

Figure 1-1:
The iPhoto
interface.

Is iPhoto a photo editor?

A common question about iPhoto concerns iPhoto's editing capabilities. iPhoto is photo-management software; it is not a true photo editor. iPhoto has an Edit mode that allows you to perform common edits, such as cropping, changing brightness and contrast, and fixing red-eye. You can even enhance the color of photos and fix little problem spots. However, iPhoto does not give you the editing features and functions of a true photo editor, such as Photoshop Elements. For this reason, many iPhoto users also use an additional software program to make major editing changes to photos, and then use iPhoto to manage their photos. The point to remember is that most quick fixes can be made directly within iPhoto. If you require more advanced editing techniques, you need another program. Chapter 7 introduces you to the world of editing beyond iPhoto.

Welcome to Digital Photography

The world of digital photography is an exciting world that frees you from the old confines of photography. You don't have to worry about buying rolls of film or the expense of developing pictures. Digital photos give you the freedom to learn by experimenting with photos. If you don't like how a photo turns out, you can simply delete it. Nothing is wasted.

In fact, the world of digital photography gives you many advantages that are not available in the film world. Here are just a few:

- **Cost:** One of the great features of digital photography is cost management. After you purchase a digital camera and the media cards/memory sticks or minidiscs the camera uses to store digital photos, you're all set. You no longer need to buy film. You can take as many photos as your memory card can hold, and then simply transfer those images to your Mac. After that's done, you can erase the memory card and start over again . . . and again . . . and again!

- **Flexibility:** Digital photography gives you flexibility. Using your digital camera, you are free to try new techniques and get instant gratification. Most digital cameras have a viewer window built right in to the camera. So you can take a photo, see how it has turned out, and decide right then and there whether or not you want to keep the photo. More advanced digital cameras offer great zoom lens modes and other shooting modes, for everything from portraits to action shots.

- **Digital editing:** In times past, you were at the mercy of your film. Maybe a photo would turn out just right — and maybe not. However, with digital photos, you can use photo-editing software to make any number of editing changes to your photos, and you can use iPhoto to fix most common problems, such as red-eye and brightness/contrast problems.

Digital photography gives you not only the power to take the photos you want, but also the power to fix them.

✔ **Electronic use:** With digital photography, you are free to print your own photos or, if you choose, have a photo-processing center print them for you. But you don't have to print your pictures: You are also open to a new world of using electronic photos. You can e-mail photos to family and friends and create online Web pages and photo albums. If your Mac is equipped with a DVD burner, you can easily make slide shows and burn them to a DVD so that you can watch them in your DVD player. Use iMovie to combine photos and digital film clips and take home movies to the next level.

In fact, there are so many features and options, it's no wonder that the world has embraced digital photography. In fact, about 10 million people purchased a digital camera last year!

Digital camera fundamentals

No, this isn't a book on digital cameras, but because I do cover digital photography and considering that new digital cameras are released virtually each month, I bet that some of you are itching for a new camera. I know I wish that I could buy every new model that appears on the market, but digital cameras are expensive and finding the one that works best for me is a lot like finding that proverbial needle in a haystack. So many options . . . so many choices.

The downside of digital photography

Are there any real negatives of digital photography? Not many. In fact, as digital photography has developed and matured over the past few years, finding negative things to say about it has become harder. In the past, digital cameras didn't take the high-quality photos that film cameras produced, but that simply isn't true anymore. Additionally, because programs such as iPhoto make digital photos so easy to use and manage, naysayers have a hard time criticizing their ease of use.

Of course, digital photography isn't perfect either. The primary drawback at this time is cost. Digital cameras are more expensive than film cameras, and in order to get all the great features you may want in a camera, you likely need to spend $300 or even much more, depending on the type of camera you purchase. Plus, you'll spend more on batteries and the memory cards. (One way to save money on batteries is to buy the rechargeable kind.) If you want to print a lot of photos, you'll also have to buy special paper to print on, and you'll spend more on printer ink. So, your film camera is initially cheaper than a digital version.

However, after you begin buying film and spending money on processing for that conventional camera, your expenses will even out over time. Parting with that hard-earned cash is a little unnerving in the beginning, but overall, it's money well spent.

As you begin thinking about buying a digital camera, you need to look at the process sort of like buying a car. You have to balance what you want and need with what you want to spend. As such, your budget may prevent you from buying the exact camera you want, but you may also discover that some of those seemingly indispensable features aren't all that necessary anyway.

Before you start shopping for a digital camera, I suggest that you first start with a pencil and piece of paper. Write down the features that you think you really want and write down how much money you can spend on a camera. Maybe you are certain that you want a really good zoom lens, or a camera that supports at least a 3-megapixel resolution. Maybe you aren't even sure what you want or need, and that's fine, too. Just try to think of the major things you want in your camera model and determine how much you are willing to spend.

Shopping for a digital camera can be very confusing, so you should have at least a few ideas to work from when you get started. You can do that by asking your friends and family for advice. Other digital camera owners are happy to share with you their trials and joys, so be sure to seek advice. Also, if you need to get a little more familiar with digital cameras and what they provide, check out www.shortcourses.com. This site has lots of introductory information and tutorials to get you started.

Understanding camera resolution

One of the main reasons people have a tough time choosing a digital camera is resolution. Resolution affects quality and file size: High-resolution photos are high-quality photos, but the file size of a high-resolution image can also grow very large very quickly. In order to print digital photos, you have to have a camera that shoots the photos at a high enough resolution for the printing process. The bigger the resolution you use, the bigger images you can print without distortion and graininess. So, if you are shopping for a camera, the resolution of the camera has to be carefully considered, along with how you intend to use your photos and how big you want to print your photos.

A camera is capable of a certain maximum resolution. With today's digital cameras, resolution is expressed in megapixels. A *pixel* is an individual unit of information in a digital camera — or more simply, a tiny dot. Pictures are made up of pixels, which, when put together, create the image you see. The more pixels a photo has, the more "information" is available to the printer, so the better it will print. In short, the more resolution you have, the better the photo.

A megapixel is equal to one million pixels. If your camera is a 1.3-megapixel camera, it is capable of taking a photo that has 1,300,000 pixels. If your camera is a 5-megapixel camera, it is capable of taking a photo that has 5,000,000 pixels. Obviously, the 5-megapixel camera can give you much greater resolution than a 1.3-megapixel camera.

When you want to take a photo, you can use the camera to choose a resolution value for the photo that you want to take. Your camera lists resolution values in terms of photo pixel height times the width. Rather than giving you the option to shoot a 1.3-megapixel image, you see the option to shoot a 1280 x 1024 shot (1280 x 1024 = 1,310,720, or roughly 1.3 megapixels). If you have a 4-megapixel camera, your highest resolution is listed as 2240 x 1680 (which equals 3,763,200, or roughly 4 megapixels).

In order to print an image, you must have a high enough resolution to recreate all those pixels in the printed image. For this reason, you cannot print an 8 x 10 photo with 640 x 480 resolution and expect good results. The pixel count is too low, and you'll see jagged lines and other print anomalies. If, however, you just want to print small images or view the images on the computer, you can shoot at 640 x 480.

So, what resolution do you really need to print the sizes you want? Table 1-1 offers general guidelines to keep in mind, and I explore this concept in more detail in Chapter 8.

Table 1-1	Minimum Resolutions for Standard Print Sizes
Print Size	*Minimum resolution*
4 x 6	1024 x 768
5 x 7	1280 x 1024 (1 megapixel)
8 x 10	1600 x 1200 (2 megapixels)
11 x 14	2048 x 1536 (3.3 megapixels)

So, when you are looking at camera models, you need to decide what megapixel support you want. The more megapixels, the more expensive the camera, of course, so this is where you have to balance your wants against the reality of your pocketbook. Many people today crave the 4-megapixel cameras because they give you complete printing flexibility. I understand because I own one of them, too, but they cost at least $400. However, if you know for a fact that you don't want to print 8-x-10s or larger photos, you really don't need a 4-megapixel camera. A 3-megapixel model can save you some money and still give you great prints up to 8 x 10. However, you will get better 8-x-10s using a 4-megapixel camera.

Because resolution is such an important issue, I refer to it time and time again throughout the book. If the resolution issue has still left you a little stumped, again, check out www.shortcourses.com for some great background material.

Other camera features

The resolution of the camera will be a big deciding factor in your quest for a digital camera. However, resolution isn't the only issue you should think about as you're camera shopping. Keep the following tips in mind as well:

- ✔ **Check out the lens.** Do you like the zoom feature? Do the lens and viewer seem easy to use?

- ✔ **Get a feel for the camera.** Does the camera seem comfortable in your hand? Does the size seem easy to use, and will the camera be easy to transport from place to place?

- ✔ **Check out the mode options.** Does the camera allow you to easily switch modes for a variety of shots and lighting conditions (action mode, portrait mode, and so on).

- ✔ **Is the display easy to use?** Do the button options make sense, or will you have to become a camera expert just to figure them out?

- ✔ **What kind of batteries and memory cards are used?** Will you have the flexibility to use memory cards from other (and often less expensive) manufacturers? Will you be able to buy batteries at the grocery store, or can you use only special rechargeable batteries that work only in that camera?

- ✔ **How does the camera connect?** Most (although not all) cameras connect to the computer using a USB port. You'll find it easier to work with a camera that connects this way.

Before you spend your hard-earned money on a digital camera, you should also check out Chapter 3 and make sure the camera you are interested in is compatible with iPhoto. Most are, so don't worry.

Finally, shop around before you buy a camera. Check your local camera and department stores, and then compare their prices with online stores, such as Amazon.com (www.amazon.com) and buy.com (www.buy.com). You can often get rebates and other freebies online, so be sure to you shop around for the best deal.

The basics of great photos

After you have your digital camera, it's time to take some pictures. As you explore your digital camera, use the camera's instruction guide to get familiar with the controls and the basic process of taking photos. All cameras work a little differently, so you need to study the manufacturer's instructions to get started.

Watch out for Internet scams!

Some small Internet-based electronics stores offer huge savings — often up to a third off the price offered by established stores such as Amazon.com and buy.com. Should you buy from these lesser-known sites? Buyer beware!

These stores advertise new cameras at great savings, but customers often complain about what they get. The cameras may be refurbished, or you may not get the camera for a long time. Many of these sites require you to call and "confirm" your order. During your call, a salesperson tries to hard sell you add-ons and other extras at marked up prices in order to recoup the discount on the camera price. In some cases, the seller won't even ship your camera to you unless you buy some of these extras.

My advice is to play it safe and buy from reputable dealers. The money you may save at the other sites isn't worth the headaches and problems you may experience.

When you're ready to start taking photos, get ready to experiment! Photography is an art form, and as such, there are no hard rules about what you can and can't do. However, you can follow some general guidelines that will help you produce great photos time and time again — and after all, great photos are what everyone wants. In the following sections, you take a look at some basics that will get your feet on solid ground when you take pictures.

Composition

Knowing a thing or two about composition can help you take great photos. In simple terms, *composition* is what you see in the picture: the main subject(s), plus everything else that you see, including other people, objects, and the background. In truth, composition can make a picture really interesting and exciting — or not.

First of all, consider the concept of the subject in a photograph. Every picture generally has a main subject. The primary exception to this rule is landscape photos, where the entire picture makes up the subject. But even landscape photos may still have one focal point. As a general rule, the main subject is the focal point of the photo, and everything else in the photo, including other objects, people, and even the background, should enhance the subject.

Unless you are using a backdrop or shooting a portrait where the background is blurred, you are likely to have some objects in each picture you take. As you are thinking about subjects and objects, memorize these two important rules and put them to work in your photos:

✔ **Objects should never overpower the main subject.** By *overpower,* I mean that the object should not get the most attention from the viewer. This concept can include placement of the objects, their color, and a number of other factors that can cause an object to get more attention in a photo than the subject.

✔ **An object should enhance the subject.** Objects should exist in the photo to enhance the main subject, or perhaps create a certain mood, theme, or interesting perspective.

Consider a couple of examples. Take a look at the following photo in Figure 1-2.

Figure 1-2: This photo has one main subject.

This close-up of an outdoor candleholder gives you an example of a primary subject. The subject is clearly the focal point of the photo. The background consists of a fence and some trees, which provide a backdrop for the main subject. As you can see, the fence and trees do not grab your attention — the main object does. The background simply backs up the subject without distracting from it.

Now, take a look at Figure 1-3.

As far as a snapshot goes, this photo is okay, but the problem is its composition. You have three people in the photo (plus another one standing in the background) and a lot of boxes, wrapping paper, and toys, all competing for your attention. This photo would be a lot better if it focused on a main subject; as it is, simply too many subjects and too many objects are cluttering up the photo. The good news is that you can often fix cluttered photos like this one by cropping away some of the unnecessary portions of the photo, which you can do quickly and easily within iPhoto. See Chapter 6 to find out more.

Figure 1-3: This photo has too many items competing for your attention.

So, the first key to great photos is to think about composition. As the photographer, give some thought to what is actually in the photo. Think about the main subject and the main subject's placement, but also take a hard look at everything else in the photo. Are the other objects and the background complementary to the main subject, or are they a distraction?

Training your eye

I know you're probably thinking, "Sure, composition is great, but how do you deal with all this when you only have a few moments to capture the pose?" A good question, no doubt. In reality, unless you are taking posed shots, you may not have as much power over composition as you may like. And in truth, capturing that moment is sometimes a trade-off between getting the perfect composition you want and getting the shot at all.

However, the more aware you are of composition, the faster you can make decisions as you take photos. As you are practicing, retrain your eye so that you are not captivated by the subject you are photographing. Practice and retrain your eye to think in terms of subjects and objects. This will help you frame subjects and control the objects around them so that you can capture really great photos.

Lighting

Lighting is a major factor in producing great photos. After all, light enables us to see the world around us, and light allows your digital camera to create the image on the storage media. Without light, you don't get a photo, and without good light, your photo will probably be lacking.

When you take a picture, the film or digital sensor is exposed to light. The amount of light that is allowed to strike the film or digital sensor determines the picture you get. Too much light equals a picture that is too bright and where the people look washed out. Too little light equals a dark picture. Your camera controls the amount of light that is exposed through two controls — aperture and shutter speed.

The actual lens opening is called the *aperture*. Aperture is measured in f-stops, which are simply numbers that determine how much light enters. A 35 mm camera lens typically provides openings for f/2.8, f/4, f/5.6, and so forth. The higher the number, the smaller the aperture, or the less light that enters. Depending on your camera, you may not be able to directly control the aperture, or your camera may handle it automatically, depending on the mode you select.

Whereas aperture is the opening size that allows light to enter, *shutter speed* determines the amount of time that light is allowed to act on the film or sensor. Shutter speed is expressed in fractions of seconds, such as $\frac{1}{60}$, $\frac{1}{125}$, and so forth. Faster shutter speeds are used for action shots, while slower shutter speeds are used for still shots. Again, depending on your camera, you may have no direct control over shutter speed, but your camera may select one for you based on the mode you choose.

As a general thought to keep in mind, remember that light affects how the photo looks. Too much light can create a harsh effect, and too little light can make a photo look dim. Light that is just right can give a photo a soft, warming feeling. Study your camera instructions and the camera itself a bit to get a feel for how your camera deals with aperture and shutter speed. If your camera provides modes that automatically select these settings, get familiar with the settings and what your camera chooses for you based on the mode. This can help you determine the best mode for the shot you are trying to get.

Outdoor lighting

To make a blanket statement, outdoor lighting is the best lighting for taking pictures. This is especially true if you are taking photos of people. Of course, taking pictures outdoors is not always practical, but natural light is the most flattering for people and most objects. That, of course, does not mean every picture you take outdoors will look great. The kind of outdoor lighting you use has a lot to do with the quality you get. The following list gives you a quick overview of the types of outdoor light and their pros and cons:

- **Direct sunlight:** Direct sunlight is the most difficult kind of light to work with. Direct sunlight creates the most shadows, and that same concept holds true when you are photographing people. Aside from your subjects squinting a lot, direct sunlight often creates shadows under eyes, noses, and chins and even makes people look older than they are. The reason is simply the harshness of the sunlight acting on the person's features. The exception to this rule is the beach or on water. Because sand and water reflect light, you can usually take photos of people on sand or water with good results in direct sunlight. You may have heard the advice to "shoot with the sun in front of the subject." The result? Squinting subjects with wrinkled faces and shadows. Despite the old saying, this approach doesn't help most of the time. Can you shoot with the sun behind the subject? Sure, but you'll most often get a bright background and a dark subject. As a rule, avoid direct sunlight. Figure 1-4 shows you some of the negative effects you can get when you shoot a photo in direct sunlight.

- **Shade:** If you are taking photos on a sunny day, your best bet for great photos is to put the subject in the shade, especially when taking photos of people and animals. The shade provides plenty of diffused light without creating all the shadows and harsh lines that come with direct-sunlight shots. However, taking photos in the shade does cause problems with color cast. A *color cast* occurs when a subject is in the shade, but objects around the subject are casting a certain color. For example, if the subject is under a yellow awning, you may get a yellow cast on the picture, or a subject under too many trees may get a green/brown cast, which tends to make the subject reflect the cast. The trick is to watch out for brightly colored objects that are in the sun.

- **Overcast:** The best outdoor light is overcast lighting. Overcast lighting occurs on days when clouds are covering the sun, but not rainy dark days. Overcast lighting diffuses the sun's rays and makes the light friendly to photography. Your subjects and objects will have rich, warm light without stark sunlight that creates shadows and lines. Overcast days provide more blue tones, which help contrast against skin tones and other natural colors, such as the grass and flowers.

Figure 1-4:
Direct
sunlight
produces
harsh
lines and
shadows.

Indoor lighting

Unless you have a professional photography studio with actual photography lights, you have to deal with some lighting problems when you take photos indoors. Of course, you can take great pictures of people indoors: You just have more problems to contend with. One of the main problems is that household lighting isn't a replacement for sunlight. Household light from standard light bulbs is *tungsten* light, which has a yellow/orange tint to it, although you probably don't notice this when you are going about your daily activities. However, your camera certainly notices, and for this reason, you often get photos that have a slight yellow or orange cast to them. To combat indoor lighting problems, here are some quick tips to remember:

- ✓ **Use overhead lighting, but try to use lamps as well.** The lamps in a room help diffuse shadows created by the overhead lighting. In short, if you want to take some photos indoors, turn on the overhead light and any available lamps.

- ✓ **Take indoor pictures near a large window if possible.** Try not to use a window that has direct sunlight streaming in, but one that provides diffused light. Make sure you use room lighting as well, or you'll get a ton of shadows.

- ✓ **Your camera likely needs to use the flash when taking pictures indoors.** Because of this, make sure no mirrors are visible in the picture because the flash bounces back, and try not to take pictures of people standing directly in front of a window, because the flash sometimes bounces off the glass in the window. Also, you may have problems with red-eye. Red-eye occurs when the flash reflects off the blood vessels and retina in a person's eye, creating the red-eye "vampire" effect. Window lighting can help this problem, and your camera may be equipped with a red-eye reduction mode. The good news is that iPhoto can easily fix this problem for you, so don't stress over it. (I show you how to use iPhoto to fix red-eye in Chapter 6.)

Taking Great Portraits

Photography encompasses a number of subjects, including photos of people, landscapes, animals, and other creative forms. However, one of the most difficult subjects to capture well in a photo is . . . well . . . us! Taking photos of people can be very difficult, due to a number of factors. For this reason, many professional photographers spend their entire career doing nothing but taking portraits and getting paid well for it.

Let's face the fact — we all like to see flattering photos of ourselves, and if you stop to think about it, those flattering photos are the ones that we like to keep out for other people to see. Yet, how many unflattering photos of family and friends do you have stuck in the closet? If you are like most people, quite a few.

The simple fact is that people are the most difficult subjects to photograph (and they are the only subjects that tend to argue with and complain to the photographer!). Yet, you'll probably spend a fair amount of time taking photos of people. The good news is that you can pull a few tricks out of your sleeve to make your portrait shots look better. This section gives you some quick tips and tricks.

Working with human subjects

One big problem with portraits plagues all photographers — even those who make their living with photography. The problem? Portraits are staged. You ask a person or group to sit or stand in a certain location in a certain way, and then you tell that person or group to say, "Cheese." Sometimes that works great, but a lot of times it doesn't. There are a few reasons why.

The good news is that portrait photography gives you total control over lighting and objects. Because you are controlling the environment, you can spend some time setting up the composition of the photo and making sure everything looks great. The only problem is that you have to deal with people who know that you're about to take their picture, which is an entirely different dynamic than capturing people "in the moment." Specifically, you may run into these problems:

> ✔ **Most adults are a little uneasy about having their pictures taken.** Even those of us who are not camera-shy still become self-conscious. We may think, "Does my hair look okay?" Or "Will my smile look natural?" Just thinking about these issues alone is enough to cause problems, so as the photographer, you have to develop some skills to combat nervous subjects. First of all, always compliment the subjects. Even if the portrait is an impromptu picture, find something good to say. Something like, "You all look great! This will be a nice picture," helps a lot with groups. For individuals, try something more specific, such as, "That shirt really

complements your skin tone," or "Your hair looks great today." Be sincere and don't overdo it. A simple compliment can give your subject confidence and help him or her relax.

- **Your subject gets stiff body syndrome.** When you start to take a portrait of someone, the person often tenses up, thinking this will make the photo look more formal. Instead you get stiff shoulders, a stiff neck, and what ultimately looks like someone who is posing for a picture. The look is unnatural and uninviting. To help subjects relax, put them in the basic position you want them for several minutes before you take the picture. For a portrait, seat the subjects or have them stand where the picture will be taken. This gives the subjects a moment or two to get used to the surroundings. Make small talk. When you get them where you want, get their attention off the task at hand. Simple conversational questions, such as "How was work today?" or "How's your family doing?" will help. This technique gets the subjects talking and helps the subject to relax. Some photographers talk to their subjects while purposely fumbling with camera equipment, just to give them a few minutes to get adjusted.

- **Your subjects may have fake or stiff smiles.** Your subject may smile too much, too little, or plaster a fake-looking smile on his or her face. This is a common problem and causes the picture to look unnatural. Keep in mind that the goal of a portrait is to capture the likeness of the person, so it's important that the subject give you a good smile. What can you do? First of all, when you have the person or group first get into place for the photo, tell them not to smile. A phrase like, "Just relax while I get everything ready" is good to set people at ease. If the person starts practicing the smile, it almost never comes out good. The old adage, "Say cheese," isn't a bad one. Use a trick like this, especially with groups, to get everyone to smile at the same time. You don't have to use the word *cheese,* but try to use some word that is one syllable and has an *ee,* such as *tree.* The *ee* naturally helps you form a smile. If the subject is having a lot of problems, try this: Tell the subject to completely relax her face. Then, tell the subject to close her eyes and count to five. Immediately after the subject says, "Five," you say, "Open your eyes and smile." Then take the shot quickly.

Unless you are a really good comedian, refrain from telling jokes to make your subject smile, especially in group shots. When you give the punch line, you tend to get different reactions (some smiles, some straight faces, some eye rolling, and so on). Jokes usually do not help you get a better picture.

Portraits of individuals

Now that you've taken a look at handling people when you take portraits, I want to move on and consider some important skills that help you take great portraits of individuals. First of all, when you take a portrait of an individual, you are working with only one subject. In this case, the single subject is the focal point of the photo. You may be taking a close-up with a diffused background, or you may have the subject posed with other objects in order to create a certain effect. Regardless, the subject is the essence of the picture.

The center of any picture of an individual is their eyes. No matter how close the subject is to you, how far away, or how many objects are in the picture, study after study has told us that people notice the eyes first in any photograph. So, when you are taking pictures of people, you must train yourself to think about the eyes. Think of the eyes as the mental "center" of your picture, even if the subject is not directly in the center of the physical picture itself.

Why? The answer is simple: The eyes reveal more feeling and personality in a portrait and in real life than we first may think. Eyes, regardless of a person's age, are beautiful in their own way. We often think of a smile as being the most important part of a portrait, but in reality, the eyes communicate more than a smile. For this reason, portraits often focus on the face and on the eyes.

Now, does this mean that all portrait photos should have the subject sitting forward, looking at the camera? No, not at all. The subject can be looking away from the camera lens, or the subject may not be looking at the camera at all. Still, always think about the eyes. Asking yourself, "What do the eyes communicate when I look through the lens?" will help you produce great portraits of individuals.

The next major issue concerning individual portraits is posing and composition. Before you think about posing the subject, first think about composition. Will the portrait be a close-up of the subject's face? Will you show the subject's head and shoulders, or more of the subject's body? Because you are dealing with a single subject, address this issue first. If you are unsure, take several different photos, everything from a close-up of the face to a wider shot of the subject's body. The variety of shots can help you find the composition that you really want.

As you are thinking about composition, the next point to consider is objects. Will you provide a nondescript background with basically no objects, or will you have the subject with objects in the picture? There is no right or wrong approach, but one word of caution — try to keep things as simple as possible. The objects, or surroundings in the photo, can keep things warm and friendly (or even cold and stark — depending on what you are trying to accomplish), and as a general rule, they should be minimal. Consider the example in Figure 1-5.

In this classic shot of a child's first birthday cake, the subject is shot in close-up. In terms of composition, you see just enough of the birthday hat without detracting from the subject's face. Notice that the subject isn't even directly looking at the lens. That's okay, though: The feeling of happiness is still communicated. And of course, the cake-smeared face and hand add to the feeling in this picture. Now, take a look at Figure 1-6.

Figure 1-5: The focus is on the child, not the objects.

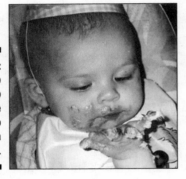

Figure 1-6: Subjects do not have to look at the camera to create a good photo.

Now, here's another shot of the same event. Notice that the subject is not looking at the camera and is not smiling. However, the intent staring at the iced fingers gives the photo that moment of wonder and awe that makes the photo a keeper. The lesson here is to keep in mind that, in great portraits of a single subject, the subject doesn't need to be looking at the camera and smiling. Remember that you are trying to capture a representation of that person, and that representation can take on many feelings and moods.

Another point to remember is that objects should enhance the subject. Keep the objects simple, minimal, and always ask yourself, "How is the object adding to the mood or feeling of the picture, and how is the object supporting the subject?" These questions can help you make good decisions about composition every time.

As you think about composition in an individual portrait, you must also think about posing. Because portrait pictures can be anything from a formal pose in front of the camera to relaxed shots of someone doing an activity, there are no hard rules about posing. The key in any portrait picture, however, is to make the subject look natural. You can give the subject great props and put the subject in the perfect place, but if the subject is stiff and unnatural looking, the picture won't look good. As with composition, the best approach to posing is to keep things as simple as possible.

Finally, I can offer you a few more words of advice as you work with taking photos of individuals. Keep these tips in mind as you take your photos:

- If your subject is wearing glasses, the glass lenses may reflect the flash. You can often fix this problem with photo imaging software, but solving the problem before you take the picture is always best. So, if the subject is wearing glasses, have him tilt his head slightly forward or a slightly to the side. This is usually enough to keep the glass lenses from reflecting the flash back into the camera.

- If the subject is bald, you may get *flash bounce*. The oily skin of the subject's head often reflects the camera light, so you see a hot spot on the film that seems shiny. Keep this problem in mind and have your subject wipe his head with a moist cloth before taking the picture.

- If you want to diminish a subject's large nose, have her look straight at the camera and try to keep the camera directly focused on the eyes.

- If the subject has a double chin, have the subject tilt his head up slightly and take the photo at a slight angle down toward the subject.

- If you are shooting an elderly person who is worried about wrinkles, try soft diffused lighting, because it tends to soften the face and make wrinkles look less distinct.

- If a person is worried about his weight, tilt his body about 45 degrees away from the camera, and then have his head turned toward the camera. This automatically makes a person look thinner.

Working with groups

For the most part, all the issues I address in the previous section concerning the photographing of individuals apply to photographing groups. After all, a group shot is simply more people. However, you have to think about some distinct issues when taking pictures of groups.

Most of the time, composition isn't that big of an issue when photographing groups, mostly because you don't have the space to use objects anyway. The exception to this rule is photographing a group doing something or involved in some occupation. In this case, objects can help communicate the message of the photograph.

Including pets

Are you taking a family group shot where you want to include the family pet? For small dogs and cats (or other small animals), have someone in the front portion of the photo hold the pet. This makes sure the pet doesn't get lost in the photo. For large dogs and other large pets, you can put the pet in the center and arrange the people around the pet, or put the pet on the left side of the photo. As you think about eye movement, don't forget to include the pet's head. When a person is viewing the photo, her eyes should naturally move to the pet just as they would to a person.

Most of the time, though, your job is to get everyone in the photograph, positioned well, and in a way that is flattering to everyone — and believe me, that can certainly be a job all by itself.

When you position people in a group portrait, you should keep in mind two main concepts at all times — eye movement and depth.

When I say *eye movement,* I am talking about the viewer's eyes, not the people in the photo. You want a person looking at the photo to naturally move from one subject to the next, so how can you pose your subjects? The old advice here is best: Think in terms of a circle. That doesn't mean that your group should actually form a circle. Rather, it means to look at the heads of the people in the group and see if your eyes tend to move in a circle when looking at them. The trick is to arrange people at different heights and in a naturally flowing pattern. Don't make people of the same height stand shoulder-to-shoulder because this arrangement makes them look like soldiers.

Aside from eye movement, the second issue is depth. When taking photos of groups, think of your arrangement in terms of layers. Group photos look best when some people are a little closer to the camera than others. This creates texture and makes viewing the individuals in the photo easier. Again, this makes the photo look more natural instead of looking like a line of soldiers.

When working with depth, keep one point in mind. The subjects should be at different depths, but they should be very close to each other. If not, your camera may try to focus the front faces and not the ones in the back. Keep the depth, but keep the group close together too.

Chapter 2

Getting to Know iPhoto

Getting to know iPhoto 2 is a lot like getting behind the wheel of a new car. Sure, you can probably figure out how to drive the car with only a few minutes of exploration, but you should know a few things before you take off down the road.

Beginning to use iPhoto is like getting ready to drive a car for the first time: The interface looks really simple, but hiding under the hood are a number of powerful features that you should know a thing or two about before you start using iPhoto. Think of this chapter as your fifteen-minute introduction to iPhoto. If you don't have iPhoto installed on your Mac, you can find out where to get iPhoto and how to install it. If you do have iPhoto, you can skip ahead in this chapter to "Opening iPhoto," which helps you get your bearings before you really start working and having fun with this cool software.

Checking Out iPhoto Requirements

Probably the best news of this chapter is simply this: iPhoto is free software that Apple gives away. iPhoto ships ready to go in Mac OS X, so you may already have a version of iPhoto. If don't already have it, you may be able to simply download it from Apple. Before you take off to use iPhoto or to download it at the Apple Web site, however, take a quick look at your computer to verify whether you have the current version, which is iPhoto 2. Click the iPhoto icon on the Dock to open iPhoto. Then, choose iPhoto⇨About iPhoto. An information page that lists the version number appears.

If you don't have the latest version, check out the following sections to see if your computer has what it takes to run iPhoto.

iPhoto demands a Macintosh computer

iPhoto works only on Macintosh systems. If you're a Windows user who has heard the talk about iPhoto, you need to get away from your Windows computer and get a Mac in order to use iPhoto. iPhoto for Windows simply doesn't exist. iPhoto is built for the Mac and lives only in the Macintosh space.

"Great," you may say, "I have a Mac. Now what?" If you recently purchased your Mac with OS X version 10.2 or later preinstalled, you may already have the current version of iPhoto on your Mac. If you purchased that Mac before March of 2003, you probably need to download iPhoto 2, because you probably have an earlier version of iPhoto. To find out how to check your version, see the previous section, "Checking Out iPhoto Requirements."

Now, what if you are using OS X, but you upgraded to it from OS 9? Before jumping ahead, stay with me a moment while I explain how to make sure your computer can handle the demands of iPhoto.

iPhoto demands OS X

Now, here's the bad news. iPhoto was built for OS X. If you are using OS 9 or previous versions of the Mac OS, you'll need to upgrade to OS X before you can begin using iPhoto 2. iPhoto 2 requires OS X version 10.1.5 or later, so if you are not using at least version 10.1.5, you need to upgrade to OS X before you can even think about using iPhoto. The good news is you'll like OS X much better than OS 9, so you'll want to upgrade anyway.

Upgrading to OS X

So, you need to upgrade to OS X, eh? Well, before doing so, I suggest you spend some time at www.apple.com/macosx/upgrade/requirements.html and do some reading. Before you buy OS X as an upgrade to your Mac, you need to make absolutely sure that your current Mac can handle the demands of the OS X operating system.

The skinny is that you need to be currently running OS 9 to upgrade to OS X. Your Mac must be a Power Mac G3 or G4, an iMac, a PowerBook G3 or G4, or an iBook. You must have at least 128MB of physical RAM. Also note that the original PowerBook G3 and processor upgrade cards are not supported under OS X.

If your machine doesn't meet these requirements, upgrading is not an option. If you want to work with iPhoto and Mac OS X, you have to buy a newer Mac, which will have OS X installed on it already.

---

iPhoto demands memory

Yes, iPhoto certainly demands memory. Memory refers to physical RAM installed on your Mac. RAM (random access memory) is basically memory that the Mac uses to store information as you work. Apple recommends that you use iPhoto 2 on Macs that have at least 256MB of RAM. Although you can work with iPhoto using less RAM (such as 128MB), less RAM causes iPhoto to run slowly, and you'll get rather aggravated. 256MB is really the lowest practical recommendation, and the more RAM you have, the better.

iPhoto is a photo-management application. If you don't have enough RAM (256MB) on your Mac to make iPhoto run nicely, don't assume you can just buy a different application and solve your RAM problems. Most photo-management applications love memory, simply because working with picture files uses a lot of it. If you don't have enough RAM, now is a good time to consider an upgrade.

iPhoto demands a fast processor

The processor is the brain of your Mac. The processor performs all calculations and runs all programs. As such, each application requires a certain processor speed in order to work and play nicely. iPhoto is no exception to that rule. Apple recommends that you use at least a 400 MHz G3 processor. You can use something slower, but you probably won't be happy with iPhoto's performance. The faster the processor, the more quickly iPhoto works, which reduces the amount of time you have to drum your fingers on the table while you wait on iPhoto.

I should also mention that a 400 MHz G3 processor is the recommended requirement, but it's not necessarily the best. You'll get much better performance from a G4 when you use applications like iPhoto. If you are thinking about buying a new Mac anyway and plan to work with iPhoto frequently, make sure you get one with a G4 processor.

iPhoto demands a few other things, too

The operating system, RAM, and processor are the main requirements of iPhoto, but you should consider a few other items as well. Before you jump into iPhoto land, consider these points:

✔ Your Mac needs built-in USB ports so that you can connect your camera directly to the Mac and iPhoto.

If you want to work only with existing photos and not actually import photos from a digital camera, you don't really have to worry about the USB ports.

✔ If you want to connect a digital camera to the Mac and download directly to iPhoto, you need a compatible digital camera. The good news is most USB digital cameras are compatible with iPhoto, and you can even see a list of them at www.apple.com/iphoto/compatibility. You can find out more about connecting your camera to the Mac and iPhoto in Chapter 3.

✔ If you are going to print photos, you need a compatible printer. Basically, any printer that works with OS X also works with iPhoto, so you don't have anything to worry about here. If you are curious, though, visit www.apple.com/iphoto/compatibility to see a list of compatible printers.

✔ iPhoto doesn't give you any specific hard disk space requirements, but as you may already know, pictures can take up a lot of room on your computer's hard drive. So, if you know you will be storing a lot of pictures in iPhoto, just be aware that you'll need plenty of hard disk space available. iPhoto can store about 1000 medium resolution photos on 1 GB of disk space, so a recommendation of 1GB of free disk space is not unreasonable.

✔ Although not required, Internet access is certainly great to have because it enables you to take full advantage of iPhoto's features. A number of iPhoto features require you to be connected to the Internet. For example, you can e-mail photos using iPhoto and your e-mail application, and you can even use your photos to create a Web page at www.mac.com. See Chapter 9 to find out more.

Downloading and Installing iPhoto

You should always get the latest version of iPhoto, and even if you have the current version, you can bet that new versions will become available from time to time. The good news is that iPhoto is free, and you can download the newest version at any time from Apple. You have to give away your name and e-mail address to download it, but that's no biggie.

At the time of this writing, iPhoto 2 is the latest version. If you bought your Mac before March 2003, you probably have iPhoto 1.1.1.

Come on down, iPhoto!

Before you begin the download process, make sure you have read the previous section about system requirements. Also, before you start the download, I should point out that iPhoto 2 is a 32MB download. If you are using a modem to access the Internet, downloading the software will take a long time (probably in the neighborhood of three to five hours). I recommend that you start the download at night and hope you awake to find the iPhoto installer waiting on you.

When you're ready to download iPhoto, just follow these easy steps:

1. **Open your Web browser and go to** `www.apple.com/iphoto/.`

2. **Choose the option to download iPhoto from this page.**

    This opens the iPhoto download page, which you can see in Figure 2-1.

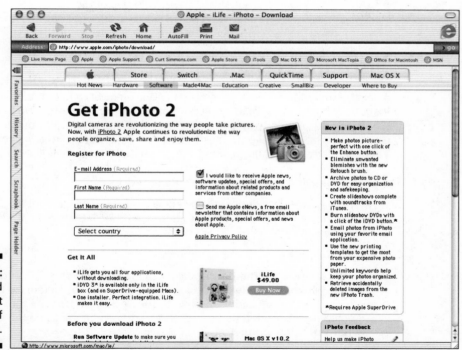

Figure 2-1:
Download the latest version of iPhoto here.

3. **In the Register for iPhoto section, enter your e-mail address, first name, and last name in the provided dialog.**

   Also note the check box options to get e-mail offers and info from Apple and the free e-mail newsletter from Apple. If you don't want these, just deselect the check boxes. If you are worried about entering your e-mail address, be at ease. Apple maintains a strict privacy policy, so you can rest assured that Apple won't sell your e-mail address or share it with other people or Web sites.

4. **Click the Download iPhoto button at the bottom of the window.**

   A Download dialog appears, showing you the status of the download. Now all you have to do is sit back and wait. If you are using a modem, the download will probably take two or three hours. If you are using a broadband (high-speed) connection (such as DSL or cable), the download takes only a couple of minutes.

After the download is complete, you see a Download icon on your desktop. All you have to do now is install iPhoto, which I explain how to do in the next section.

Installing iPhoto

After the download is finally complete, you're ready to install iPhoto. Installing iPhoto is a real snap, so you have no worries here. The Download icon that automatically appeared on your desktop after you downloaded iPhoto represents the setup files that install or update iPhoto on your Mac. This is called a Disk Image (.dmg) file. To install iPhoto, follow these steps:

1. **Double-click the iPhoto icon your desktop.**

   The files are decoded, and you see a disk copy progress bar. After the decompression process is complete, an iPhoto drive icon appears on your desktop.

2. **Double-click the iPhoto drive icon.**

   In the window that appears, shown in Figure 2-2, you see a folder called Read Before You Install and an iPhoto.pkg icon. You can open the Read Before You Install folder and locate the version of this file that is in your language; it simply tells you about the requirements to install iPhoto and what's new in the version.

3. **When you're ready to install, double-click the iPhoto.pkg icon.**

4. **In the dialog that appears, enter the OS X administrator name and password and click OK.**

   You must be the computer administrator in order to install new software.

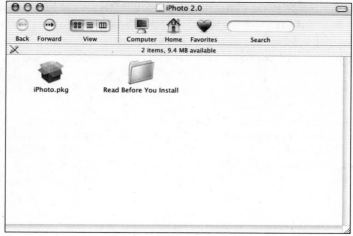

Figure 2-2:
The iPhoto
2.0 drive
contains the
iPhoto setup
package
and a Read
Before
You Install
folder.

5. **In the Welcome screen that appears, read the welcome and click the Continue button.**

6. **The Read Me file appears again; just click Continue to move on.**

7. **The licensing agreement appears; read it and click Continue.**

8. **In the Select a Destination dialog that appears (shown in Figure 2-3), select the appropriate option and then click Continue.**

   If you have only one hard disk, it is selected for you. If you have more than one hard disk, click the disk on which you want to install iPhoto.

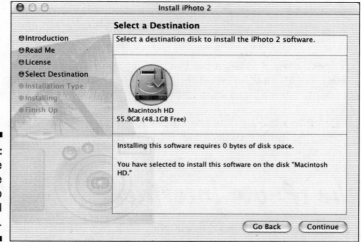

Figure 2-3:
Select the
disk where
you want to
install
iPhoto.

9. **In the Installation dialog that appears, select what kind of installation to perform by clicking the corresponding button.**

   You can choose to customize the installation, perform a full installation, or upgrade (if you currently have an older version of iPhoto). After you click a button, iPhoto is installed on your Mac.

10. **When the installation process is done, simply click Finish.**

Sometimes, downloads get fouled up. If you start the installation and it fails, or if you get weird error messages or nothing seems to happen, your download likely experienced a bit of turbulence that corrupted the files or left you with an incomplete download. In this case, exit the setup program (click the Red X to close the installer window), go back to the Internet, and download iPhoto again.

Opening iPhoto

You can open iPhoto in one of two main ways. The easiest is to simply click the iPhoto icon that resides in the Dock, shown in Figure 2-4. The iPhoto icon looks like a picture and a camera, and if you just click the icon, iPhoto comes to life.

Click to start iPhoto.

Figure 2-4:
Click the
iPhoto icon
in the Dock
to open it.

If iPhoto doesn't seem to be in the Dock or if you prefer the longer route, double-click the Macintosh HD, double-click the Applications folder, and then double-click the iPhoto icon. Either way, iPhoto opens and is ready to use.

You can also press ⌘-Shift-A in the Finder to go directly to the Applications folder. Then, just double-click on the iPhoto icon.

Touring the iPhoto Interface

As with any software, you have to get your bearings before using iPhoto, and the following sections in this chapter point you in the right direction.

When you first open iPhoto, you see the primary interface, which is made up of two major window panes, some buttons, and a mode area that appears in a box at the bottom, shown in Figure 2-5.

As you can see, the iPhoto interface contains a few primary parts, which you can take a quick look at in the following sections.

Keep in mind that the following sections (and the rest of this chapter) are designed to get your feet wet with iPhoto. You can explore all the features and usage options in iPhoto in detail throughout the rest of this book.

Source pane

The Source pane of the window, shown in Figure 2-6, gives you access to your Photo Library, the place where all your photos are stored, as well as the last imported film roll, any albums that you have created, as well as the iPhoto Trash. If that seems like gibberish, here's a quick explanation:

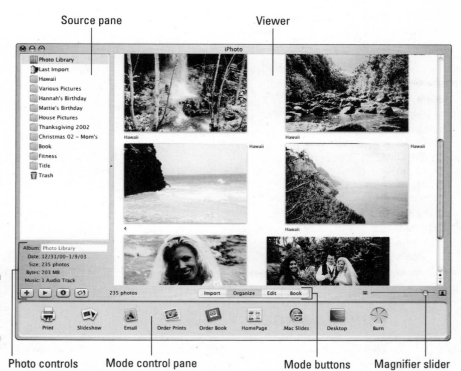

Figure 2-5:
The iPhoto
interface.

Source pane   Viewer

Photo controls   Mode control pane   Mode buttons   Magnifier slider

✔ **Photo Library:** The Photo Library contains all the photos that you have imported into iPhoto. You can select the Photo Library icon in the Source pane and see all your photos appear in the Viewer pane.

✔ **Last Import:** iPhoto keeps track of the last import you have performed. This organization feature just gives you a quick way to see the most recent photos you have imported. Click the Last Import icon in the Source pane to see your photos in Viewer pane.

✔ **Albums:** You can organize your photos into albums so that they are easier to find and work with. All albums you create appear in the Source pane. Select an album icon in the Source pane to see its contents in the Viewer pane. You find out all about creating and managing albums in Chapter 4.

✔ **Trash:** iPhoto contains its own Trash. If you want to remove a photo, just drag it to the Trash icon.

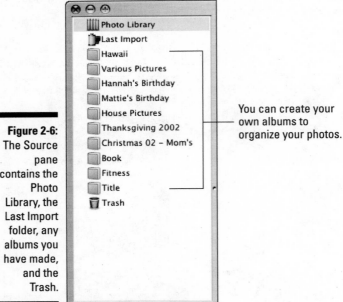

Figure 2-6: The Source pane contains the Photo Library, the Last Import folder, any albums you have made, and the Trash.

You can create your own albums to organize your photos.

Viewer pane

The Viewer pane shows you the collection of pictures you have selected from the Source pane. If you are editing a picture or want to work with it in any way, you simply double-click the picture in the Viewer pane. Notice the Magnifier slider bar just below the Viewer pane, shown in Figure 2-7. You can move the slider bar to the left to see thumbnails of the pictures, or move the slider bar to the right to its maximum magnification to make each picture fill the Viewer pane.

Figure 2-7:
Move the
slider bar
to change
the magnifi-
cation of the
pictures in
the Viewer
pane.

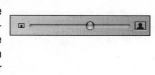

Photo controls

On the left side of the iPhoto interface, just below the Source pane, are a few photo controls. When you select the Photo Library, Last Import, or an album, you see the name of the album and the date it was created, along with number of photos and the total amount of disk space that is being used as well as the default music that is selected (in case you want to view the album as a slide show — see Chapter 11 to find out more). If a specific photo is selected in the Viewer pane, you see the name, date, the actual size of the photo (such as 4 x 6), and the file size of the photo (such as 100 KB), along with the default music selected for the photo.

Also on the left side, you see four button controls:

Button Control	*Name*	*What It Does*
➕	Create a New Album	Creates a new album, which then appears in the Source pane. You can also create a new album by choosing File⇨New Album.
▶	Play the Slide Show	iPhoto automatically creates slide shows from the pictures in the Photo Library, Last Import, and your albums. If you click this button, the interface changes to a full screen slide show with music. Check out Chapter 11 for more details.

(continued)

Button Control	Name	What It Does
![Show Information button]	Show Information about Selected Photos	If you select a photo in the Viewer pane, you can click this button to get the name, date, size, and bytes (amount of space that the photo takes up on the disk).
![Rotate button]	Rotate the Selected Photos	This option lets you select and rotate a photo or several photos at once.

Mode buttons

In the middle, lower portion of the iPhoto interface you see a collection of mode buttons. iPhoto is designed to help you manage your photos, and in doing so, it gives you four different modes that do different things: Import, Organize, Edit, and Book. By simply clicking the mode button you want, as shown in Figure 2-8, you can switch to a different mode. (The choices in the Mode Controls pane at the bottom of the interface vary, depending on which Mode button you click.) To find out what's available in each mode, see the "Meddling with Modes" section later in this chapter.

Controls here change...   ... depending on which button is clicked.

Figure 2-8:
Click a mode button to change modes.

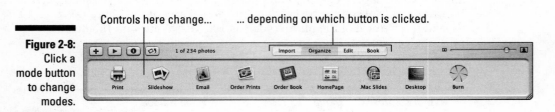

Mode Controls pane

Finally, at the bottom of the iPhoto interface resides a Mode Controls pane. When you click a mode button, the contents of the Mode Controls pane change, depending on the mode you select. When you select a mode, the mode pane gives you the controls you use when working in that mode. You can explore the mode options in the next section, "Meddling with Modes."

Meddling with Modes

iPhoto is designed to be a full-service, photo-management system. For the most part, everything you need is included in iPhoto. However, to keep the interface from becoming one big mess, iPhoto provides you with four different modes: Import, Organize, Edit, and Book. You can shift into the different modes at any time, depending on what you want to do at the moment. This feature keeps iPhoto powerful, but keeps the interface simple and uncluttered.

So, what can you actually do with each mode? The following sections give you a quick look at each mode's major features, and of course, you delve into all these modes in later chapters, as you explore using iPhoto in more detail.

Import mode

If you click the Import button, you see the Import controls in the Mode Controls pane, shown in Figure 2-9. These controls enable you to connect your digital camera and then import the pictures from the camera to the Photo Library quickly and easily. As you can see in Figure 2-9, an import from a camera is currently in progress.

Figure 2-9:
Import mode allows you to import from a digital camera.

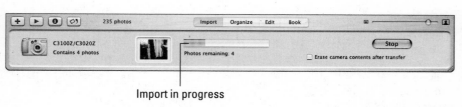

Import in progress

The Import pane gives you the option to import photos from your camera only. In reality, though, you can import photos from anywhere — another folder, a network share, a CD-ROM, or whatever. To import from another source besides a camera, you have to choose File⇨Import. See Chapter 3 for details on all types of importing.

Organize mode

If you click the Organize mode button, the Organize mode controls appear in the box at the bottom of iPhoto, as shown in Figure 2-10. Here are the features you can find in Organize mode:

- ✔ **Print:** Use this button to set up the print settings and to print your pictures.

- ✔ **Slideshow:** Use this button to view any slide shows you have created.

- ✔ **Email:** Use this button to e-mail photos to others.

- ✔ **Order Prints:** Use this button to access the Internet, where you can order prints of photos in your Photo Library.

- ✔ **Order Book:** Use this button to order from Apple an iPhoto book that you have created yourself.

- ✔ **HomePage:** Use this button to create a HomePage, which is a standard Web page at Mac.com.

- ✔ **.Mac Slides:** Click this button to share your photos on the Internet by creating a slide show page at Mac.com.

- ✔ **Desktop:** Use this button to make one of your photos the desktop picture.

- ✔ **Burn:** Burn photos directly to a CD or DVD using this feature.

Figure 2-10:
Organize
mode
allows you
to manage
your photos
in a number
of ways.

I explore these features in-depth throughout the rest of the book.

Edit mode

Edit mode allows you perform some basic editing functions on your photos. When you click the Edit button, the Edit controls appear in the bottom pane of the iPhoto interface, as you can see in Figure 2-11. Using the Edit mode, you can constrain photos so that they adhere to standard sizes, crop the photo, enhance photos, fix red-eye, retouch photos, change a photo to black and white, and adjust the brightness and contrast of a photo. You can also move through a list of photos in the Viewer using the Previous and Next buttons. You find out how to use these features in Chapter 6.

Figure 2-11:
Edit mode allows you to fix photos.

Book mode

Book mode enables you to assemble an iPhoto book. You can then use the Organize mode to upload your newly created book to Apple, so that the book can be printed, bound, and mailed to you (for a fee, of course). The iPhoto book is a hardcover book containing your photos, professionally printed and bound on glossy photo paper. You can even include your own captions.

When you click the Book mode button, the Book controls appear, as shown in Figure 2-12. Here's what they do:

- **Theme:** You can use the drop-down list to choose a preset theme for your book, such as Classic or Story Book. The Story Book theme, for example, allows you to create a story book with captions for your photos.

- **Check boxes:** Use the check boxes to apply titles, comments, and page numbers to your book.

- **Page Design:** You can use this drop-down list to manage the design of individual pages, including the number of photos you put on each page of the book.

✔ **Preview:** Click the Preview button to preview your book as you work on it.

✔ **Order Book:** After you have finalized and previewed your book, click here to order it.

Figure 2-12:
Use Book
mode to
create your
own book.

You can find more details about creating a book in Chapter 10.

Chapter 3

Importing Photos

After you've done the photography thing, you're ready to get your photos into iPhoto. You probably have numerous pictures you want to manage with iPhoto. The pictures may be in a number of locations, such as your digital camera, a storage folder, a CD-ROM, Zip disk, or even a network share. You may even have pictures stored on the Internet at a free online storage center. Your digital photos may be neatly organized, or they may be a jumbled mess of pictures and file types — after all, getting organized is why you want to use iPhoto in the first place. You can't do anything with iPhoto until you import some pictures, but never fear: The act of importing pictures to iPhoto is a rather simple process. This chapter covers just about every kind of import scenario you may run into, and I show you how to get around any aggravations or problems along the way.

Importing Photos from a Digital Camera

You are probably going to be importing photos from a digital camera directly to iPhoto. That's cool, and iPhoto is designed to make this process quick and easy. However, you may need to import photos from other locations as well. In fact, you may not even be using a digital camera, and that's fine too. If that's the case, see the section titled "Importing Photos from Other Locations," later in this chapter, to find out more. But if you are importing digital photos from a camera, read on.

Making the connection with your camera

Digital photography and digital cameras have come a long way in the past few years. Digital cameras do more than ever, and compatibility between digital cameras and the Mac is better than ever before. In fact, importing is so easy that the process is almost foolproof . . . well, almost.

Here's the deal: Your camera has to connect to your Mac, and your Mac has to detect the camera's presence in order for iPhoto to import your pictures. iPhoto isn't a magical application that resides in its own universe. It is a Mac application, and when you want to import photos from a digital camera, that camera must first be detected by your Mac.

Connecting with USB

Most digital cameras connect to computers by using a USB port, although some digital cameras can also connect to a Mac's FireWire port, assuming that the Mac is equipped with one. In fact, your digital camera probably came to you with its own USB cable. Your Mac can automatically detect the camera after you plug it in to the USB port and turn the camera on — most of the time.

Before going any further though, you may want to check out iPhoto's digital camera compatibility list at www.apple.com/iphoto/compatibility. The iPhoto Device Compatibility site, shown in Figure 3-1, lists the names of the camera manufacturers that produce cameras compatible with iPhoto. As you can see when you scroll through the iPhoto Device Compatibility page, a bunch of cameras from well-known manufacturers, such as Canon, Olympus, Sony, Nikon, Kodak, and so forth, appear on the list.

So, what should you do if your device isn't listed here? First of all, don't panic. The cameras listed here have been tested with iPhoto and are guaranteed to work, but this list isn't all-inclusive. Your camera may work just fine, even if it doesn't appear on the list. In fact, if your camera is a newer model that uses a USB port, the odds are good that it will work just fine.

However, do check your camera's instruction booklet to check Mac compatibility. You may need to install some software to get things working right, so refer to your camera's instruction booklet to find out more.

Connecting if your camera doesn't use USB

Most all cameras today use the USB port for picture transfer to a computer, whether you're using a Mac or not. USB is today's standard. However, a number of cameras don't use a USB port, but instead use some other method of transferring pictures to a computer. In this case, you may need to find a work-around so that your photos end up in iPhoto. Here are three common scenarios:

But . . . I don't have any extra USB ports!

You'll probably find two or three USB ports on the back of your Mac where you can plug in your keyboard, printer, or another USB device, such as a scanner, and you'll probably find two on your keyboard as well. If you already have several USB devices connected to your Mac, you may simply be running out of ports. One solution is to plug in and unplug stuff every time you need an extra port, but that's a real pain.

So, what to do? The answer is to get a USB hub. A USB hub plugs into one of your USB ports and then simply provides three or more additional ports on the hub. You can then begin plugging USB items in to the hub to extend your USB ports. A standard four-port USB hub should cost less than $50 at your local or online computer store, and these USB hubs can save you a lot of hassles.

However, I should mention one important issue. USB hubs are sold as *self-powered* or *bus-powered*. A self-powered hub has its own AC connection. You plug the hub into your Mac; then you plug the hub's power cord into a wall outlet. A bus-powered hub gets its power from the USB bus or from inside of the Mac. The hub simply plugs in to the Mac, and that's it. So, which one is best? For most devices, such as digital cameras, a bus-powered hub is fine. However, if you want to plug in a printer, scanner, external hard drive, or other power-draining device, you may need to get a self-powered hub; otherwise, those devices may not work at all when plugged into the hub. The moral of the story is to think carefully about what you will plug into the hub and then make a wise decision. When in doubt, get a self-powered hub to make sure that you don't have any power problems.

✔ **If your camera uses a serial port:** Some older cameras use a serial port for transfer instead of USB. Serial ports are commonly found on PCs, but they are as slow and as painful as a root canal. Your Mac probably doesn't have a serial port, so what can you do? You have your choice of two work-arounds. First, if the camera uses a removable memory card, see if you can buy a compatible memory card reader. You can take the memory card out of the camera and insert it into the reader, which then connects to your Mac via a USB port. See the "Importing using a memory card reader" section, later in this chapter, for more info. Second, you can always use a PC to transfer the pictures from the camera; then you can put the pictures on a disk or CD and take them to your Mac. A pain, yes, but you *can* do it this way. See the "Importing Photos from Other Locations" section, later in this chapter, for more info.

✔ **If your camera stores photos on a floppy disk:** Some digital cameras do not connect to a computer at all. Rather, they use a standard 3½-inch computer floppy disk to store the photos. When the disk is full, you simply eject the disk and pop it into the computer. Now, if your Mac didn't come with a floppy disk drive (which newer models do not), you have to buy a USB floppy disk reader so you can get the photos into your Mac. You can get a USB floppy disk reader at any computer store for around $50. (Check www.macwarehouse.com.)

Here's where I get on my soapbox. Okay, I'm not knocking these cameras (well, I guess I am), but a floppy disk can only hold a little over 1 megabyte (MB) of information, whereas standard memory cards in other cameras can hold 16MB, 32MB — even up to 128MB and more, depending on what you buy. For this reason, cameras that use a floppy disk don't give you very good resolution quality because the floppy disk doesn't have enough storage room to hold high-resolution picture files. If you are serious about your photography, consider using the $50 you would have spent on a USB floppy disk reader and apply that to a new camera. End of my soapbox speech.

✔ **If your camera stores pictures on a minidisk:** Some camera brands are now using minidisks to store pictures. These cameras should function like a USB camera because you can still connect the camera to the computer by using a USB port. Of course, just because you can connect the camera to your Mac with a USB port doesn't guarantee that you can directly import your pictures into iPhoto. If the camera works with the Mac, though, you can simply import the pictures to the Mac and then manually import them to iPhoto. I deal with this subject in more detail in the "Importing photos from folders, CDs, and other locations" section later in this chapter.

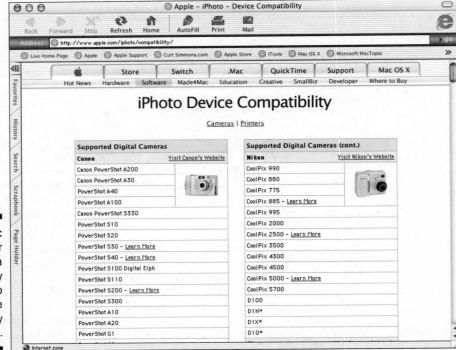

Figure 3-1:
Check for camera compatibility at the iPhoto Device Compatibility site.

Importing to iPhoto with your digital camera

After you know that your camera is compatible with iPhoto and will talk to your Mac, you are ready to transfer pictures to iPhoto. To transfer pictures to iPhoto from your digital camera, follow these steps:

1. **Connect your camera to a USB port on your Mac.**

   Your USB cable probably has an A to B connection. An *A to B connection* means that one end of the cable is small and square-shaped, and the other end is flatter and more rectangular. The small square end connects to your camera, and the rectangular end connects to your Mac. The connection on your camera may be hidden under a cover panel, so see your camera's instructions if you have problems finding its USB connection. Keep in mind that the USB cable you are using is not a standard USB cable that you can pick up at any old computer store — it is a specific cable for your camera. Don't lose it: Replacements are expensive!

2. **Turn on the camera.**

   Your camera may require a certain mode selection setting for camera-to-computer transfer, so see your camera's documentation for more information. If iPhoto is open when you plug in the camera, it detects the camera and is ready for transfer. If not, ImageCapture may come to life and ask you how you want to download your pictures. ImageCapture is a default program on the Mac used to transfer photos from a camera, If ImageCapture opens, just click File⇨Quit to exit image capture, and then click the iPhoto icon in the Dock to open iPhoto.

   If your Mac doesn't seem to detect your camera, leave your camera plugged in to the Mac; then turn the camera off and turn it back on. You probably had the camera on when you originally plugged it in. This action doesn't hurt anything, but the Mac may not detect the camera if it is on when you plug it into the USB port.

3. **To open iPhoto, click the iPhoto icon in the Dock or open Macintosh HD⇨Applications and double-click the iPhoto icon.**

4. **In iPhoto, click the Import button, shown in Figure 3-2, to switch to Import mode.**

   iPhoto switches to Import mode and you see the name of your camera listed in the Import pane.

Figure 3-2:
Click the
Import
button.

5. **(Optional) In the Import panel, as shown in Figure 3-3, select the Erase Camera Contents After Transfer check box.**

   This option erases all the pictures on your camera's memory card after the photos are transferred to iPhoto, saving you the hassle of doing it yourself on the camera. Of course, the process should be totally safe, but if you want to ensure that nothing happens to your photos, import them first, check to be sure that they transferred properly, and then erase them from the camera. This process ensures that you have the photos in a safe place before you erase them.

Figure 3-3:
Select the
Erase option
if you like.

6. **Click the Import button (refer to Figure 3-3).**

   The photos are imported. You can see a minipicture of each in the Import control box as the import takes place, as shown in Figure 3-4.

Figure 3-4:
An import in
progress.

Your photos are previewed as they are imported.

7. **Now that your photos are imported to iPhoto, minimize iPhoto by clicking the yellow minimize button in the left upper corner of iPhoto (it looks like a minus sign).**

   Depending on your camera, you may see a drive icon for your camera's memory card. It may say Unlabeled, as the one shown in the following figure does, or it may have some name that seems to make no sense at all. Some camera cards don't even show up on the desktop, so don't worry if you don't see it there.

8. **You can drag the drive icon to the Trash to eject the camera from the system; then turn off your camera and unplug it.**

    If you do not see a drive icon on the desktop for your camera's memory card, simply unplug the camera from the computer and click OK to the warning message that appears.

Two quick notes about the drive icon and ejecting the camera. First of all, if you simply want to get photos from your camera to your Mac without using iPhoto, you can simply open the drive icon, select the pictures, and then drag them to your desktop or another folder. You can also drag pictures back to the Drive icon to put them back on your camera. However, don't do these actions if you are using iPhoto at the same time, or you'll totally confuse iPhoto as it tries to import pictures. Keep in mind, however, that if you want to want to work with your pictures in iPhoto, you'll still need to import the photos into iPhoto.

Second, you don't have to go to the hassle of dragging the Drive icon to the Trash to eject the camera from the Mac — you can just unplug the camera. However, if you do, you see a warning message, as shown in Figure 3-5. Although the message sounds sinister, unplugging your camera doesn't actually hurt anything, so just click OK.

Figure 3-5:
This warning message looks troublesome, but don't worry about it.

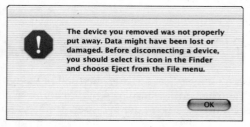

Changing the default ImageCapture preferences

By default, OS X opens ImageCapture when a camera is connected to the Mac. ImageCapture is a handy program you use to import photos to your Mac, but of course, if you use iPhoto, you don't need ImageCapture jumping to life. When you first opened iPhoto, you should have received a message asking if you want iPhoto to be your default image management software. If you clicked Yes, iPhoto jumps to life when you connect your camera. If you clicked No, ImageCapture opens, leaving you thinking that you are forever stuck in ImageCapture land. Not so.

In fact, you can easily fix this annoyance by following these steps:

1. **Open Macintosh HD⇨Applications⇨ImageCapture.**

2. **Click ImageCapture⇨Preferences.**

3. **In the Preferences dialog that appears, shown in Figure 3-6, select iPhoto from the When a Camera Is Connected, Open drop-down menu.**

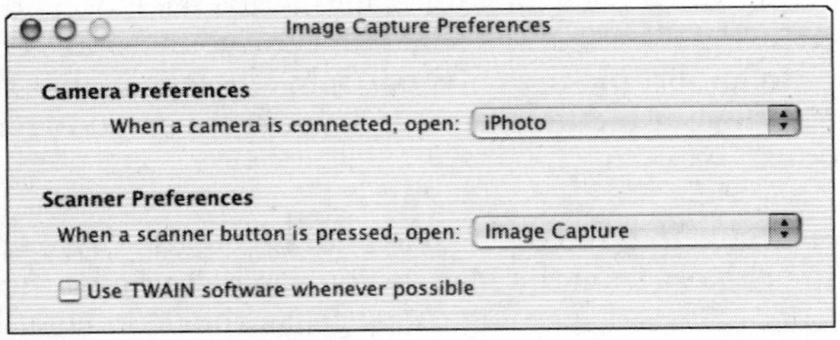

Figure 3-6: Choose iPhoto from the drop-down menu.

4. **Close the dialog and then quit ImageCapture by choosing File⇨Quit.**

The next time you connect your camera, iPhoto will come to life automatically and be ready to import.

Importing using a memory card reader

Many people prefer to use a memory card reader instead of using the camera for picture import. Why? The answer is simple — digital cameras love to suck up batteries, and using a memory card reader requires none. As an added benefit, the memory card reader usually works faster than importing directly from the camera. A memory card reader is a simple little device that connects to your Mac's USB port. You take the memory card out of your camera (follow the camera's instructions) and insert it into the memory card reader. iPhoto then comes to life, and you can import the images directly to iPhoto without any additional grief, just as you would if the camera were directly connected.

iPhoto is compatible with most major memory card readers from such manufacturers as Sony, SmartDisk, ImageMate, and a number of others. Most memory card readers cost $30 or less, so the cost of owning one isn't prohibitive. Before you run out and buy a memory card reader, do the following:

- ✔ **Check your camera's documentation to make sure that the card reader you buy will work with your camera's memory cards.** Many memory card readers can read more than one kind of card, but it is always better to be safe than sorry.

- ✔ **Check** `www.apple.com/iphoto/compatibility` **to make sure that the memory card reader is compatible with iPhoto.** When you find a match for both your camera's memory card and iPhoto, you're good to go.

After you have your memory card reader, the process is basically the same as importing pictures directly from your camera. Insert the card into the card reader, iPhoto comes to life, and you can then transfer your pictures using iPhoto's Import pane. That's all there is to it. As with most cameras, the memory card reader will probably mount on your desktop. You can eject it when you are done by dragging it to the Trash.

Importing Photos from Other Locations

You may be thinking, "Hey! I don't live in the USB world with a spiffy new camera — shouldn't I be able to use iPhoto too?" Sure you should, and you can. Or you may think, "Importing from my camera is great, but what about the other two hundred pictures I have stored on my Mac, Zip disks, CDs, and other places? Wouldn't it be great if I could use iPhoto to manage all those?" Yes, it would — and you can.

In fact, importing from a digital camera is only one way to get photos into iPhoto. iPhoto's Import feature doesn't make this readily apparent in the interface, but you can easily import picture files from other locations without too much trouble.

Before we get into the task of importing photos from other locations, you should be aware of two major issues you should keep in mind at all times.

First of all, iPhoto never *moves* photos — it only imports or copies them. This statement is true for digital cameras as well. When you import any photo into iPhoto, the file is copied to the iPhoto Library, which is simply the place on your computer where iPhoto stores all your pictures and the information about them. Your original file remains safely in its original location where you can leave it, move it elsewhere, delete it, or do whatever you want to with it. The point to remember here is that iPhoto only copies picture files — it never moves them.

The second thing to remember is that iPhoto can read most major picture file formats, but it can't read everything. A *picture file format* is simply a *kind* of picture file. Some file formats are common and can be read by many different programs; other formats are specific to certain kinds of photos. iPhoto can import the following kinds of picture file formats to its library:

- ✔ **JPEG:** JPEG is the most popular kind of picture format used today. Many images you see on the Internet are JPEG files, and many, many different programs (such as Web browsers, e-mail applications, photo imaging software, and yes, iPhoto) can use JPEGs. In fact, most digital cameras take JPEG pictures by default. JPEG, a universal file format, provides compression features that keep files smaller while retaining good photo quality. By the way, JPEG files may also be called JPG or JFIF, but they are all the same thing.

- ✔ **TIFF:** Another kind of universal file format is TIFF. Many different programs, including iPhoto, can use TIFF files. TIFF files are typically high-resolution image files and can be quite large in terms of megabytes (many of them are well over 1 MB) in size. Many people prefer to work with TIFFs because they can give you great print quality. Most cameras can also shoot pictures in the TIFF format.

- ✔ **GIF:** GIF picture files are most often used for graphics you see on the Internet, such as backgrounds, banners, buttons, and other graphics features that aren't expressly pictures. iPhoto can use GIF files with no problem.

- ✔ **PDF:** PDF files are primarily used by Adobe Acrobat Reader. Most of the user manuals and other documentation you may get on a CD are PDF files. iPhoto can display and store PDF files, but if the PDF file is a multi-page document, iPhoto only opens and stores the first page.

- ✔ **BMP:** The BMP, or bitmap, file format is used on Windows PCs and produces high-quality (and large file size) pictures. iPhoto can use BMP files, too.

- ✔ **PICT:** PICT files were originally used as the default picture file format in Mac operating systems before OS X. iPhoto can read PICT files.

- ✔ **FlashPix:** This is another Web picture file format that iPhoto can use, and like PNG, it is not as popular as JPEG and GIF.

- ✔ **SGI/Targa:** These picture file formats are used by certain high-end video systems. You are not likely to run across them, but iPhoto can use them.

- ✔ **MacPaint:** The very old MacPaint program stored photos in its own MacPaint file format. Although not really in use today, iPhoto can use this file format should you wish to import any old MacPaint files.

- ✔ **Photoshop:** Adobe Photoshop and Photoshop Elements are overwhelmingly popular photo imaging software products. The good news is you can directly import Photoshop files into iPhoto without having to resave them as another file format.

- ✔ **PNG:** This newer file format, designed for portable image files, can also be used by iPhoto.

iPhoto cannot read any other kinds of picture files besides those in the preceding list. For the most part, that's fine, considering that the major ones you'll likely import are JPEG and TIFF anyway. However, if you try to import a picture file that is not supported, you get a message telling you that the photo is unreadable, as shown in Figure 3-7.

If you really need to get an unreadable photo into iPhoto, you may be able to use a shareware plug-in to help you. See Chapter 14 for details.

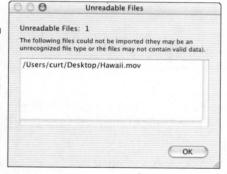

Figure 3-7: You'll see this message if you try to import an unreadable file format.

Unreadable Files

Unreadable Files: 1

The following files could not be imported (they may be an unrecognized file type or the files may not contain valid data).

/Users/curt/Desktop/Hawaii.mov

OK

Importing photos from a nonsupported camera

As I mentioned in the preceding section, your Mac may be able to read your digital camera files, but iPhoto may not. Although this problem doesn't happen too often, you may have a camera that came with Mac software. You installed the software, and you can see the camera's drive icon on the desktop. However, iPhoto acts like the camera is not there. What can you do?

In this case, you can simply import the photos into iPhoto by using the Import command, or you can just drag and drop them. To import a file or a collection of files, follow these steps:

1. **Open iPhoto and click File⇨Import.**

   The Import Photos dialog appears, as shown in Figure 3-8.

2. **Select the files you want to import in the right pane and click the Import button.**

   You can import several photos at the same time by ⌘-clicking them before clicking Import.

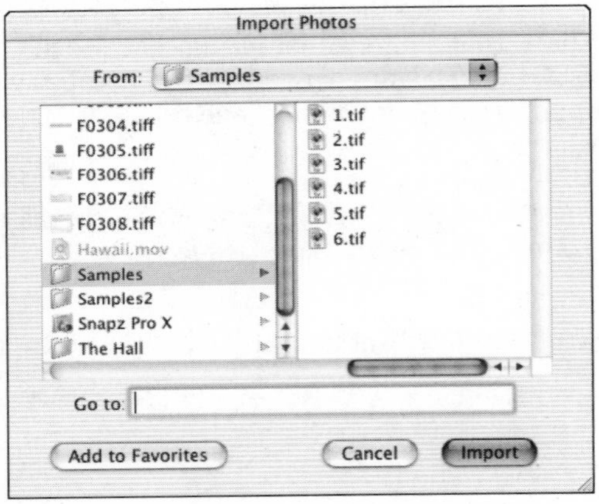

Figure 3-8:
Select the
pictures you
want to
import and
click the
Import
button.

That's one perfectly viable way to import, but here's an easier way: Just drag and drop the picture files you want to import from the camera's drive on the desktop. Follow these steps:

1. **Click the drive icon on your desktop to open it.**

   You see the pictures stored on the camera's memory card.

2. **Click a desired photo to select it (or select two or more of them by ⌘-clicking them).**

3. **Drag the photos to the iPhoto Viewer pane, as shown in Figure 3-9.**

   The photos are automatically imported into the iPhoto Library.

You can also drag and drop entire folders of pictures. iPhoto imports the pictures into the Photo Library and creates a new film roll for the folder of pictures. Or if you want the folder to function as an album, just drag it into the Source pane, and a new album is created from the folder. You can find out more about film rolls and albums in Chapter 4.

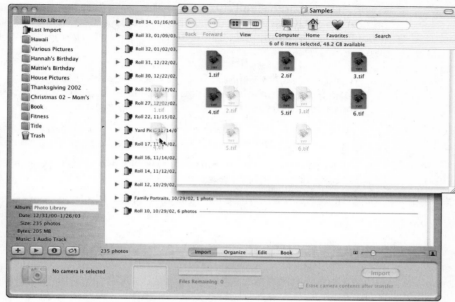

Figure 3-9:
You can simply drag and drop photos into the Viewer pane to auto-matically import them.

 By the way, what if you have a folder that contains pictures and other files, such as documents? No problem — you don't have to sort through every-thing. Just drag and drop the folder, and iPhoto will import only the picture files.

Importing photos from folders, CDs, and other locations

Just as you can manually import pictures from a nonsupported camera, you can do the same thing from practically any other location by using the File⇨Import command or just by dragging and dropping the pictures into iPhoto. This includes pictures stored in folders on your Mac, on a network volume, on a disk, CD, Zip disk, the Internet, or wherever. The process is exactly the same as explored in the preceding section. Just drag and drop to your heart's content.

Checking Out the Photos You Import

After you import pictures into iPhoto, you can then check out those pictures using the Viewer. All photos that you import into iPhoto are stored in the Photo Library. The *Photo Library* is simply a big storage area where iPhoto keeps all your photos. You can manage the library and create albums from pictures in the library, and I cover those details in Chapter 4. For now, though, you can simply use iPhoto to take a look at what you have imported. Just follow these steps:

1. **When you select the Last Import option in the Source pane, the pictures from the last import you performed appear in the Viewer, as shown in Figure 3-10.**

   If the pictures in the Viewer are too small to see clearly, keep in mind that you can adjust the size of the pictures by using the Magnifier slider bar.

2. **If you want to see everything in your Photo Library, just click Photo Library in the Source pane.**

   Every picture you have ever imported into iPhoto appears in the Viewer pane, as shown in Figure 3-11.

Click to view recently imported pictures.

Figure 3-10: Select Last Import in the Source pane to see your most recently imported pictures in the Viewer pane.

Adjust magnification here.

Click here to view all the pictures you have imported.

Flippy triangle

Figure 3-11:
Select
Photo
Library
to see
everything
you have
imported.

Now you may be wondering what all this business about *film rolls* is about — and rightly so. If you look in Figure 3-11, you see different film rolls. Beside each film roll, you see a *flippy triangle*. If you click the flippy triangle, the triangle flips downward and the pictures in the film roll appear before your eyes. To hide the pictures, click the flippy triangle again to make it point to the right.

Now, here's the deal. When you work with digital pictures, obviously you have no actual film. You don't use film, and you certainly have no film roll. So the film rolls you see here are just an organizational method that iPhoto uses to keep track of your various imports. You can see each roll has a name and the date that you imported it. Think of film rolls as folders that keep pictures organized so you can more easily find them, based on the date that you imported them into iPhoto.

However, what if you don't want to see film rolls? What if you want to scroll through your entire library picture by picture? No problem. Click the Organize mode button, and then click View⇨Film Rolls to clear the option. Now, you simply see all your pictures in the library. You can find out more about film rolls in Chapter 4.

If you have a bunch of pictures in the Photo Library, you can scroll them by using the scroll bar. However, what if scrolling takes too long? Option-click the portion of the vertical scroll bar where you want to move to jump to that location. You can also just grab and move the slider bar to the portion of the library you want to see.

As you may imagine, film rolls can be very helpful for finding the things that you want. The good news is that you can customize the film rolls so they make more sense to you, and you can find out all about that feature in Chapter 4.

Part II
Organizing with iPhoto

The 5th Wave   By Rich Tennant

"...and here's me with Cindy Crawford. And this is me with Madonna and Celine Dion..."

In this part . . .

In this part, you take a look at organizing with iPhoto. iPhoto is some of the best photo-management software around, and in Chapter 4, you see how to work with the Photo Library and albums. Then, in Chapter 5, you find out how to use titles and labels on your photos so that you can catalogue them more easily. You also find out how to use iPhoto's quick search feature so that you can find photos quickly.

Chapter 4

Managing Your Pictures in iPhoto

• •

• •

After you import photos into iPhoto, you need to think about how you want to organize them so that they don't get lost amid all the photos you already have (or will have). If you use iPhoto to manage only a small number of photos, you may not need to do anything at all. However, as you work with iPhoto, you're likely to begin accumulating a lot of photos. You may constantly import new photos, and you may decide to import a bunch of existing photos from a folder or CD into iPhoto.

Managing all these photos can become quite a challenge, but it doesn't need to be. In this chapter, I explain how you can organize photos in a logical way. You'll also see how to use albums, how to delete photos you no longer want, and even how to export photos out of iPhoto.

Using the iPhoto Library Folder

Every photo, without exception, goes to the Photo Library that you use with the iPhoto interface. The Photo Library is iPhoto's management system, and it holds every single photo that you import. What you may not realize is that the Photo Library is closely connected to another library, the iPhoto Library folder. The iPhoto Library folder keeps track of your photos and everything you do through the interface to make sure that your photos are neat and organized.

In iPhoto, you can scroll through every picture using the Photo Library. Just select Photo Library in the Source pane, and every picture in the library appears in the Viewer pane. Of course, if you have a lot of pictures, you need to do quite bit of scrolling to see them all, but the point is that your photos are all there, safe and sound. Within iPhoto, you work with pictures in the Photo Library. You can arrange them, delete them, and export them — all issues you explore later in this chapter.

You don't really do much with the iPhoto Library folder that hangs out in the background, but you do need to know a bit about the folder so that you can back it up, divide your pictures into separate libraries (if one library becomes too big), create individual libraries for each user on your computer, or share a library among users.

You may want to set these folder options before you start importing pictures, but you don't have to. If you are just getting started with iPhoto, consider skipping to the "Working with Albums" section in this chapter.

Accessing your iPhoto Library folder

Your personal iPhoto Library folder is stored in your Pictures folder under your user account. Keep in mind that OS X is a multiuser operating system. This feature allows different users to start OS X and log on to the system as a unique user, keeping his settings and files separate from others who may log on to the system. With this design, several different people can log on and use iPhoto, and each user's photos and settings are kept separate.

Your personal iPhoto Library folder is stored in your Pictures folder under your user account. Open Macintosh HD⇨Users⇨*Your user account short name*⇨ Pictures⇨iPhoto Library. As you can see in Figure 4-1, the iPhoto Library folder isn't anything particularly exciting. It consists of folders and library files that aren't intended for you to read. Keep in mind that the iPhoto Library folder is a database of pictures that iPhoto uses to keep track of your picture files — not a place for you to manage pictures.

Do not change the names of folders or move items around in the iPhoto Library folder. Doing so creates havoc in the iPhoto Library folder and may prevent iPhoto from displaying some or possibly even all your pictures. In fact, if you mess with the contents of the iPhoto Library folder too much, iPhoto can even crash. You should manage pictures only through the iPhoto interface.

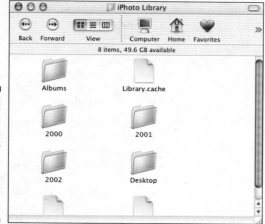

Figure 4-1:
iPhoto uses
the iPhoto
Library
folder to
keep track
of your
picture files.

Backing up the iPhoto Library folder

As with any data, photo files can get corrupted or accidentally deleted from iPhoto. For this reason, you should periodically back up the iPhoto Library folder. Of course, you may have copies of all your photos on CDs or whatever source you imported your files from originally because iPhoto only copies photos when it imports them (it doesn't move them). Still, if something happened to your iPhoto Library folder and you hadn't backed it up, you would have to completely start over with iPhoto, importing all the original photos again (whew!).

The quick moral to this story is to treat your photos like any other data on the Mac that you can't live without, and back up the iPhoto Library folder — especially if you have a lot of photos in iPhoto. Should the Mac ever crash and you have to reinstall, you can simply copy the backed-up library to your Pictures folder and keep working with iPhoto like nothing ever happened.

How often should you back up the iPhoto Library folder? That all depends on how often you use iPhoto. If you are editing a lot of pictures and importing pictures regularly, you may consider backing up once a week. If you casually use iPhoto, once a month is probably fine. The bottom line is that you can't restore what you haven't backed up. If you import a lot of photos or make a lot of changes, a backup is usually in order.

What are all those folders?

In case you're the curious kind, you may wonder how iPhoto manages and keeps track of your pictures. iPhoto does this through a few database files found in the iPhoto Library folder, such as `Library.cache`, `Dir.data`, and `Library.data`, but it also uses a number of folders to store information:

✔ **Albums:** The Albums folder holds information about the albums you have created (see the "Working with Albums" section in this chapter). Albums are simply groups of photos. If you haven't created any albums, all you see is picture files. After you start creating albums, the files that iPhoto uses to keep track of what albums you have and what pictures are in what album are stored in this folder.

✔ **Picture:** You'll see several Picture folders, such as 2000, 2001, 2002, and so forth. Inside the Picture folders, you can find additional folders that are organized by date. For example, in your 2002 folder, you may see a 10 folder (October). Inside the 10 folder, you may see any number of other dated folders, such as 19, which refers to the day of the month on which the file was imported.

Inside those folders, you can find additional folders and pictures. iPhoto manages your pictures by date of import, such as October 19, 2002, in this example.

✔ **Data:** The Data folders don't actually hold picture data. They contain iPhoto files that keep track of data on pictures, such as keywords used, titles, and so forth. (For more on keywords, see Chapter 5.) Information about the size of the image, when the photo was taken, the camera used, and the exposure settings are also kept in this folder.

✔ **Originals:** The Originals folders contain original images that you imported. When you edit a picture, a copy is edited and the original picture is stuck here. This feature allows you to "revert to original" if you don't like the editing work you have done. See Chapter 6 to find out more about editing images in iPhoto. By the way, you'll only see an Originals folder if you have actually edited some images in iPhoto.

✔ **Thumbs:** The Thumbs folders contain the thumbnail images of your pictures that are used to display pictures to you in the Viewer pane.

The cool thing is that iPhoto allows you to directly burn your iPhoto Library to a CD or DVD for safe storage. Just follow these steps:

1. **Insert a blank, writeable CD or DVD into your CD/DVD drive.**

   If a dialog appears asking what you want to do with the blank CD/DVD, just choose the Open Finder drop-down menu option, give the disc a name in the Name dialog, and click OK.

2. **In iPhoto, select the Photo Library in the Source pane.**

3. **Click the Organize button to switch to Organize mode, and then click the Burn icon that appears in the Organize pane.**

   The Burn icon opens and begins to glow.

4. **Click the Burn icon again.**

5. **In the Burn Disk dialog that appears, click the Burn button.**

   iPhoto will now burn the Library onto the disc for safekeeping. This
   process may take several minutes, depending on the number of photos
   that need to be burned.

If your iPhoto Library folder is brimming with photos, albums, and the like,
you may have trouble fitting it onto a CD or DVD. In this case, you can copy
the library to another hard disk, or if you don't have another hard disk, your
best bet is to copy the individual folders to different CDs. For example, you
can copy the Albums folder and a Picture folder or two to one CD and the
rest of the folders to another. (See the sidebar, "What are all those folders?"
for details about the folders in your iPhoto Library folder.) If your iPhoto
Library folder is extremely large, you may need several CDs to copy everything. The important point is that you copy everything in the iPhoto Library
folder (all files and subfolders).

In the event that you do have a catastrophic failure and have to reinstall
OS X, all you have to do is drag the iPhoto Library folder back to your Pictures
folder. Then open iPhoto. iPhoto sees the existing library, and you can continue with business as usual.

 Of course, you don't have to use iPhoto's burn feature to burn photos to a
CD. You can also open your Pictures folder, and then burn the iPhoto Library
folder to a disc manually. The choice is yours, but you'll probably find that
using iPhoto's burn feature is easier.

Using multiple Library folders

Say you're a really active photographer. You keep storing more and more pictures in iPhoto. According to Apple Computer, you can store as many pictures as you want in iPhoto — thousands upon thousands of them even,
assuming you have the hard disk space to hold that many pictures. However,
the burden of too many pictures eventually starts to tax your system. Your
RAM (random access memory) can't keep up, and iPhoto starts to run so
slowly that you feel like you've settled to the bottom of the ocean. If this is
happening to you, you can use multiple iPhoto Library folders so that iPhoto
doesn't have to mess with all your photo data at once. Of course, doing this
may make life more difficult because you can only work with one Library in
iPhoto at one time. This means you'll be limited when creating albums of different photos. If your Mac seems to run slowly when you use iPhoto in general, you probably need more RAM — not more iPhoto libraries.

Creating multiple library folders

Adding a new library folder is actually pretty simple: You just drag the existing iPhoto Library folder out of your Pictures folder and store it somewhere else. In fact, you can even leave the iPhoto Library folder in your Pictures folder; you just have to rename it something else so that iPhoto thinks the Library folder is gone. When you restart iPhoto, it checks to see if a library folder is in the Pictures folder. Because iPhoto thinks the library folder is gone, it creates a new library, and you can move on your way.

When you want to return to the old library folder, you can do the same thing in reverse. Close iPhoto, rename the existing library folder something else, and then rename the old library folder iPhoto Library (if you moved the library folder, drag it back to the Pictures folder). When you reopen iPhoto, it sees the library folder and starts using it again.

Switching between libraries with iPhoto Library Manager

If switching between libraries manually seems aggravating and a little scary, well, it is. However, there is an easier way to switch between libraries. Brian Webster, a Mac enthusiast, wrote a cool little program called iPhoto Library Manager. You can get this free program by downloading it from Brian's Web site at homepage.mac.com/bwebster. Click Mac Stuff⇨Software⇨iPhoto Library Manager. Read the information about it and download the software. To install the iPhoto Library Manager, follow these steps:

1. **Double-click the** iPhotoLibraryManager.dmg **file on your desktop.**

   The file expands, and a drive icon appears on your desktop.

2. **Double-click the iPhoto Library Manager drive on your desktop.**

   Inside, you see a ReadMe file and the iPhotoLibraryManager icon.

3. **Drag the iPhotoLibraryManager icon to your Applications folder, found inside your Macintosh HD.**

   Now, you have the software installed, and you can open it by double-clicking the iPhoto Library Manager in your Applications folder. You get a single, easy-to-use interface, shown in Figure 4-2.

The program allows you to easily select and switch between libraries. Note, however, that the New Library option doesn't create a new library — it allows you select one that already exists (only iPhoto can create libraries). See the information earlier in this section about creating a new library. After you have multiple libraries, you can then use this handy feature to simply switch between them.

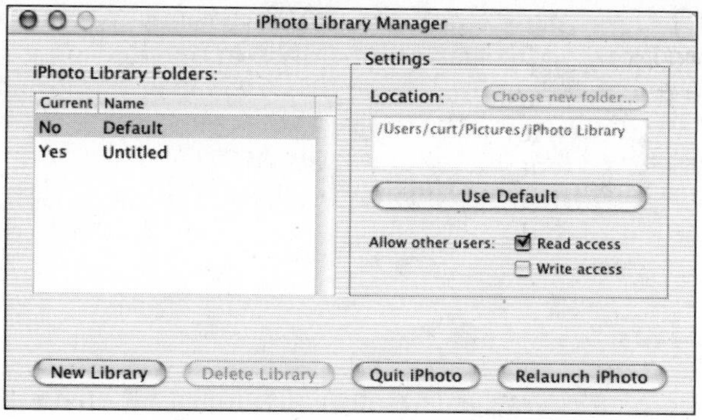

Figure 4-2:
iPhoto
Library
Manager.

Sharing a Library folder among multiple users

Each user on the Mac gets his or her own iPhoto Library folder, which means that multiple people can use the same computer and each one get his or her own Library folder.

However, if you want all users on the Mac to use the same iPhoto Library folder, you can set this up in one of two ways: by using OS X's Shared folder or using Brian Webster's iPhoto Library Manager.

You just have to make the iPhoto Library folder accessible from the Shared folder. (All users have access to the Shared folder.) Here's how:

1. **Log on with an administrator account and then open Macintosh HD⇨ Users⇨*Your user name*⇨Pictures.**

2. **Drag the iPhoto Library folder to the desktop.**

3. **Navigate to Macintosh HD⇨Users⇨Shared.**

4. **Drag the iPhoto Library folder to the Shared folder.**

5. **In the Shared folder, Control-click the iPhoto Library folder and click Make Alias.**

6. **Drag the iPhoto Library alias to *Your user account*⇨Pictures folder.**

7. **Repeat Steps 5 and 6 for all other users.**

   Now, each user can access the same library. When a user opens iPhoto, it checks the user's Pictures file for the library. The alias redirects iPhoto to the Shared folder.

If all that sounds aggravating, you can go the easy route, using Brian Webster's iPhoto Library Manager, as described in the preceding section, "Switching between libraries with iPhoto Library Manager." Using this handy program, you can simply select the desired library and select the Allow Other Users check boxes for Read Access and Write Access. This effectively does the same thing as the preceding steps, without all the headaches.

Managing Film Rolls

A film roll in iPhoto, of course, isn't really a film roll at all: Film rolls don't exist in digital photography. In reality, a roll is a group of photos that you imported all at once (see Chapter 3 for more on importing). The film roll is labeled with a number and the import date, and when you view the Photo Library in Organize mode or view an album using film rolls, you see the rolls listed, as shown in Figure 4-3. To see the contents of the roll, just click the triangle next to the roll.

Figure 4-3: Film rolls are used to organize photos by import date.

Click to view contents of a film roll.

Film rolls only apply to the Photo Library. They are not used in albums.

For the most part, film rolls are pretty static entities. They exist for organizational purposes so that you can find pictures more quickly. You do have a few options for how you view your rolls:

✓ **Using the roll number and date:** Rolls are organized by roll number and date of the import. Rolls group photos by import so that you can see those photos together. You can't move a photo from one film roll to another.

If you don't see film rolls when you are in Organize mode, click View⇨Film Rolls. If you clear the Film Rolls option, you see that photos are simply listed by roll number and picture number, which can be more confusing than helpful, as shown in Figure 4-4.

Figure 4-4: Clear the Film Rolls option to see pictures listed by roll number and picture number.

✔ **Using your own names:** If the film roll numbers don't work for you, you can change them to any name that you want. Just select the film roll icon in the Viewer pane. Then type a new title and date, if desired, in the Title and Date Info boxes, shown in Figure 4-5. If you don't see the Info boxes, click the Show Information about Selected Photos button. See Chapter 5 to learn more about working with titles, dates, and comments.

✔ **Organizing by date:** If you don't want to use film rolls at all, you can arrange photos by date instead. In Organize mode, choose View➪Arrange Photos➪By Date. This action arranges all the photos in the Photo Library by the date they were imported. This view can be helpful if you want to see all your photos in the Photo library arranged over the course of your imports, rather than in film rolls. Again, you can change this view back to Film Rolls by simply clicking View➪Film Rolls.

You can also export entire film rolls so that you can use the pictures in another way. For example, you can export a film roll so that the photos can be shared over a network, or if you need to use the photos in another application. See the "Exporting Photos" section later in this chapter for details.

Figure 4-5:
Type a new name and date in the Info boxes.

Title and Date info boxes

Working with Albums

An album is simply a way to organize pictures. When you create an album, you drag photos from the Photo Library to your album. You can then click through albums to use and edit pictures instead of having to wade around through all the photos in Photo Library. An album can contain photos from any location in your library. In other words, the idea of film rolls and import dates doesn't mean anything in an album. Just as you can assemble all kinds of photos taken at different times in a paper album, you can do the same thing in an electronic photo album. In short, use albums to bring photos from different film rolls together. You can have as many photos in an album as you like and you can create as many albums as you like.

An important point to remember is that iPhoto doesn't move or copy anything out of the Photo Library. Rather, it creates links to your photos when you drag them from the Photo Library to the album. If you don't believe me, just create an album, put some photos in it, and then check your Photo Library. The photos you put in the album are still there. You can have the same photo in more than one album, and deleting an album doesn't actually delete any photos from your photo library — it just deletes the way you had them organized.

An album is a way to organize pictures so they are easier to find and work with. You can create albums using any names you want. You may create albums to hold vacation pictures, Christmas or birthday pictures, or pictures that reflect some other theme. The choice is entirely up to you. Think of the album feature as file folders in a filing cabinet where copies of pictures can be organized and kept (while the originals safely remain in the Photo Library).

If it helps clarify the concept in your mind, try this analogy: Think of the Photo Library as the place that holds "negatives." The "prints" are in the album, but the "negatives" remain in the Photo Library where you can use them over and over again. Of course, with digital photography, negatives don't exist, but the analogy may help you keep things straight.

Any albums that you have created appear in the Source pane of iPhoto, as shown in Figure 4-6. They appear under the Photo Library and Last Import film roll. (If you haven't created any albums yet, of course, you won't see any albums here.)

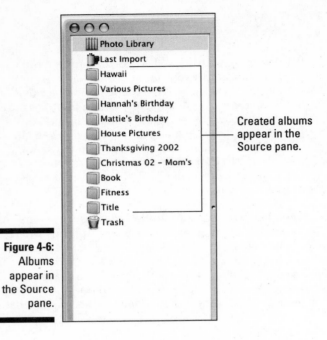

Created albums
appear in the
Source pane.

Creating an album

 Creating an album is really easy. All you have to do to create a new album is choose File⇨New Album, press ⌘-N, or click the Create a New Album button in iPhoto.

No matter how you get there, a little dialog appears asking for a name of the new album. Enter the name you want and click OK. The new album appears in the Source pane.

If at any time you want to rename an album, just double-click its title and type a new name. In the next section, I show you how to begin adding pictures to an album.

Adding pictures to an album

After the album is created, it is simply an empty container because no pictures are in the album. To add pictures to the album, all you have to do is select the Photo Library in the Source pane, locate in the Viewer the picture that you want to put in the album, and drag the picture to the album, as shown in Figure 4-7.

TIP

As you are dragging a photo, notice that a number appears on it. This reflects how many photos you are adding to the album. (In Figure 4-7, you see the number 1, which indicates that I am adding one photo to the album.)

Adding a photo to an album

Figure 4-7:
Click and
drag a photo
to add it to
an album.

As you add pictures to an album, keep the following points in mind:

TIP

✔ You can only put a picture in an album one time. In other words, an album can't hold the same picture over and over. If you try to drag a picture to an album twice, the picture jumps back to the Viewer pane. To find out how to get around this fact, see the sidebar, "But . . . I need two of the same picture in an album."

✔ You can drag entire film rolls to an album.

✔ You can use ⌘-click to select multiple photos and then drag them to an album all at once. Also, you can click on a photo and then shift-click on another photo to select those two photos and all the photos in between them.

✔ To copy a photo to another album, just drag the photo from one album to the other. This creates a copy of the photo in the second album.

✔ You can move a photo from one album to the next. Select the photo and choose Edit➪Cut. Then, click the destination album's icon and choose Edit➪Paste.

✔ You can't store an album within an album.

✔ You can delete a photo from an album by first selecting the album in the Source pane, and then selecting the photo in the Viewer pane and dragging the photo to the Trash in the Source pane. When you delete a photo from an album, the photo is not deleted from the Photo Library itself.

Notice that when you drag a picture from the Photo Library to the album, the picture remains in the Photo Library. Remember that iPhoto maintains internal *links* to keep track of which photos belong in which albums, but it doesn't actually *move* or *copy* pictures out of the Photo Library.

After you've added pictures to an album, just select the album in the Source pane to see the pictures in the Viewer. Note that the Photo Library doesn't let you rearrange pictures, but an album does. Just drag them around in the Viewer pane to rearrange them, as shown in Figure 4-8. This is very useful when creating an iPhoto book, which you can find out more about in Chapter 10.

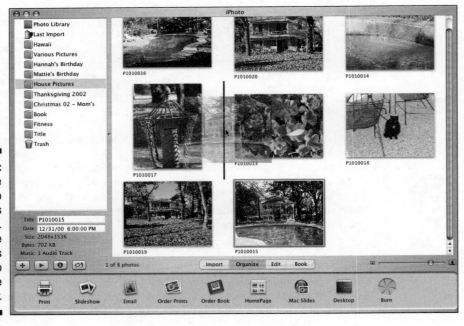

Figure 4-8:
Select the album to view its contents. Drag the pictures around to change the order.

But . . . I need two of the same picture in an album

iPhoto doesn't let you drag the same picture into an album twice. This is because iPhoto is really maintaining links to the real pictures in the Photo Library, and it doesn't allow you to create the same link twice. However, if you need the same picture to appear in an album for some purpose (such as the beginning and ending of a slide show, a book, or for some other reason), here's what you need to do. First, duplicate the photo in the Photo Library by selecting the photo and choosing File➪Duplicate. A duplicate of the photo now appears in the Photo Library with the word "copy" attached to its file name. Now, you can move the original photo and the copy into the album. Because the word "copy" is now

included in the file name, the photos no longer have the same name, and iPhoto does not realize that they are duplicates.

However, if you want to save a little disk space, open an album, select the photo you want to copy, and click File➪Duplicate. This makes an additional copy of the photo in the album only instead of the actual Photo Library. In tech-talk, this just creates an *alias* to the single original file in the Photo Library, instead of actually creating a duplicate of the photo. If you do this often enough, you'll save disk space because you are not really creating copies of photos, but rather creating aliases.

Duplicating and deleting an album

Say you have created an album of a favorite vacation trip. You have even used the album to create a slide show (see Chapter 11). Maybe you want use the album to create a book as well (see Chapter 10). But, for the book, you need to reorganize the photos and make some changes.

Rather than changing your original album or creating a brand new one, you can just duplicate the original album. This basically lets you have two albums that have different names but the same content. You can then edit them as you like.

To duplicate an album, just select it in the Source pane and then choose File➪Duplicate. A new album appears in the Source pane, titled Album-1. (If you already have an Album-1, it will be named Album-2, and so forth.) If you select this new album, you'll see the same pictures in the Viewer pane. Just double-click the album's name to select it, and then type in whatever name you want (but two albums can't have the same name).

Finally, you may eventually want to delete an album. Perhaps you are done with the pictures, or maybe you've reorganized your album structure. Regardless, all you have to do is drag the album to the Trash icon in the Source pane. Keep in mind, however, that only the album is deleted — not the original pictures, which are kept safe in the Photo Library.

Deleting Photos

Not all photos are good photos, and after you import photos from your camera, you may decide that you want to get rid of some of them. That's no crime, and iPhoto gives you a quick Trash option. Keep in mind that photos are deleted from iPhoto only through the Photo Library. You can't delete a photo from the library by deleting its thumbnail found in an album because an album is only a reference to the photo — not the real photo itself.

To truly delete a photo, follow these steps:

1. **Select Photo Library in the Source pane.**

2. **Locate the photo you want to delete and then drag the photo the Trash in the Source Pane.**

3. **When you are ready to permanently delete the items in the Trash, select the Trash icon in the Source pane and click File⇨Empty Trash.**

   An alert message appears asking if you are sure.

4. **Click OK.**

   After you click OK, the photo is deleted permanently. Of course, you can always reimport it into iPhoto at a later time if you still have the original photo stored somewhere else.

Exporting Photos

iPhoto holds your photos for as long as you want. You can print them, e-mail them to friends, create Web pages, and utilize a variety of other features that you can explore throughout this book.

However, from time to time, you need to get a photo out of iPhoto, perhaps to use in some other way or with some application. That's why iPhoto gives you an export feature. With this feature, you can export a copy of the file to your desktop or some other folder and even choose the file format that you want for the export.

When you export a photo, keep in mind that any titles, keywords, and comments you may have added do not go with the photo when it is exported. You can, however, choose to use the title for exporting instead of the name. (See Chapter 5 for more about these features.) Any edits you have made to the photo do go with the exported file.

You can export several photos at the same time by simply selecting them (⌘-click them), and then following the export options mentioned in the following list.

Here are the two basic ways to export a photo:

- **Drag the photo from an album or the Photo Library to your desktop.** This copies the file and retains its current file format (JPEG, TIFF, and so on). Keep in mind that the export process only copies the file; it does not remove it from your albums or Photo Library.

- **Select a photo and choose File⇨Export, or just press ⌘-E.** This opens the Export Photos dialog, shown in Figure 4-9. When you export this way, you can select the file format by choosing the Format drop-down menu and selecting Original, JPEG, TIFF, or PNG. You can also choose whether to use the file name or the title for the export. Also, you can export the full image or scale it to a certain size, using the provided radio buttons, which is a really handy feature when you need to use the figure at a certain scale.

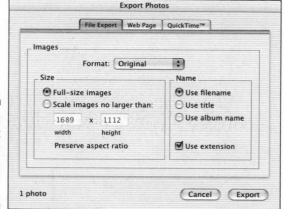

Figure 4-9:
The Export Photos dialog gives you several options.

You may have noticed the Web Page and QuickTime tabs of the Export Images dialog shown in Figure 4-9. These tabs are for exporting photos in a Web page format or as a QuickTime movie, and we'll explore these options in Chapters 9 and 11 respectively.

Note that you can also export entire film rolls and albums at once. Just drag them to the desktop or use the File⇨Export command. This feature simply exports all the actual pictures in the film roll or the album — not the film roll or album itself because those features are specific to iPhoto.

Chapter 5

Titles, Labels, Searches, and More

. . . .

In This Chapter

▶ Finding info about your photos

▶ Adding titles and comments

▶ Working with keywords

▶ Searching iPhoto

▶ Managing view appearance

. . . .

When you import photos from your digital camera, they end up in iPhoto with some ridiculous name, probably something like DS1054785x. Your digital camera has its own way of naming files on the camera media. Some cameras enable you to customize the naming feature, some don't; but no matter what, they often end up in iPhoto with some name that isn't very meaningful.

Relax. iPhoto lets you customize all the names of your photos and customize the information about them; you can even use some handy keywords to keep track of your photos. You may ask yourself, "Why should I care?" The answer is simple — for organization purposes and to help you find your photos.

Face the facts: The more photos you import into iPhoto, the more difficult specific photos are to locate. If you are a really busy shutterbug, you may end up with a few thousand pictures in the Photo Library. Without good names and keywords that can help you organize and find the photos you need, you're going to do a lot of scrolling to try and find them.

In this chapter, I show you the cool organizational techniques and tricks that iPhoto gives you, as well as information about a few photo-management-related issues.

Finding Info About Your Photos

I'll tell you a little secret — iPhoto knows more about your pictures than you think that it does. For example, with photos that you import from a digital camera, iPhoto typically knows the size, the original date, the camera type, the shutter speed, the aperture, the focal length, the light source, and so on. How is iPhoto that clever? Well, it's really not. iPhoto is getting this information from the picture itself. Most digital cameras record information about each picture right onto the picture file itself. This information is saved in a standard format called the Exchangeable Image File (EXIF) format. When iPhoto imports the photo from the digital camera, it reads the EXIF information and plugs that data into the Show Info window.

Of course, if you import a photo from another location, such as one that has been scanned and saved as a file, little or none of the imported photo's EXIF information will be available because the file didn't directly come from a digital camera.

Now, if you look at the iPhoto interface, you don't readily see this EXIF information in front of you, but it is hiding directly below the surface, just ready for you to take a look.

To get the info, just follow these steps:

1. **Select Photo Library in the Source pane and then locate the desired photo.**

2. **Select the photo by clicking it in the Viewer.**

3. **Then click File⇨Show Photo Info, or just press ⌘-I on your keyboard.**

   The Photo Info dialog (refer to Figure 5-1) appears. The Photo tab gives you information about the image (width, height, original date, and digitized date), the file (name, size, modified date, and imported date), and the camera (maker, model, and software).

   On the Exposure tab, you can find information about these categories: Shutter, Aperture, Max Aperture, Exposure Bias, Exposure, Exposure Index, Focal Length, Distance, Sensing, Light Source, Flash, Metering, Brightness, and ISO Speed.

Notice, in Figure 5-1, that some of the information is not provided. Again, iPhoto simply reads the EXIF data from the photo and plugs the values into the fields on this window. If the photo doesn't provide EXIF data for all of the values, you see the double dash to note that the data is missing.

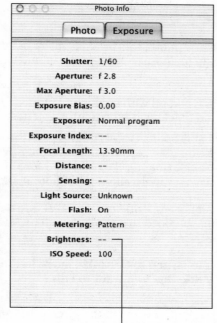

Figure 5-1:
The Photo
Info window
provides
EXIF data
from your
picture.

The double dash indicates that your camera
did not provide this information to iPhoto.

Of course, you can't do anything with this data directly — after all, it's just
provided for your information. However, if you can't remember how you shot
a particular picture or you want to know its size, modification date, and the
like, this is the place to snoop around.

Adding Titles and Comments

As I mentioned in the introduction to this chapter, your digital camera probably gives your pictures some arbitrary names that only make sense to the
camera — not to you. That's fine, because you can easily change the *title* of a
photo, which you can also think of as the photo's *name*. You can also change
the date and add comments to your photos.

Changing the title

If you don't care about the title of a photo, this practice may not seem that useful to you, but before you skip to another page, wait a minute! Keep in mind that titles

- ✓ **Make searches easier:** If you end up with a bunch of photos in iPhoto, you can search for titles and quickly find the photos you need.

- ✓ **Make creating Web pages and books easier:** iPhoto uses the titles you give to your pictures when you post pictures in a Web page or when you are creating an iPhoto book. See Chapter 9 to find out more about Web pages and Chapter 10 to discover more about the iPhoto book.

The good news is that you can change the title of a photo at any time without any grief, so this isn't something you need to spend a bunch of time doing. It's quick and easy, and here's how:

1. **Click the Organize button to switch to Organize mode in iPhoto, and then select a photo with a title that you want to edit.**

   In the area just below the Source pane, you see Title, Date, Size, Bytes, and Comments areas. If you don't see any of these, click the Show Information about Selected Photos button.

2. **Click inside the Title area, as shown in Figure 5-2, and type the desired title.**

Dealing with the details . . .

Before you get carried away with new titles for your photos, think carefully first. Remember that titles are a great way to keep photos organized and a great way to find photos that you want. For this reason, try to be as specific as possible, but use words that will most likely help you find the photo you want. For example, my wife and I were married in Hawaii. Naturally, we have a bunch of pictures from our wedding and honeymoon, and I keep them stored in an iPhoto album. I could simply title each photo *Hawaii,* but when I search for *Hawaii,* guess what? I get all the pictures! Instead, I've used specific titles, such as *wedding, beach, ocean,* and so forth. When I'm searching for a particular picture, these specific titles help me find what I want more quickly. Also, keep in mind that titles can contain more than one word. For example, I can title some photos *wedding ceremony* and some photos *wedding reception.* These titles are more specific and help me search for the photos I want more quickly.

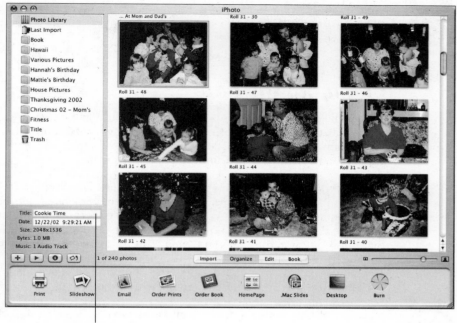

Figure 5-2:
Type a new
title in the
Title field.

Type a new title here.

Aside from simply being able to change the title of a photo in the Title area, iPhoto also has a few other tricks up its sleeve.

You can give several photos the same title from a list of preset options (you cannot type in a customized title for several photos at once, unfortunately). Follow these steps:

1. **Locate your photos in the Viewer pane.**

2. **Hold down the ⌘ key and select all the photos that you want to give the same title.**

3. **Click Edit⇨Set Title To, and in the submenu that appears, choose Empty, Roll Info, Filename, or Date/Time.**

   The suboptions are to use Empty titles (no title at all), Roll Info (which gives each photo a title made up of the roll name and an image number within the roll), Filename (which is the default already), and Date/Time (which is the date and time the photo was taken).

Unfortunately, you can't select multiple photos and type a new title for them all in the Title field. The Title and Date areas are grayed out when multiple photos are selected.

Changing the date

Just below the title of each photo, you see a date. That date is the date the photo was taken. (If the photo is a scanned image instead of coming from a digital camera, the date the file was created is used instead.) The Date appears in the Date box just under the Source pane.

Say that you saved your money, bought several extra memory cards, and took off to Europe for a month. When you return, you have hundreds of pictures to import into iPhoto. As you import those pictures, iPhoto stores them all by the date the photos were taken. However, if your camera doesn't put that information in the EXIF data, then iPhoto will use the import date.

To change the date of a photo, select the photo in the Viewer pane, and then click inside of the Date field and enter the new date.

As you probably noticed, the date and time are displayed by default in a certain format, but you can change this default format if you want.

1. **Just click Edit⇨Set Title To⇨Date/Time.**

   A Set Title To Date/Time dialog appears, as shown in Figure 5-3.

2. **Just use the check boxes and radio buttons to select the date/time format that you want.**

   An example of the date and time that you currently have selected appears at the preview area at the bottom of the dialog.

3. **When you are satisfied, click OK.**

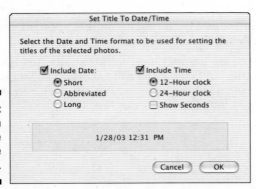

Figure 5-3:
You can change the date/time format here.

Adding comments

Along with the Title and Date boxes, you have a Comments field just beneath the Source pane as well. (If you don't see it, click the Show Information about Selected Photos button.) The Comments field provides a place for you to enter any additional information about the picture that you may want. It's really just a way to keep some personal notes about the photo. You can simply type any information you want (such as locations, names, events — anything at all — you can even write a paragraph) that can be used when you search for pictures, or you can use the Comments field to type explanations about the picture or fun memories — again, anything that you want.

The Comments field is, of course, optional, but it can hold anything from a few words to several paragraphs. You can practically write an exposé about the picture and store it in the Comments field if you want. To add comments, just type them in the Comments field, and iPhoto will keep those comments for you.

One navigation note I would like to point out is that you can greatly enlarge the size of the Comments field by changing the size of the Title/Date area and Viewer pane. As you can see in Figure 5-4, click and drag the small buttons on the divider bars to expand or shrink the existing panes so that the Comments field is the size you want. Then, just type away.

Click and drag these buttons to resize the iPhoto panes.

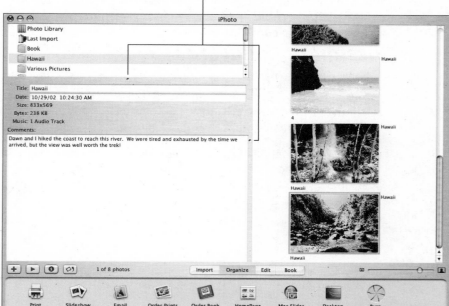

Figure 5-4: Grab the buttons and move your mouse to resize the panes.

When you have finished typing your Comments, you can also check your spelling if you like. Just click Edit⇨Spelling⇨Check Spelling.

Also, you can copy and paste text from any text editor or word processor directly to the Comments field.

Finally, as with title and date, you can't add comments if multiple photos are selected. You must add comments to one photo at a time.

Working with Keywords

Besides titles or information you place in the Comments field, you can also assign predefined keywords to photos. When you assign keywords, you can then search for photos based on those keywords so that the photos are easier to locate. Select the Photo Library or an album in the Source pane, click the Organize button to switch to Organize mode. To access keywords, choose Edit ⇨ Keywords or press ⌘-K to bring up the Keywords/Search dialog, shown in Figure 5-5.

iPhoto gives you a few keywords (such as Favorite, Family, Kids, and the like) to get you started. You can also add some of your own, which I show you how to do in the "Changing keywords and creating your own keywords" section, later in this chapter. The Keyword feature has some useful functions, and the judicious use of keywords can certainly make finding photos easier.

Assigning keywords

To assign a keyword, all you have to do is select the photo to which you want to assign the keyword, and then press ⌘-K. In the Keywords/Search dialog, select the desired keyword and click the Assign button. The keyword appears to the right of the photo, as shown in Figure 5-6. To remove a keyword, just select the photo, press ⌘-K to bring up the Keywords/Search dialog, select the keyword, and then click the Remove button. You can also hold down the ⌘ key, select several photos, and click the desired keyword buttons to assign keywords to several photos at the same time.

Figure 5-5:
Use the Keywords/ Search dialog to assign keywords or perform a search.

Figure 5-6:
Keywords appear beside the photos in the Viewer pane.

 If you don't see the keywords on your photos, as they appear in Figure 5-6, click View⇨Keywords to make them appear on your photos. Likewise, you can add as many keywords to a single photo (or group of photos) as you want.

Changing keywords and creating your own keywords

The Keywords/Search dialog is rather versatile: You can use the existing keywords, edit them, or create your own. This gives you the flexibility you need when assigning keywords. To edit the keywords, follow these steps:

1. **In Organize mode, click Edit⇨Keywords.**

   The Keyword/Search dialog appears.

2. **Select the keyword you want to edit, and then in the drop-down menu, choose Rename.**

   Type over the existing keyword to rename it as you prefer.

3. **To delete a keyword, select it and choose Delete from the drop-down menu.**

   When you're done, just close the dialog.

As you are editing keywords, keep a couple of things in mind:

✔ First, remember that keywords should apply to your entire Photo Library. Try to use words that you'll use most of the time. In other words, *family, vacation, nature,* and the like are general keywords that are useful. Keep the keywords helpful, but not too specific.

✔ After you edit your keywords, try not to change them. For example, say you have a keyword called *portraits* that you have assigned to a number of pictures. If you later edit the *portraits* keyword to *vacation,* all the pictures previously assigned the keyword of *portraits* will now be labeled *vacation.* As you can see, editing keywords after they have been used can create a lot of confusion.

About that Checkmark option

As you are working with keywords, you notice a Checkmark option. If you are editing keywords, you have probably also noticed that you can't edit the Checkmark option either.

The Checkmark button is a permanent fixture in Organize mode, and it is simply there to help you work with photos. If you select a photo and click the Checkmark button, a check mark appears in the lower-right corner of the photo, as you can see in Figure 5-7.

Figure 5-7: The check mark appears on the photo.

The Checkmark button enables you to put a temporary check mark on a photo. This feature can be helpful if you are working with a large number of photos and you want to keep track of which photos have been edited. If you are working on a book, for example, you can use it to keep track of which photos are to be included. You can then use the Search feature to find all your photos that have check marks. The Checkmark button doesn't serve any purpose other than organizational, so feel free to use it in a way that is useful to you — or don't use it at all.

After you have put a check mark on a photo, you can easily remove it by selecting the photo, clicking Edit⇨Keywords, selecting the check mark in the list, and clicking the Remove button.

Searching in iPhoto

All this talk about keywords, comments, and even titles comes down to one thing — finding the photos you want to find. To find photos, you have to use the keywords, comments, or titles to give your photos the labels they need so that iPhoto can find them. From that point, you can use the Search feature to round up the photos you want. The Search feature is quick and easy and can save you a lot of time. Here's how you do it:

1. **In Organize mode, click Edit⇨Keywords.**

2. **In the Keywords/Search dialog, enter the keywords or text you want to search for and click the Search button.**

   As shown in Figure 5-8, the photos that match your keyword search appear in the Viewer. Keep in mind that if you enter multiple words, you'll only see photos that have keywords matching all the words you entered.

Figure 5-8:
Photos that
match your
search
appear in
the Viewer
pane.

If you want to confine your search to a particular album, just select the album in the Source pane, and then click Edit➪Keywords and perform the search. The results of the search will be limited to the album you selected.

Changing the Appearance of the Viewer

You can also make a couple of basic changes to the way photos appear in the Viewer pane. If you click iPhoto➪Preferences, you see a couple of options under Appearance, as shown in Figure 5-9.

The options are

- **Drop Shadow, Border, or No Border:** By default, the Shadow feature is used. Photos appear on a white background, and they have a shadowing effect around them. However, you can choose Background slider bar to adjust the background of the Viewer between white and black. You can also choose to use a Border around the photos, or no border at all.

- **Align to Grid:** This option, which is selected by default, keeps photos lined up on an imaginary grid, regardless of their position. In other words, horizontal and vertical images will all line up in rows when you are viewing them. However, if you choose to use keywords and titles on photos, images will not line up, even if the Align to Grid option is selected.

✔ **Place Most Recent Photos at the Top:** This option places the most recently imported photos at the top of the Viewer.

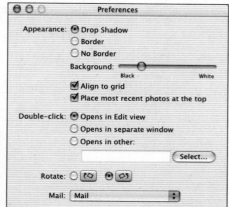

Figure 5-9:
Photo
options in
Preferences.

Part III
Editing Photos

The 5th Wave   By Rich Tennant

"THAT'S A LOVELY SCANNED IMAGE OF
YOUR SISTER'S PORTRAIT. NOW TAKE
IT OFF THE BODY OF THAT PIT VIPER
BEFORE SHE COMES IN THE ROOM."

In this part . . .

*i*Photo is photo-management software, but it also gives you some quick editing tools so that you can fix common problems with your photos. In Chapter 6, you discover how to crop photos, adjust brightness and contrast, use one-click enhance, fix red-eye, and convert photos to black and white. In Chapter 7, you find out what other photo-editing software can do when you edit beyond iPhoto.

Chapter 6

Fixing Photos

· ·

· ·

I'll tell you a secret up front: iPhoto is photo-management software; it isn't a photo editor. "But wait!" you may say, "I thought you could edit photos with iPhoto." Yes, you can — in a limited manner, anyway.

iPhoto provides you with a number of tools to do the things you most likely want to do with your photos, and this includes some basic editing features. You can use iPhoto to quickly perform some standard fixes, but iPhoto doesn't have the features of other major, photo-editing software programs. For example, in iPhoto, you can't

✔ Change a photo's background.

✔ Work with layers.

✔ Use special-effects tools.

✔ Add text.

✔ Edit two pictures together.

✔ Cut and paste.

✔ Adjust the color.

In fact, most photo-editing software on the market today provides tons of editing features that iPhoto simply does not give you. True, iPhoto gives you some common editing features that you'll use time and time again, which you can explore in this chapter, but iPhoto doesn't give you any editing capabilities beyond those basics.

Now, don't get bummed out or become disappointed. After all, iPhoto wasn't designed for this purpose. It was designed to be a full-featured photo-management system, which it is. But, if you want to do a lot of editing work on your photos or use special effects, you need to buy additional software. For example, I use iPhoto to manage my photos and fix basic problems. However, if I really want to make some editorial changes to a photo, I export the photo from iPhoto, open it in Adobe Photoshop Elements, make my edits, and then drag the photo back into iPhoto. No problem.

If you are wondering about additional editing features and software available for your Mac, I cover that in Chapter 7. In this chapter, you can explore what iPhoto can actually do in terms of editing, and you'll probably see that these basic editing techniques are all you need most of the time anyway.

Getting Ready to Edit a Photo

Before you edit a photo using the iPhoto software, the first question you should ask yourself is, "Do I really need to edit this photo?" Because photo editing has become so popular and cool, many photographers assume that they need to edit every photo they take. However, this simply isn't the case. In many circumstances, you can simply import the photos you take on your camera into iPhoto, where you can begin using them in any way you want. Just because you *can* edit a photo doesn't mean that you *need* to edit a photo. So, what are the indicators that a photo needs to be edited? Here are some common problems iPhoto can fix:

- ✔ **Cropping:** Sometimes, photos have extra stuff that distracts from the main subject of the photo, or makes the photo look more cluttered. For example, consider the following photo.

  The focus of this picture is the birdbath and the flower bed, but as you can see, the picture was taken too far away from the subject, leaving a bunch of unnecessary stuff in the picture. I can crop out the unwanted outer edges to bring the subject into better focus and make the picture look great.

- ✔ **Brightness/Contrast:** Some pictures come out either too light or too dark. You may have a great picture otherwise, but poor lighting has basically ruined it. You can use iPhoto to fix this problem using iPhoto's Brightness/Contrast controls or the Enhance tool.

- ✔ **Red-eye:** You've seen it a million times before — those glaring red eyes that make your subjects look like vampires. This is an aggravating problem, but you can easily fix it with iPhoto.

- ✔ **Spots:** Sometimes photos have small, unwanted spots on them, or even blemishes on a subject. You can use iPhoto's Retouch tool to easily fix these problems.

- ✔ **Black and white:** Some pictures may look better as black and white photos, or maybe you want to create that vintage look. You can easily transform a color picture to a black and white one.

iPhoto can easily fix these problems, so train your eye to watch for these issues in your photos. When you see a photo with one of these problems, or if you have a photo that you would like to make black and white, you know it's time to edit the photo.

Of course, your photos may have other problems that need to be fixed as well. If iPhoto can't fix the specific problem, you'll need to turn to some additional software, which I talk about in Chapter 7.

So, when you determine that a photo needs some editing work, what do you do to turn iPhoto into a photo editor? It's really easy, and here are the quick steps:

1. **Open iPhoto by clicking its icon in the Dock, or from the Macintosh HD, choose Applications and then double-click iPhoto.**

2. **In iPhoto, locate the photo you want to edit by browsing through the Photo Library or an album.**

3. **Double-click the photo, or select the photo and click the Edit button.**

    iPhoto is now in Edit mode, shown in Figure 6-1.

Now you're ready to edit your photo. Before you jump feet first into editing, though, let me point out something else you might like to know. When you want to edit a photo, you can also have iPhoto open the photo in its own window, with your editing tools right along with it. Many people find it easier to work with a photo when it is opened in its own window. Here's how you can make sure all your photos open in their own windows:

Figure 6-1:
Double-click
a picture to
go into Edit
mode, or
select the
picture and
click the
Edit button.

Editing controls   The Edit button

1. **In iPhoto, choose iPhoto➪Preferences.**

2. **In the Preferences dialog, shown in Figure 6-2, in the Double-Click area, select the Opens in Separate Window radio button.**

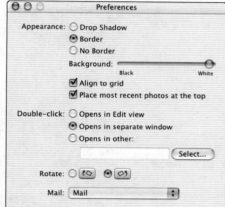

Figure 6-2: Choose the Opens in Separate Window radio button.

3. **Close the Preferences dialog.**

4. **Double-click the photo you want to edit.**

   As you can see in Figure 6-3, the photo opens in its own window with your editing controls in the top toolbar.

Okay, that was the long way to open a photo in Edit mode. However, you can also use one of a few shortcuts:

✔ If you have selected the Opens in Edit View radio button in the Double-click area under Preferences, you can hold down the Option key when double-clicking to open the photo in its own window.

✔ If you have selected the Opens in Separate Window radio button in the Double-click area under Preferences, you can hold down the Option key when double-clicking to open it in Edit view.

✔ If you have selected the Opens in Other radio button in the Double-click area under Preferences and specified another application in the box, the photo opens in the other application you specified, regardless of whether you hold down the Option key or not.

Figure 6-3:
The photo
now
appears in
its own
window.

Guess what? You can also customize your editing toolbar when a photo is opened in its own window. See the "Customizing the Edit Toolbar" section later in this chapter for the details.

Cropping Photos

The word *crop* means that you cut away some portion of a photo. Typically, you crop a photo to trim away excess portions of the photo to make the primary subject look better, or to remove unnecessary distractions. Return to the previous example of the birdbath and the flower bed. The original picture, shown on top, has extra stuff in the picture. The extra items do not help this picture and distract from the main subject. With a quick crop, I can simply cut away the extra stuff, leaving only the main subject, as you can see on the bottom. The cropped picture is much better than the original.

Retraining your eye

The crop tool in iPhoto will be one of the tools you use most often, primarily because many of your pictures will benefit from some cropping work. Everybody takes pictures that need a little trimming.

However, if you want to avoid the cropping tool as much as possible, you can crop with your camera instead, by teaching yourself a thing or two about composition. The *composition* of a photo refers to everything that you see — the main subject(s) in the photo, plus everything else that ends up there, such as furniture, trees, sky, and whatever else. All these elements, when you put them together, are the composition of the photo. In other words, the elements in the photo compose it. You end up cropping photos to adjust the composition when the photo contains objects that don't help it or that simply do not belong.

As a photographer, you can reduce the amount of cropping work you have to do by training your eye to pay attention to composition. The best way to do that is to look at a photo in terms of subjects and objects. Generally, every photo contains something or someone that is the main subject. Everything else in the photo can be thought of as objects. The objects you see should always support the subject(s). When they don't, you end up with a cluttered photograph that you have to fix by trying to crop out the objects.

For example, take a look at this picture:

This is an older photo that I scanned and imported to iPhoto. This is me (no, I'm not that young now) and my grandmother at an informal Christmas party. I love this picture because of its informal look, but the composition is terrible. There is too much space around us and that beautiful metal chair really ruins the picture. Unfortunately, lack of attention to composition ruins many photos. I can use iPhoto to crop this photo, as I have done in the following illustration, but I can't fix everything.

The moral of the story is that iPhoto can help you fix composition problems, but it can't fix everything: Your best bet is to train your eye so that you look at a photo in terms of subjects and objects. Ask yourself, "Do the objects in the photo help the subject(s)?" If not, try to get rid of them before you take the picture. Of course, when you are quickly trying to capture movement, you don't always have this luxury, but the more you think about composition as you take pictures, the more sensitive you become to it and the faster you can make decisions. Often, just the effective use of your camera zoom can fix a world of problems.

While we are on the subject of retraining your eye, I would like to point out another creative issue. Sometimes, when you take a photo, you may have an entirely new photo residing in the original. "What?" you may ask. Here's the deal. If you train your eye to carefully look at your photos, sometimes you see something more interesting in the photo than the original subject.

Let me offer an example. Consider this photo:

As you can see, this is a picture of some trees, a brick wall, and a house beyond the wall. Nothing too interesting, right? No doubt, you have taken photos like this one before. They don't really do anything, and you normally end up discarding them.

However, be careful. Train your eye to think of a photo in terms of what you can crop. In the picture, did you notice the old birdbath against the brick wall? It is just sort of sitting here alone in an overgrown flower bed. Hmmm. . . Could the birdbath make an interesting picture?

As you can see, I've cropped away everything but the birdbath. Now, I have an interesting picture of a forgotten, lonely object.

The trick is to simply train yourself to look critically at your photos. Sometimes, you find something interesting that you didn't even notice at first — something creative and beautiful!

Pixel panic

In the previous section, I discussed how to find a picture within in a picture, which sounds great. You simply open the picture in iPhoto, crop away, and have a great picture, right? Not really.

The truth of the matter is that every time you crop a photo, you cut away portions of it. This means that you cut out pixels, the individual units of color that make up the photo. That may not be such a big deal, but it can be when you try to print your photo.

For example, say you have 5 x 7 photo. It prints beautifully from iPhoto as a 5 x 7. Now, you decide to crop away some of the photo. After cropping, you print it again as a 5 x 7, but guess what? The photo is no longer a 5 x 7 because you cut some of it away. Because the printer is trying to print it as a 5 x 7, the printer has to stretch the pixels to make up the difference, and you end up with jagged lines and print anomalies.

The issue with pixels all comes down to resolution. The more pixels a photo has, the higher the resolution, which means the more cropping freedom you have to make it turn out right. Remember the original birdbath picture from the previous section? I shot that photo as a 3.2-megapixel image in the TIFF file format: The photo was 9MB in size! Because the resolution is so high, I can crop it down to a small portion (the birdbath) and still get great print results, but if I had shot the picture at the low resolution setting, the cropped picture wouldn't have turned out well.

Cropping is always a tradeoff between getting the picture you want and dealing with size when you try to print. This is one instance where having a good digital camera that can shoot 3 to 4 megapixels can save your neck.

Cropping your photos

Okay, after you've realized what cropping can do for your photos, you're probably ready to get started. Here's how to crop a picture:

1. **Open iPhoto by clicking the icon in the Dock, or in the Macintosh HD, choose the Applications folder, and then double-click the iPhoto icon.**

2. **In the iPhoto Viewer, double-click the picture you want to edit.**

   iPhoto switches to Edit mode and displays the picture in the Viewer pane.

3. **Move your mouse pointer over the photo.**

   Notice that the mouse pointer becomes a + sign.

4. **Position the mouse in the upper-left corner of where you want to crop, and then click and drag the mouse button to the lower-right corner where you want to crop.**

   As you can see in Figure 6-4, a box is created where everything inside of the box is kept in the picture. Everything outside the box is dimmed, meaning that it will be cropped away.

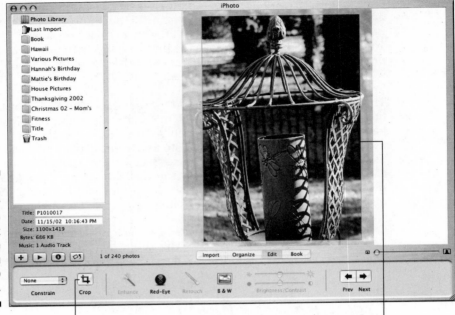

Figure 6-4:
Drag your
mouse to
create a box
around the
area you
want to
keep.

Click to crop.   Everything outside this box will be cropped away.

5. **If you like, click and drag the sides of the box around to adjust the cropping field.**

   Keep in mind that everything outside the box will be cut away.

6. **When you are happy with the crop box, click the Crop button in the editing tools box at the bottom of iPhoto.**

   The area outside the crop box is cut away, leaving you with the cropped photo, shown on the following page.

Constraining the photo

In Edit mode, you may have noticed the Constrain option that appears in the
lower-left portion of iPhoto. You see a drop-down box that has choices such
as 1024 x 768, 4 x 3, 4 x 6, 5 x 7, and so forth. What does all this mean, and
does it have anything to do with cropping?

When you crop a photo, you may not end up with a standard photo size. So, if you send the photo off to be printed, you get back a print that may contain white margins around it because the cropped photo isn't a standard size. The Constrain feature lets you choose a size that you want to adhere to, and then when you crop the photo, the box you draw sticks to that size. This obviously doesn't give you as much cropping flexibility, but it makes sure the photo stays the size you want it to. For example, let's say you are creating an iPhoto book or preparing pictures to be burned onto a DVD. You can select the 4 x 3 (Book, DVD) option to make certain the cropped photos all adhere to the necessary 4 x 3 size.

Note that the Constrain feature doesn't actually give you a photo of the size you constrain to — it simply keeps the aspect ratio correct. This way, if you decide to print a 5 x 7 or whatever size you chose, the aspect ratio of the photo is correct so that it can be printed at that size.

If you are interested in constraining a photo to your own customized size, Option-click the picture to open it in a separate window. On the toolbar, you can find an option to enter your own custom Constrain size.

Fixing a cropping mistake

If you make a mistake cropping a photo (such as cutting off someone's head), don't worry. iPhoto is very forgiving. After cropping the photo, just choose Edit⇨Undo Crop Photo, and the photo returns to its original state.

What if you have done something else to the photo, such as fix red-eye too? No problem — you can step backwards several steps in a row. Just click Edit⇨Undo Crop Photo repeatedly to begin undoing your changes back to when you cropped the photo.

What if a week goes by and you decide you don't like the cropping job? You can fix this, too. Whenever you crop a photo, iPhoto keeps a copy of the original in the Photo Library just to be safe. So, all you have to do is locate your cropped photo in the Photo Library or album you may have it in, select the photo, and then choose File⇨Revert to Original.

Note, however, that when you choose to Revert to Original, *everything* you have done to the photo is wiped away. This includes any other edits you may have made to the photo other than cropping.

Adjusting Brightness and Contrast

Another common photography problem occurs when pictures are taken in too much light or too little light. The result is a picture that is too light or too dark. iPhoto gives you the editing power to adjust the brightness of a picture, as well as the contrast, which refers to the color saturation in the picture.

It is important to note, however, that iPhoto (or any photo software for that matter) can't fix serious brightness or contrast problems. The real trick is to try to take pictures that need only a little touch up. Also, you can't spot-fix brightness or contrast problems in iPhoto. For example, say that you take a photo where part of it is in full sun and part of it is in shade. You can't brighten up the shady part of the photo or tone down the sunny part; the changes apply to the whole photo.

More advanced photo-editing software products, such as Photoshop or Photoshop Elements, do let you spot-fix brightness and contrast problems, although the process is a bit complicated.

Your best bet is to work on your photography skills and try to avoid overly bright or dark photos. Here are two quick tips to help you practice:

- ✔ When shooting indoors, make sure there is plenty of overhead light as well as lamplight to brighten the entire room. Also, try to shoot in a room that has diffused light coming through a window.

- ✔ When shooting outdoors, keep in mind that direct sunlight creates the most problems because portions of the photo may turn out too dark and too light. Overcast days are often the best days to take pictures outdoors. Color tones tend to look better in softer, overcast light, so don't let those overcast days pass you by!

The process for making slight brightness or contrast adjustments in iPhoto is simple. Just follow these steps:

1. **Open iPhoto by clicking the icon in the Dock, or in the Macintosh HD, choose the Applications folder and then double-click the iPhoto icon.**

2. **In iPhoto, double-click the picture you want to edit.**

   iPhoto switches to Edit mode and displays the picture in the Viewer pane.

3. **Carefully move the slider bars for brightness and contrast until the picture looks the way you want, as shown in Figure 6-5.**

   Keep in mind that slight movements of the slider bars are typically all you need. Moving the contrast slider to the right increases the color saturation in the photo.

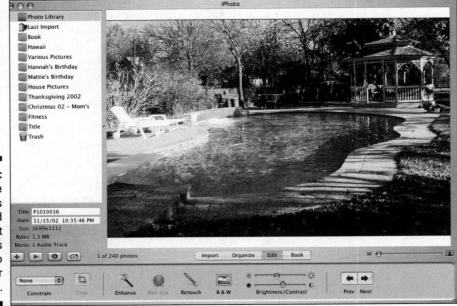

Figure 6-5:
Move the
Brightness
and
Contrast
sliders
slightly to
make your
edits.

As you are working, hold down the Control key to toggle between the original photo and the edited photo. This helps you see the changes you have made and whether or not they are better.

Move the slider bars around as much as you like to find the right combination. At any time, you can click Edit⇨Undo Brightness/Contrast to return to the original photo, or simply press ⌘-Z.

Using the Enhance Tool

iPhoto gives you another editing tool called Enhance. It appears on the Edit pane and it looks like a magic wand. The Enhance tool is a one-click option that tries to automatically enhance the colors of the photo for you. This tool basically brightens up a dull-looking photo.

The good news is that Enhance can brighten up your photos automatically. Just click the Enhance button on the Edit pane — that's all you need to do. If your photo needs more enhancement, you can click it several times to get more color enhancement. The bad news is that this tool works wonderfully on some photos and not very well at all on others. Sometimes the colors you get back are too bright, making the photo look artificial. If you don't like the changes the Enhance tool has made, simply click Edit⇨Undo Enhance Photo. If you want to see the changes that Enhance has made to your photo from your original, you can toggle between the enhanced photo and the original by pressing the Control key on your keyboard.

Fixing Red-Eye

If you like people in your pictures to look like vampires, you can skip this section. If not, read on. Seriously, red-eye is one of the most aggravating problems that occurs when taking pictures of people. In the past, red-eye was something you had to live with, but with digital photography and programs such as iPhoto — no more! In fact, you can easily fix red-eye in iPhoto with just a few simple steps.

Red-eye typically occurs when you take indoor shots. Because the lighting is lower, the eyes are dilated. When the flash fires, the flash hits the subject's retina and bounces a red color back to the camera from the retina and the blood vessels around the retina. The result is red-eye.

You can avoid red-eye by taking photos in well-lit rooms or outdoors. Also, some film and digital cameras offer a red-eye reduction mode, which helps eliminate the problem, too.

However, if you end up with red-eye in pictures, you can easily fix the problem in iPhoto, and here's how:

1. **Open iPhoto by clicking the icon in the Dock, or in the Macintosh HD, choose Applications and then double-click the iPhoto icon.**

2. **In iPhoto, double-click the picture you want to edit.**

   iPhoto switches to Edit mode and displays the picture in the Viewer pane.

3. **Use the Magnification slider to move in closer on the subject's face, if necessary.**

   You may have to use the side and bottom scroll bars to center the subject's eyes on your screen as well.

4. **When you are zoomed in on the face, hover your mouse pointer over the picture.**

   The mouse pointer turns into cross hairs.

5. **Click and drag the mouse pointer to create a box around the eyes, as you can see in Figure 6-6.**

   After you draw the box, the Red-Eye button becomes active in the bottom dialog.

6. **Click the Red-Eye button and the red-eye disappears.**

The Red-Eye removal feature removes anything in the selection that is red. As such, just draw a box around the eyes. If you include the whole face or any red clothing, those items turn black as well!

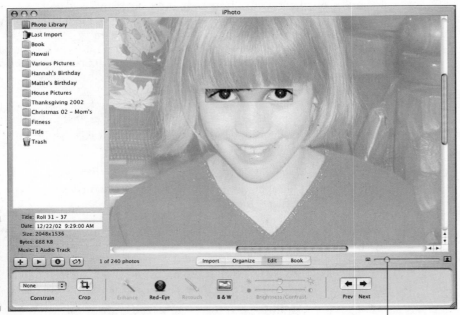

Figure 6-6:
Create a box
around the
person's
eyes.

Zoom to the subject's eyes with the Magnification slider.

Converting a Photo to Black and White

iPhoto includes a quick tool that lets you convert color photos to black and white photos for artistic flair. Black and white photos often have an interesting texture. They can make certain photos look older than they are and even bring on an air of mystery.

You can play around with turning photos to black and white quickly and easily, and you undo the black and white conversion just as easily. Follow these steps:

1. **Open iPhoto by clicking the icon in the Dock, or from the Macintosh HD, choose the Applications folder and then double-click the iPhoto icon.**
2. **In iPhoto, double-click the picture you want to edit.**

   iPhoto switches to Edit mode and displays the picture in the Viewer pane.
3. **In the editing controls at the bottom of iPhoto, click the B & W button.**

   The photo automatically converts to black and white.
4. **If you don't like the conversion, just choose Edit⇨Undo Convert to B & W.**

Retouching a Photo

With any photo, you may end up with a small blemish or mark that you want to fix. This is especially true with scanned photos. Also, if you take a close-up of someone's face, you may see a facial blemish or some other discoloration you would like to remove.

No problem — iPhoto to the rescue. You can use the Retouch tool in Edit mode to make small changes to a photo in order to blend blemishes away. This tool doesn't work on big spots or blemish problems — it is designed to fix small problems by blending the blemish into the color around it. If you use it on a big spot or blemish, your fix will look discolored and will be noticeable.

However, for small blemishes and spots, the Retouch tool works great. Just follow these steps to use it:

1. **Open iPhoto by clicking the icon in the Dock, or from the Macintosh HD, choose the Applications folder and then double-click the iPhoto icon.**

2. **In iPhoto, double-click the picture you want to edit.**

   iPhoto switches to Edit mode and displays the picture in the Viewer pane.

3. **Use the Magnifier slider bar to zoom in on the portion of the photo that needs retouching.**

   Figure 6-7 contains a white spot on a shirt that I want to blend away.

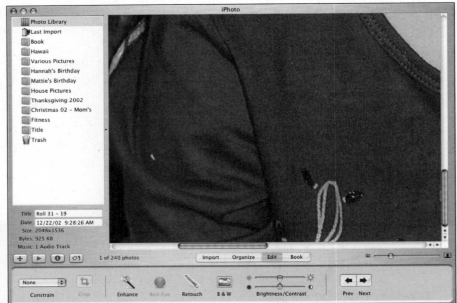

Figure 6-7: Zoom in on the spot you want to fix.

4. **Click the Retouch icon on the Edit pane, and then move your mouse pointer to the spot you want to fix.**

   The mouse icon turns to cross hairs.

5. **Hold down your mouse button and make small strokes across the spot or blemish until it is blended away, as shown in Figure 6-8.**

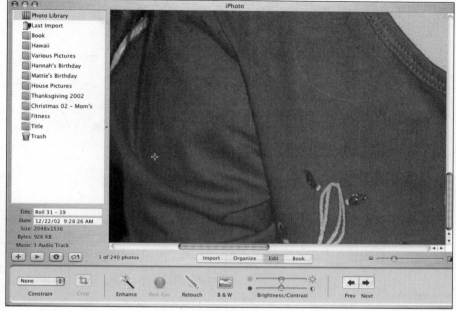

Figure 6-8:
Hold down
the mouse
button and
make small
strokes to
blend away
the spot.

Customizing the Edit Toolbar

As I mentioned earlier in this chapter, you can choose to view and edit a photo in its own window. (See "Getting Ready to Edit a Photo" for more information.) If you choose this option, you can also customize the toolbar with some interesting options. Note that toolbar customization is only available when you're working with a photo in its own window. You can't customize the toolbar in the main iPhoto interface.

Here's how to customize the toolbar in the window:

1. **Locate a photo you want to edit, and then hold down the Option key and double-click it.**

   The photo opens in its own window.

   If you have already configured preferences to always open the photo in its own window, you don't have to hold down the Option key.

2. **At the top of the window, choose Customize, as shown in Figure 6-9.**

Click to customize the toolbar.

Roll 31 – 9 (36%)

Zoom Fit Rotate   Constrain Custom Crop   Red-Eye Brightness/Contrast **Customize**

Figure 6-9:
Choose
Customize.

A pull-out window, shown in Figure 6-10, appears with a listing of icons. Notice that most of these are available on the toolbar by default (the default set appears at the bottom of the window, as you can see in Figure 6-10).

3. Drag the icons you want to use to the toolbar.

Some helpful icons you may want to add to your toolbar are the icons labeled 4 x 6 (P), 5 x 7 (L), and so on, which represent the different constrain sizes that iPhoto offers.

4. Drag any icons that you don't use often off the toolbar.

The unwanted icons disappear in a cloud of smoke.

For example, if you mostly take nature photos and simply don't use the Red Eye tool, just drag it off the toolbar.

5. When you are finished, just click the Done button.

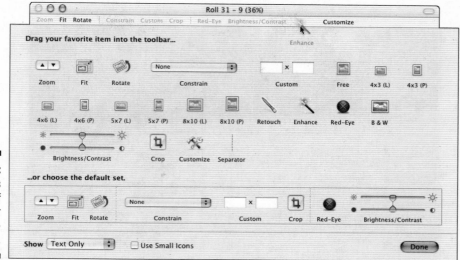

Figure 6-10:
Drag icons
on and off of
the toolbar
to cus-
tomize.

Notice the Show drop-down menu at the bottom of the Customize window. This allows you to display toolbar items as icons, text, or icons and text. Try the Text Only option in order to save some space on the toolbar.

When you're done, you'll notice that if you have added a lot of icons, they can't all fit on the toolbar: Some are hidden. To access the hidden icons, just click the double arrow at the end of the toolbar, and the additional menu that pops out lists the icons.

Finally, if you monkeyed around with the toolbar a lot and want to return to the default set, just return to the Customize window and drag the entire default set back to the toolbar. You'll be right back where you originally started.

Rotating Photos

When you take portrait pictures on your camera and import them, they usually are displayed sideways in iPhoto because they were imported that way. However, you can easily rotate photos so they are right side up, or you can even rotate existing photos so that they are sideways, upside down, or whatever you want.

A sideways photo appears in Figure 6-11. To rotate the photo, all I need to do is select the photo and click the Rotate button.

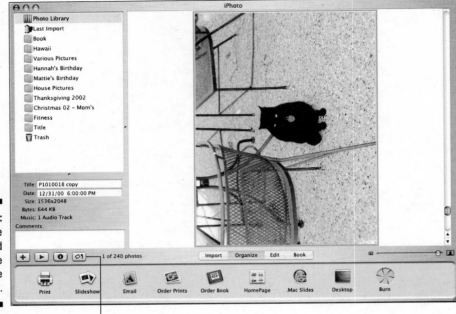

Figure 6-11:
Select the
photo and
click the
Rotate
button.

Click to rotate a photo.

You can rotate photos any way, and if you feel frustrated by the way iPhoto
rotates them, you can change that, too. By default, iPhoto rotates photos in a
counterclockwise motion. You can change that to clockwise if you like. Click
iPhoto⇨Preferences to bring up the Preferences dialog. Under Rotate, select
the radio button on the left, which features an arrow pointing in a clockwise
direction. Changing your Preferences affects how all your photos are rotated.

If you want to change the way just one of your photos is rotated, hold down
the Option key while you click the Rotate button — this will reverse the order
of the rotation.

Chapter 7

Editing Beyond iPhoto

• •

In This Chapter

▶ Fixing common photo problems

▶ Doing advanced editing

▶ Working with text

▶ Having fun with special effects

• •

If you read Chapter 6, you're probably well aware that, in addition to photo management, iPhoto enables you to do basic editing. For example, you can adjust the brightness and contrast of a photo, fix red-eye, and crop a photo. However, you probably noticed right away that iPhoto doesn't give you a lot of editing features. In fact, you are really limited to the most basic of the basics.

Remember that iPhoto is designed to be primarily photo-management software, not a full-fledged editing program. Because of this, many iPhoto users also use additional photo-editing software to make changes to photos before importing them into iPhoto. You don't have to do this, of course, but if you want more control over your photos, an additional program can give you the capabilities that iPhoto doesn't.

So, when I say, "editing photos," what exactly do I mean? Well, when you edit a photo, you simply make changes to it. This can include fixing red-eyes, changing the background, working with *layers* (which allow you to combine different picture elements into one photo), and even adding text. Because you can't do many of these actions with iPhoto, you'll need some additional software.

The software you choose to purchase and use is up to you, but one of the most popular programs as I write this book is Adobe's Photoshop Elements. Photoshop Elements gives you a full plate of editing features and is reasonably priced (around $80). Photoshop comes in both Mac and PC versions. Entire books are devoted to using this complex program and its many features. In this chapter, I show you some of the cool image-editing features that Photoshop Elements provides. Use this chapter as a primer to Photoshop Elements, or if you aren't sure which photo-editing program you want to use,

use this chapter to get an idea of everything you can do with programs like Photoshop Elements. Obviously, I can't cover in one chapter *everything* Photoshop Elements does, but I give you plenty of examples and step-by-steps to get you started.

In this chapter, I use Photoshop Elements 2.0. If you don't have Photoshop Elements, consider downloading a free trial version from www.adobe.com. In case you are wondering, Photoshop is a professional editor's program, whereas Photoshop Elements 2.0 is a downscaled version of Photoshop, designed for the rest of us.

Of course, you are free to try other programs available, such as Paint Shop Pro, which also works great. But because Photoshop Elements is the most popular today, I'll stick with it as the example in this chapter.

Fixing Common Problems

We all have to face the fact that none of us, as photographers, is perfect. Sometimes we get great shots, and sometimes we get shots that could be great if we could just fix a few problems. The good news is that digital photo-editing software products such as Photoshop Elements give you the power to do just that — in most cases anyway. In this section, I take a look at some of the common problems you may encounter and how to solve those problems using Photoshop Elements.

Using the Quick Fix window

Most of your photos won't require extensive editing. The photos you take with your digital camera are typically just fine the way they are, or maybe you need to make only a few simple changes to them, such as adjusting the brightness, color correction, rotating the photo, and so forth. You can perform these actions quickly and easily in iPhoto, but you can also quickly perform them in Photoshop Elements. Photoshop Elements gives you a Quick Fix feature that enables you to quickly make these standard changes. The Quick Fix feature doesn't give you as much control over some of the fixes, but it's the easiest way to make quick changes to a photo.

The following steps show you how to use the Quick Fix feature:

1. **Open Photoshop Elements by opening Macintosh HD⇨Applications⇨ Photoshop Elements.**

2. **Choose File⇨Open.**

   This brings up the Open dialog, which you use to navigate to the folder where the picture you want to edit is stored.

3. When you find the picture you want to edit, select it and click OK.

The picture opens within Photoshop Elements, as shown in Figure 7-1.

An easier way to open a photo is to open Photoshop Elements, and then drag the photo to the Photoshop Elements icon in the Dock. Your photo will open automatically.

Tool Palette   Main toolbar

Figure 7-1:
Your image
is ready to
be edited in
Photoshop
Elements.

4. Choose Enhance⇨Quick Fix from the main menu.

This brings up the Quick Fix window, shown in Figure 7-2.

5. In the Quick Fix window, use the radio buttons to select the category of adjustment, the specific adjustment, and more details about that adjustment.

For example, in Figure 7-2, I am correcting the photo's color. Under the Select Adjustment Category, I have chosen Color Correction. Under Select Adjustment, I chose Hue/Saturation, and under Apply Hue/Saturation, I have used the three sliders to change these values. The Before and After photos show me how my changes look.

If at any time you want to erase your changes and revert to the original image, click the Reset Image button.

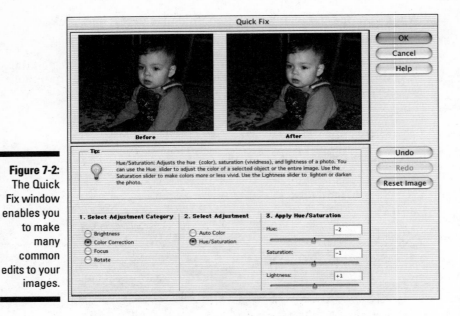

Quick Fix

Figure 7-2:
The Quick
Fix window
enables you
to make
many
common
edits to your
images.

6. **Continue making selections and editing the photo until you are satisfied.**

7. **When you are done, just click OK.**

Not sure what you are doing in Quick Fix? Check out the Tip box. For each radio button item you select, the Tip box tells you what changes that selection makes to your photo. Don't like the change you just made? No problem — just click the Undo button to undo the most recent edit. Don't like any of the changes you made? Just click the Reset Image button to return it to its original state and remove all editing. You can also click Cancel to remove all changes and close the Quick Fix window.

Rotating a photo

Rotating a photo is a simple task that you can also perform in iPhoto, but performing this function in Photoshop Elements gives you more choices. To rotate an image, open the photo in Photoshop Elements and choose Image⇔Rotate. A pop-out menu appears with several options: You can rotate 90 degrees left or right, 180 degrees, choose a custom rotation, or even flip the image vertically or horizontally. You can also use the Straighten and Crop Image or Straighten Image options to fix crooked shots automatically. Just select the option you want, and Photoshop Elements applies the changes to the image.

Cropping a photo

The Crop feature in Photoshop Elements basically works the same way it does in iPhoto. The purpose of cropping is to cut away unnecessary portions of the photo or border areas that do not add to the overall effectiveness of the photo. Cropping is a good way to clean up the photo and draw more attention to the main subject(s).

To crop a photo in Photoshop Elements, follow these steps:

1. **Open the desired photo in Photoshop Elements by choosing File⇨Open.**

2. **On the Tools palette, shown in Figure 7-3, click the Crop tool.**

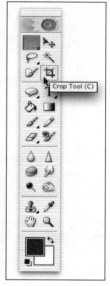

Crop Tool (C)

Figure 7-3:
Use the
Crop tool to
eliminate
extraneous
parts of your
image.

3. **Hover your mouse pointer over your image.**

   Your mouse pointer changes to the Crop tool, which looks like a box with a line through it.

4. **Position the Crop tool in the desired location, and then hold down the mouse button and drag to create the crop box, as shown in Figure 7-4.**

   All portions of the photo outside the crop box will be cropped away. Notice that the outside portion becomes darkened.

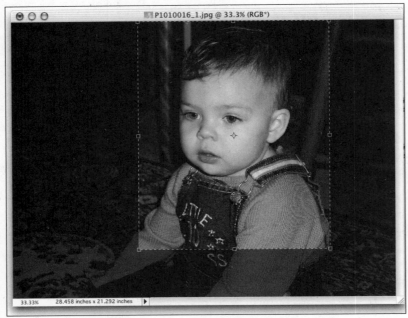

Figure 7-4:
Drag to
create the
crop box.

5. **Choose Image⇨Crop, or just double-click inside the crop box to crop the photo.**

   You can also just press Return or double-click inside the crop box to crop the figure.

6. **If you are not happy with the crop, just choose Edit⇨Undo.**

You don't have to save your changes as you are working on a photo until you are finished and ready to close the file. If you are making several edits, however, you may consider saving from time to time in case of a power failure or a Mac crash that may cause you to lose your changes. To save, just click File⇨Save or File⇨Save As.

Resizing a photo

Many times, you may want to resize the photos that you have imported from your camera or scanned in. They may be too big or too small for your purpose, or you may want to constrain a standard print size. You can easily resize a photo in Photoshop Elements, but keep in mind that, if you increase the size of a photo, you will probably lose some quality. However, you can experiment with resizing as needed to find the sizes that work best for you.

To resize a photo in Photoshop Elements, follow these steps:

1. **Open the desired photo in Photoshop Elements by choosing File⇨Open.**

2. **Choose Image⇨Resize⇨Image Size.**

   The Image Size window appears, as shown in Figure 7-5.

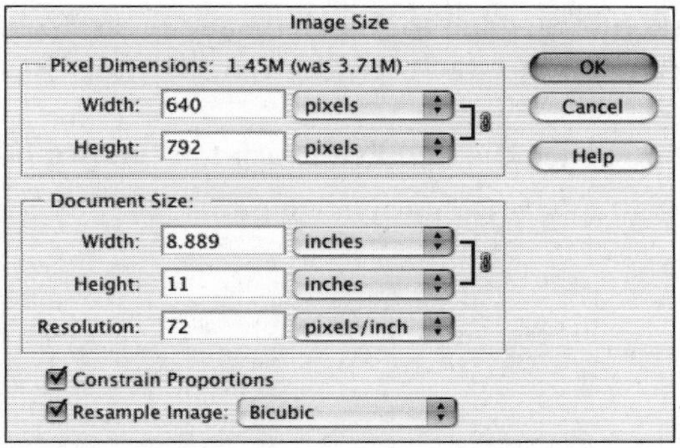

Figure 7-5:
Resize your
image in the
Image Size
window.

Image Size

Pixel Dimensions: 1.45M (was 3.71M)

Width: 640 | pixels
Height: 792 | pixels

OK
Cancel
Help

Document Size:

Width: 8.889 | inches
Height: 11 | inches
Resolution: 72 | pixels/inch

☑ Constrain Proportions
☑ Resample Image: Bicubic

3. **In the Pixel Dimensions area, type the desired measurements (in pixels) in the Width and Height boxes to get the size photo you want.**

   If you select the Constrain Proportions check box at the bottom of the window, Photoshop Elements automatically changes the height when you change the width. Using Constrain Proportions keeps the same width to height ratio as your original image. Note that you can also resize your image using a percentage instead of pixels by using the drop-down list boxes, but you'll find it easier to work with the pixel resize option.

4. **Click OK when you are done.**

Notice the Document Size option on the Image Size box. This changes the window size that your photo sits on in Photoshop Elements. It's called a Document, but resizing here just gives you the chance to make the window easier to work with — it doesn't change the actual size of your photo.

Fixing red-eye

I'll be honest: Red-eye is easier to fix in iPhoto than it is in Photoshop Elements. The process in Photoshop Elements has the same result, but it is a bit more labor intensive and a little confusing at first. Still, if you are making other edits to a photo in Photoshop Elements, you probably do not want to stop and edit the picture again in iPhoto, so here's how you fix red-eye in Photoshop Elements:

1. **Open the desired image in Photoshop Elements by choosing File⇨Open.**

2. **To make your subject's eyes more visible, zoom in on the image with the Zoom tool.**

   The Zoom tool is found on your Tools palette and looks like a magnifying glass. Click the tool to select it, and then begin clicking your photo to zoom in to the desired level.

3. **On the Tools palette, click the Red Eye Brush tool, shown in Figure 7-6.**

   The Red Eye toolbar appears, shown in Figure 7-7.

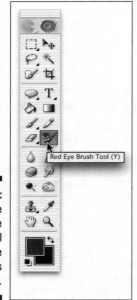

Figure 7-6:
Choose the Red Eye Brush tool from the Tools palette.

Red Eye Brush Tool (Y)

Figure 7-7:
Use the Red Eye toolbar to select a brush and pixel size.

Choose a brush size.

Choose a brush style.

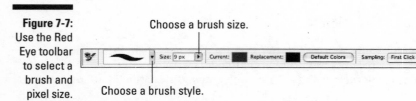

4. **On the Red Eye toolbar, choose a brush style and brush pixel size.**

   A soft brush that is about 65 pixels is often a good choice. The brush size you choose depends on the size of the eyes in the photo — use a smaller brush size for smaller eyes. Current shows you the current color of the eye area as you move your mouse over it, and the Replacement color shows you the color that will be used to replace the red. The Default Colors, Sampling, and Tolerance are fine at their default levels. The Tolerance setting determines how "fuzzy" the color will be. Obviously, you may need to do some experimenting to determine the settings that are good for your photo.

5. **Using your mouse pointer, begin clicking away at the red pupils of your subject's eyes, shown in Figure 7-8.**

   The red changes to the default black color.

Figure 7-8:
Click your image with your mouse pointer to eliminate red-eye.

Sharpening a blurry photo

In some cases, a photo comes out looking a little blurry. You can use Photoshop Elements to fix blurry photos, at least to a degree. (The software can't fix a very blurry picture.) You can use some Photoshop Element tools, however, to sharpen a photo and make the photo seem more in focus.

In Photoshop Elements, you sharpen a subject using a sharpen filter, or actually a collection of filters. (In Photoshop Elements, a *filter* is a process that is applied to a photo.) Simply open the photo in Photoshop Elements, choose Filter⇨Sharpen, and then choose one of the available filters from the submenu that appears. You have the following options:

✔ **Sharpen:** This filter performs an overall sharpening to the entire photo.

✔ **Sharpen Edges:** A sharpening trick is to sharpen the edges around objects in the picture. Photoshop Elements can detect the edges of objects and sharpen those edges only, making the photo look sharper.

✔ **Sharpen More:** This option applies a stronger filter. Be careful, though, because you may start to see a grainy look on the photo if you use this filter incorrectly.

✔ **Unsharp Mask:** The Unsharp Mask is a great tool that gives you a lot of control. When you select this option, the Unsharp Mask window appears, shown in Figure 7-9. Type **100** in the Amount box, and type **12** in the Threshold box. (These values control the pixel sharpness and the pixel radius applied when Unsharp Mask filter is used.) The Amount and Threshold values generally are your best options when trying to clear up a blurry photo. Then, move the Radius slider back and forth and watch the Preview monitor until you are happy with the results. Click OK when you're done.

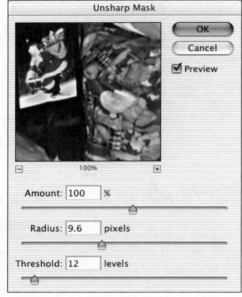

Figure 7-9:
The
Unsharp
Mask
window.

Fixing color problems

Sometimes, when you take a photo, the picture turns out to have a color cast. A *color cast* occurs when a certain color reflects too much in the lens, shading the overall photo a certain color, such as yellow or red. You may also encounter situations when the color seems dull or just doesn't look as good as you want it to.

Aside from the Quick Fix solutions (see the section, "Using the Quick Fix window," earlier in this chapter for more information), you can also use Color Variations in Photoshop Elements to apply a variation to your photo. The good news is that this tool is very easy to use and shows you exactly what the color variation does before you apply it to the photo.

To use the Color Variation feature, follow these steps:

1. **Open the desired image in Photoshop Elements by choosing File⇨Open.**

2. **Choose Enhance⇨Adjust Color⇨Color Variations.**

   The Color Variations window appears, shown in Figure 7-10.

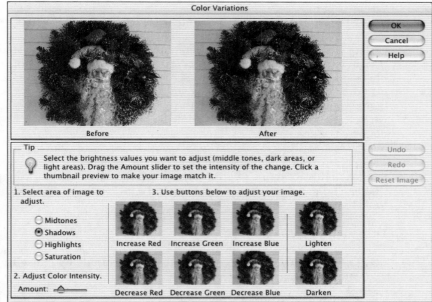

Figure 7-10: Use the Color Variations window to correct color casts.

3. **In the Select Area of Image to Adjust part of the window, use the radio buttons to indicate what type of color you want to modify.**

   The Midtones settings adjust the midtone colors in a photo, the Shadows setting adjusts the darker colors, and Highlights adjusts the brighter colors in a photo.

4. **Use the slider in the Adjust Color Intensity area to choose the intensity value.**

   The intensity determines how each click will impact the photo — low intensity creates slight changes, whereas high intensity provides significant changes. In the Use Buttons Below to Adjust Your Image area, several thumbnails of color correction options appear.

5. **Click a thumbnail to see its effect applied in the After photo.**

If you don't like the result, click Reset Image and try again until you find the color variation that looks good. You can also click the Undo button to undo your last change and Reset Image to undo all changes you have made in color variations. (Alternatively, just click the Before image to reset the image.)

6. **When you are satisfied with your image, click OK.**

Removing scratches, dust, or noise

If you are like me, you have hundreds of older photos that you have scanned into your computer (or want to scan). With these scanned photos, you often end up with distortion elements, commonly called *scratches, dust,* or *noise.* (On an image shot with a digital camera, scratches, dust, and noise on the photo generally aren't problems.) Scratches and dust come from the original photo, or from dust on the scanner bed. They end up as little particles on the digital photo. Noise occurs when the original print was of poor quality, or when the photo was scanned at a low resolution. Noise has a grainy look that distorts the image.

Using Photoshop Elements, you can clean up a number of these problems and make the photo look better. Photoshop Elements offers a couple of tools that can help, but you may need to spend a little time working with these tools to get the results you want.

The following steps show you how:

1. **Open the desired image in Photoshop Elements by choosing File⇨Open.**

2. **Choose File⇨Noise⇨Despeckle.**

This applies the Despeckle filter to your image, which removes some basic dust and specks in the image. If you look closely, you can see this is accomplished by slightly burring the image while keeping the lines sharp. For some photos, the Despeckle filter works well, but if it doesn't work for your image, choose Edit⇨Undo from the main menu and move to Step 3.

3. **To begin removing dust and scratches, choose the Lasso tool on the Tools palette, shown in Figure 7-11.**

Your mouse pointer turns into a Lasso tool, which looks like a rope.

This is the first step in using the Dust & Scratches filter. For this filter to work well, you need to apply it to selected areas of the photo only. (You *can* apply the filter to the entire photo, but this usually results in a blurry photo.)

Figure 7-11:
Choose the
Lasso tool
on the Tools
palette.

4. **Trace around an area of the photo that you want to remove dust and scratches from by holding down the mouse button as you move the Lasso tool, as you can see in Figure 7-12.**

   In this figure, I have used the Lasso tool to trace around the background in this old 1940s photo. You see the dust and scratches in the background, which I'll fix in the next step.

Figure 7-12:
Use the
Lasso Tool
to select an
area to
clean up.

5. **Choose Filter⇨Noise⇨Dust & Scratches.**

   The Dust & Scratches window appears.

6. **In the Dust & Scratches window, use the Radius slider to select a radius value of about 4 or 5, type 0 into the Threshold box, and click OK.**

   Take a look your photo. You'll see that most of the dust and many of the scratches are now gone. You can run the filter again with a higher Radius value, but the higher value you use, the more blurring effect you'll get.

7. **Continue this process with other portions of the photo as needed until you get the desired result.**

   Figure 7-13 shows the edited photo with dust and scratches removed.

Figure 7-13:
Use
Photoshop
Elements to
spruce up
old photos.

Advanced Editing Tricks

Okay, are you ready to have a little fun with Photoshop Elements? This section focuses on a few advanced editing techniques that you are likely to use time and time again. Why? The answer is simple: These tricks can fix common aggravating problems in a photo, and they can even make a photo and the people in a photo look better than they do in real life! As you read, you'll quickly discover that I'm just getting you started with advanced tricks. Photoshop Elements (and other editing programs) can do a myriad of cool things, but these will definitely whet your appetite!

Fixing a blemish

We've all taken pictures where something doesn't quite come out right on the subject's face. Perhaps the subject has a glaring pimple that ruins the picture, or some other blemish that mars the image. The good news is that you can use Photoshop Elements to remove blemishes like these from people's faces, and here's how:

1. **Open the desired image in Photoshop Elements by choosing File⇨Open.**

   Figure 7-14 is a picture of my daughter having fun with some makeup. I like this picture, but the sparkles on her forehead are a little much. What I need to do is simply copy a small (nonsparkling) portion of her forehead and paste it over the sparkle areas.

Figure 7-14: The sparkles on the forehead are too intrusive on this photo.

2. **On the Tools palette, click the Lasso tool button.**

   Your mouse pointer turns into a Lasso tool.

3. **Click and drag the mouse pointer to lasso a small portion of the forehead that has roughly the same color you want to fix.**

4. **Choose Edit⇨Copy to copy the area.**

5. **Once again using your Lasso tool, lasso around the area you want to replace, and then choose Edit⇨Paste.**

6. **Repeat the process until you have fixed the blemishes, as shown in Figure 7-15.**

Figure 7-15:
The blemishes have been removed.

Here's another quick way to fix a blemish: In the Tools palette, choose the Clone Stamp tool (it looks like an ink stamp). Position the tool on the part of the photo that you want to copy and Option-click it. Then, hover the mouse pointer above the blemish you want to hide and click. The cloned portion will be stamped over the blemish!

You can also sometimes remove small blemishes using the Smudge tool found on your Tools palette. Simply select the tool and brush over the blemish to smudge it away. This option, of course, doesn't work well on large areas.

Changing someone's eye color

You can have a little fun with eye color using Photoshop Elements. For example, say you would like to have crystal blue eyes instead of green eyes in a photo. No problem. Here's how you do it:

1. **Open the desired image in Photoshop Elements by choosing File⇨Open.**

2. **Use the Zoom button, which looks like a Magnifying glass, to zoom in on the photo to make the eyes larger.**

3. **Select the Red Eye Brush tool from the Tools palette.**

   The Red Eye Brush toolbar appears (refer to Figure 7-7). At first blush, this choice of tool may seem odd, but the Red Eye Brush tool is really just a color replacement tool.

4. **On the Red Eye toolbar, from the Size drop-down list box, choose a brush size that is right for the irises of the eyes you'll be working on.**

   A five-pixel brush is usually a good starting point.

5. **On the Replacement color, click the color block and choose a new color from the color palette that appears.**

6. **Choose 30% in the Tolerance drop-down list box.**

7. **Click and drag the brush over the irises of the eyes to change their color to the color you chose in the Replacement box.**

Removing an object from a picture

Sometimes, you may shoot a picture that would otherwise be great, but there is some object in the way, or something unsightly in the photo (maybe, say, your ex-boyfriend or ex-girlfriend). To remove unwanted items from a photo, you can use the Clone Stamp tool to copy part of the image and paste that over the content that you don't want. Of course, depending on what you want to remove, you may need a little practice to get good results, but the basic process is pretty easy.

Here's how to remove content using the Clone Stamp tool:

1. **Open the photo in Photoshop Elements by choosing File⇨Open and selecting the image file.**

   For this example, I am working on the photo shown in Figure 7-16. I am going to remove the top portion of the fountain so that it does not block the window.

2. **Click the Zoom tool on the Tools palette, and then click on the image to zoom in as needed.**

3. **Click the Clone Stamp tool on the Tools palette.**

   The Clone Stamp toolbar appears, as shown in Figure 7-17.

Figure 7-16:
The top
portion of
the fountain
blocks the
window.

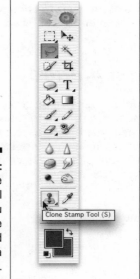

Figure 7-17:
The Clone
Stamp tool
allows you
to remove
unwanted
portions of a
photo.

Using brush selection and size drop-down lists, you can adjust the brush and pixel size on the toolbar as needed. Because the object that I'm removing in this example is small, I am using a smaller brush and pixel size. You can adjust the brush and size to meet your needs.

4. **Position your mouse on an area of the photo that you want to copy and Option-click the selection.**

   This action selects the area of the photo and copies it so it can be stamped in another location. You will stamp this copied portion of the image over the area you are trying to blot out.

5. **Use the tool to carefully begin blotting out the object.**

   As you can see in Figure 7-18, I am simply blotting away the portion of the fountain that I don't want.

Figure 7-18:
Using the Clone Stamp tool to erase a part of an image.

6. **Repeat the process to remove additional objects or to change the clone selection as needed.**

   You may also need to experiment with brushes to get the effect that you want.

For small objects that you want to block out, the Copy and Paste method works well. For example, in Figure 7-19, notice that black stick coming out of the water in the left portion of the photo.

You can get rid of this stick using the Clone Stamp tool, but you can also just copy and paste as well. Click the Lasso tool button on the Tools palette and use the Lasso tool to select a small portion of water next to the stick. Then, choose Edit⇨Copy. Select the stick with the Lasso tool and choose Edit⇨Paste. If the paste leaves some unwanted lines, just select the Smudge tool from the Tools palette to smooth out the lines. As you can see in Figure 7-20, the stick is now gone!

Figure 7-19:
You can
erase a
small object
using Copy
and Paste.

Remove this stick with Copy and Paste.

Figure 7-20:
The stick is
now gone
from the
photo.

Making teeth whiter

Yellow or discolored teeth can mar what may otherwise be a great photo, especially when that photo is a close-up of a face. Using Photoshop Elements, you can make teeth whiter using the Dodge tool on the Tools palette. The Dodge tool looks like a sucker on the tools palette, and it is used to gradually change the shading of an object on a photo.

You'll have to work carefully here, or you'll lose the natural texture and shape of the teeth, but with a little practice, you'll be a pro in no time. Here's how you do it:

1. **Open the photo in Photoshop Elements by choosing File➪Open and selecting the image file.**

2. **Use the Zoom tool on the Tools palette to zoom in on the subject's teeth.**

3. **On the Tools palette, select the Dodge tool, as shown in Figure 7-21.**

   The Dodge toolbar appears.

4. **On the Dodge tool toolbar, choose Midtones from the Range drop-down menu and choose a smaller, softer brush on the Brush and Size drop-down menu. For the Exposure setting drop-down menu, select 50%.**

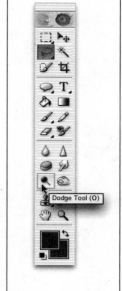

Figure 7-21:
The Dodge tool allows you to make subtle changes.

5. **Drag the brush over the teeth in short strokes, as shown in Figure 7-22.**

   If you don't see a noticeable improvement, try the highlights setting from the Range drop-down menu on the toolbar. Continue the process until you have whitened the teeth, but don't do too much or the teeth will start to look unnatural.

You can use this same process to brighten up someone's lips!

Figure 7-22:
Drag the
brush in
short
strokes to
whiten the
teeth.

Blurring a background

When you take a close-up photo of an object, such as a person, sometimes
the photo is much more dramatic if you blur the background. This feature
brings the main subject to more life. For example, consider the two photos in
Figure 7-23. The image on the left has the original background; the image on
the right has the blurred background.

Figure 7-23:
The blurred
background
creates a
dramatic
effect.

See the difference? It's easy to blur the background. Here's how:

1. **Use the Lasso tool on the Tools palette to select the background of the
   photo.**

2. **Choose Filter➪Blur➪Smart Blur.**

3. **In the Smart Blur window that appears, increase the radius and threshold values until you see the blur that you want in the preview window.**

   You can apply the filter several times until you get the effect that you
   want.

Cutting and pasting objects

You can do a number of exciting things when you begin to think of your photos as being made up of *layers*. Your original picture is one layer, but you can then place additional items or effects on different layers, and then merge the picture together to create a new picture. You can cut and paste people and objects around between photos and generally create fun and interesting photos. I'll leave the experimentation to you, but here are the quick steps for cutting and pasting objects from one photo to a layer on another photo.

1. **Open a photo in Photoshop Elements that you want to cut or copy something from.**

2. **Use the Lasso tool on the Tools palette to carefully draw around the object you want to cut, as shown in Figure 7-24.**

3. **Choose Edit⇨Cut or Edit⇨Copy.**

4. **Open the photo onto which you want to paste the object, and then choose Edit⇨Paste.**

5. **Click the object you pasted to select it, and then drag the object to the desired location.**

   If you need to move the layers around more, just select the Move tool on the Tools palette (it looks like an arrow). You can then use the tools discussed throughout this chapter to clean up the pasted object, resize it, or whatever you need to.

6. **When you're done, choose Layer⇨Merge Layers.**

   You now have a new photo, as you can see in Figure 7-25. Make sure you are done editing your photo before you merge the layers. After you merge the layers, you will no longer be able to make changes to individual layers.

Figure 7-25:
The merged
layers
become
one photo.

Working with Text

One of the great things about using any photo-editing program, such as
Photoshop Elements, is the ability to put text on your pictures. You can use
Photoshop Elements features to add titles and text to your photos, and even
paste graphics onto a photo, following the same steps as cutting and pasting
in the previous section.

Adding text to an image is really easy, and you can do some fun things to customize your text as well. First, however, here are the basic steps:

1. **Open a photo in Photoshop Elements by choosing File⇨Open.**

2. **On the Tools palette, click and hold the Text button, which appears
   in Figure 7-26, and choose either the Vertical Type Text tool or the
   Horizontal Type Text tool, depending on how your want to orient
   your text.**

3. **Click the photo and type the text you want.**

4. **Choose Image⇨Transform⇨Free Transform.**

   This setting will now allow you to drag the wording around and stretch it
   to any desired size, as you can see in Figure 7-26.

After you have stretched the wording as desired, just click the Text button on
the Tools palette again. This makes a Text toolbar appear. Use the Text toolbar to change the fonts, size, bolding, italics, underlining, and so on. You can
change the color, and even create warped text using the Warp Text button, as
shown in Figure 7-27. The trick here is to have fun and experiment!

Figure 7-26:
You can place lettering anywhere on your photo.

Figure 7-27:
You can apply many different effects to your text, including warping.

Letting Your Imagination Run Wild

As you can imagine, I have touched only the tip of the image-editing iceberg in this chapter. You can do many, many other things using programs such as Photoshop Elements. You can create panoramic views, make new photos look like antiques, and apply all kinds of special effects filters to photos. You can even mix and match portions of photos together for a mosaic effect. Figure 7-28 is an example of a photo of the Hawaii coastline with a Mosaic tile effect applied to it.

Figure 7-28:
This decorative design was created by applying a Mosaic effect to a coastline photo.

The best way to continue finding out about these features is to invest in one of these programs and start working with some photos. For more information on Photoshop Elements, pick up *Photoshop Elements 2 For Dummies,* by Deke McClelland and Galen Fott (Wiley Publishing, Inc.), and start having fun!

Part IV
Sharing with iPhoto

The 5th Wave   By Rich Tennant

"Why don't you try blurring the brimstone and then putting a nice glow effect around the hellfire."

In this part . . .

Sharing your photos with others is perhaps the best thing about taking digital photos in the first place! The good news is that iPhoto helps you share your photos easily. In Chapter 8, you see how to use iPhoto's feature to print your photos in the size and manner you want. In Chapter 9, you find out how to use photos electronically. You see how to e-mail and scale your photos from within iPhoto, and you find out how to create your own home page at Mac.com. You also see how you can export photos for other uses.

Chapter 8

Printing Photos

- -

- -

*W*hen personal computers first came on the scene in the home and office, many people believed that printers would one day become obsolete. After all, you can work with electronic files, send them over a network, store them — whatever you want. Why would you need to print anything at all?

That forecast was certainly incorrect. Printing and printers are as popular as ever. With programs such as iPhoto, you can even bypass the traditional film developing shop and simply print your photos at home. In fact, printing photos directly from your computer has become so popular that many printers are advertised as photo-quality printers, and the wide variety of photo paper choices often takes up an entire aisle at office supply or discount stores.

In fact, most people who use photo-management software, such as iPhoto, consider printing photos to be one of the major tasks that they do regularly. You may want to put printed pictures in a hardback photo album, frame them, give copies away, or just about anything else that you would typically do with printed pictures. The good news is that printing photos is easier than ever. You may, of course, encounter some problems along the way, and in this chapter, I explore these issues and show you how to get your print output looking the way that you want it to.

Printing Basics

Most people think that they know what printing entails: shove some paper in the printer, choose the photo that you want, and click Print — right? The process of printing photos from within iPhoto is almost that easy, but getting the photo quality that you want when you print your photos is another story. In fact, many newcomers to iPhoto are stunned when they try to print their photos and get really bad results. Before you start blaming iPhoto for the bad print jobs, I'll tell you a secret: iPhoto cannot make your printed photos look great all by itself. Getting great-looking photos depends on three major factors: the printer, the resolution, and the paper. I explore these issues in the next three sections.

Getting the right printer

If you want to print great photos, you need a good inkjet printer. If you're still dragging around that older printer, I'm sorry to tell you that you just won't get good print output for photos. Older printers simply weren't equipped to print great photos. After all, none of us were printing our own photos back in those days.

You may need to buy a new printer. The great news is that photo-quality printers are very inexpensive these days. You can typically get a decent photo-quality printer for as little as $99. Epson and Hewlett-Packard (HP) both make great models that they advertise as photo quality, as do other major manufacturers such as Canon and Lexmark. In fact, most all inkjet printers sold today are geared for photo-quality printing, which should tell you a thing or two about how popular printing photos has become.

The Epson Stylus Photo series of printers is designed specifically for printing photos. Of course, you'll find comparable models produced by HP and even Canon. OS X already has drivers installed for most inkjet printers, so installing the printer is a real snap.

If you're in the market for a new printer, be sure to visit your local computer store to see what is available. You can also visit www.epson.com, www.hp.com or www.canon.com for more information.

And now the bad news . . .

Printing photos from your printer is great fun and really convenient; however, don't assume that the photos are free. True, you don't have to pay for any developing or processing charges, but you do have to pay for paper and ink. Inkjet printers use ink cartridges especially designed for your printer, and they can cost anywhere from $20–40 each. And when you print photos, you burn a lot of ink; so if you print a lot, you'll find yourself replacing the ink cartridges fairly often. Also, to get quality printed photos, you need to use special paper designed for photo printing (which I discuss later in this chapter), and that paper costs you more than standard copy paper that you may use for printing text.

Dealing with resolution

The word *resolution* often strikes fear into hearts of digital photo enthusiasts — and with good reason. The concept of resolution can be difficult to understand at first, and figuring out what resolution is needed in what situation can be dizzying. I teach an online digital photo class, and issues with resolution are always the most troublesome to my students.

My goal in this section is to slay the resolution beast and make resolution easy to understand once and for all.

A digital photo is made up of pixels. A *pixel* is basically a dot of color. One by one, these tiny dots of color are pushed against each other to create the picture that you see before you. The more pixels that a picture contains, the higher the resolution of your photo; the fewer pixels, the lower the resolution. If the pixel count isn't high enough, the pixels are stretched to fit the size of the photo that you want, which creates jagged lines and other print quality issues.

Your digital camera can probably shoot photos at different resolutions, depending on your model. For example, you may notice that your digital camera can shoot at 1024 x 768 or 1600 x 1200. These values represent the vertical and horizontal pixel values, respectively. A 1024 x 768 photo contains 786,432 pixels ($1024 \times 768 = 786,432$). A 1600 x 1200 photo contains 1,920,000 pixels, also called 1.9 megapixel ($1600 \times 1200 = 1,920,000$). In short, the more pixels that reside in a photo, the larger the photo that you can print without losing any image quality.

What resolution do you need to shoot your pictures at? That all depends on the size that you want to print. If you want to print larger photos, such as a 5 x 7 or an 8 x 10, you should shoot at higher resolution (say, 1600 x 1200) so that the pixel count is high enough for your printer to reproduce images of this size.

Here's the deal with iPhoto and resolution: iPhoto cannot give you more pixels in a photo. In iPhoto, you can reduce the number of pixels by cropping the photo, but after you shoot a picture with your camera, the photo is stuck at the resolution at which you originally shot it. So when you're choosing the resolution settings on your camera, you must think about how you're going to output your pictures.

You may think, "Well, I'll just shoot everything at the highest resolution possible." That's true — you can do that, but keep in mind that high-resolution photos are big in terms of bytes. A typical memory card may be able to hold 30 or 40 300K images, but may only hold 2 or 3 high-resolution images (they can be several megabytes in size each), so resolution is always a trade-off between file size and what image quality you need for your purposes. If you know that you need to print a lot of 5 x 7 or 8 x 10 photos, you should shoot at higher resolutions. Table 8-1 gives you a general guideline of the minimum resolution that you need to shoot at to print the size pictures that you may want.

Table 8-1	Resolution and Print Sizes
For This Print Size	*Shoot at This Resolution*
Small prints for computer viewing and online sharing	640 x 480
4 x 6 prints	1024 x 768
5 x 7 prints	1280 x 1024 (1 megapixel)
8 x 10 prints	1600 x 1200 (2 megapixel)
11 x 14 prints	2048 x 1536 (3.3 megapixel)

You may be thinking, "Great — now I know how to set my camera to get the print output that I want, but I already have a bunch of photos in iPhoto — what can I do with those photos that I've already shot?" Again, you need to know the resolution of your existing photos and compare the resolution with the guide in Table 8-1 to know what size pictures you can print. iPhoto easily tells you the resolution of your photos that you've imported.

 In the iPhoto Viewer, select the desired photo that you want to know the resolution of. The Size field just below the Source pane shows the resolution of your photo. (If you don't see that information, click the Show Information about Selected Photos button.)

The photo's size, as shown in Figure 8-1, is listed as a height-times-width value. In the example in Figure 8-1, the size of this picture is 2048 x 1536. This is the pixel value of the photo. Thus, $2048 \times 1536 = 3,145,728$, or 3.1 megapixel. Referring to Table 8-1, you can see that this photo has a high enough resolution to print up to an 8 x 10.

Consider one more example. In Figure 8-2, you see another image. The size of this image is only 279 x 253, which equals 70, 587 pixels. Because the pixel count is so low in this image, even a 4 x 6 print would probably appear grainy or blurry when printed.

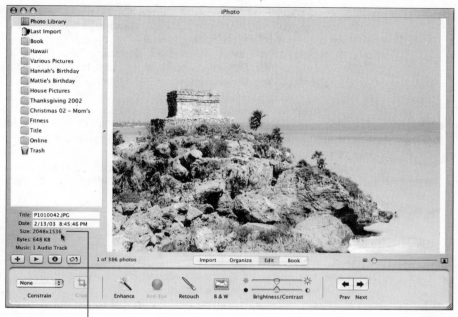

Figure 8-1:
The Size
information
gives you
the number
of pixels in
the photo.

The photo size

Figure 8-2:
Lower-
resolution
images
don't
produce
good print
quality.

Keep in mind that higher resolution values are needed when printing larger sized photos. Study your camera settings, consider your printing habits, and then shoot at resolutions that are generally right for your needs. If your model of digital camera can't shoot at a high enough resolution to print a good 8 x 10 and printing 8 x 10s is really important to you, you should probably think about buying a new camera.

Here's one other quick issue that I'd like to mention: Digital photos typically don't adhere to standard print sizes, such as 4 x 6, 5 x 7, and so forth. If you are printing photos on 8½ x 11 photo paper, this doesn't matter so much. But if you're printing on precut paper, or if you want to make sure that a printed photo fits correctly in a standard size picture frame, you need to edit the photo and use the Constrain feature to crop it to the correct size. Chapter 6 shows you how to constrain a photo.

Choosing the right paper

The printer and the resolution have a great effect on the quality of your photos, but I'll give you one stern warning: The right paper is crucial, too. You may have the best printer and high-resolution photos for printing, but if you don't use the right paper, your photos won't look good.

The dpi value: Muddying the waters a bit more

Dots per inch, or dpi, is the value used with printers. This value represents the number of ink dots that can be used per inch of the photo. This goes back to resolution of the photo; printers just express resolution in dots rather than pixels. What does this really mean to you? In order for a printer to effectively re-create an image, your photos need to meet a certain dpi value — generally around 250 or higher. If you keep your mind set on pixels and resolution as I discuss in this section, you really don't have to worry about dpi; your photos will turn out great. But if you're curious, you can figure the dpi of a photo by dividing what size photo you want to print by a photo's resolution. For example, say you have a 2048 x 1536 resolution photo. You want to print the photo as a 5 x 7. Divide the height by the photo size. In this example, divide 2048 by 7, which equals roughly 292. (Digital photos are measured in width by height, whereas printed photos are measured in height by width. This is why you divide 2048 by 7 — ugh!) Because you need around 250 dpi or higher to get a good quality print, the value of 292 tells you that you're good to go.

Again, my advice is to stick to resolution in terms of your pictures. Think of your camera resolution and compare it against the chart in Table 8-1: This will keep you on the right resolution track and keep you from muddying the waters with dpi values.

You don't have to worry about the 250 dpi value when you buy a printer. All inkjet printers sold today support much higher values than the 250 dpi minimum, so you don't have to worry if the inkjet printer has a high enough dpi to print images.

Photo-quality paper is a must. Regular copy paper that works great for text doesn't work for printing photos: It absorbs too much ink and gives you blurry prints and dull colors, as shown in Figure 8-3.

Figure 8-3:
Copy paper doesn't produce good photo print output.

To print great photos, use glossy photo paper. This paper is heavier, provides a glossy or matte finish (just like you get from a photo developer), and is sold at almost any office supply store or online seller. A sample glossy photo package is shown in Figure 8-4. As you can imagine, you have many brands to choose from — some are more expensive than others, and some even allow you to print on both sides of the paper.

Figure 8-4:
Find many brands of photo-quality paper at any office supply or discount store.

Photo paper is generally sold packages of 12–20 sheets, which will cost you somewhere around $12–20 dollars at the time of this writing. As a general rule, each sheet will cost you around 80 cents but be sure to shop for bargains. You can often find sales and good deals.

Printing with iPhoto

After you have your printer, resolution, and paper issues squared away, you're ready to start printing with iPhoto. Just like iPhoto helps you manage the electronic photos on your Mac, iPhoto can help you easily print those photos as well.

Before you jump feet first into printing, you must understand one important issue: iPhoto has its own printing control window that appears when you choose to print a photo from within iPhoto. This window is different than the standard Mac OS X printing window that you see if you simply print a document or photo from within another program. The standard Mac OS X printing window, shown in Figure 8-5, allows you to choose the printer that you want to use, the presets for the printer, and some additional options, such as the number of copies and pages that you want to print.

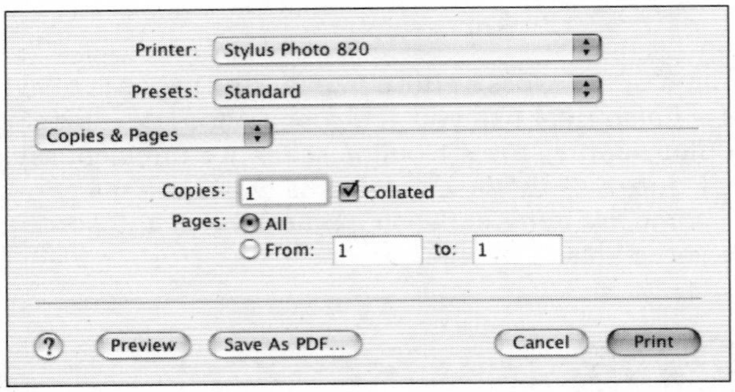

Figure 8-5:
The
Standard
Mac OS X
Print
window.

Printer: Stylus Photo 820

Presets: Standard

Copies & Pages

Copies: 1 ☑ Collated

Pages: ⦿ All
○ From: 1 to: 1

(?) (Preview) (Save As PDF...) (Cancel) (Print)

Again, from within iPhoto, you don't have to do anything with the standard printing window. However, you may need to take a look at some settings specific to your printer to make sure that you get the best print output possible. If you click the Copies & Pages drop-down menu (see Figure 8-5), you can choose Print Settings. This shows an expanded view of the window, shown in Figure 8-6, where you may be able to choose photo-quality printing from the Print Quality drop-down menu. Check your printer documentation to make sure that your printer is configured at a high enough dpi value for photo printing before you move to printing with iPhoto. Just click Print to print from this window, or Cancel to leave it.

To print a photo from within iPhoto, simply click Organize mode. In the Viewer, select the photo that you want to print and click the Print icon on the Organize pane, or choose File➪Print. See Figure 8-7.

If you want to print multiple images, select them in the Viewer by ⌘-clicking them, and then click the Print icon on the Organize pane. Either action brings up iPhoto's Print dialog, which I discuss in the following sections.

When you click Print, you see the iPhoto print dialog. You can choose a few different settings in this box, and the following sections explain them.

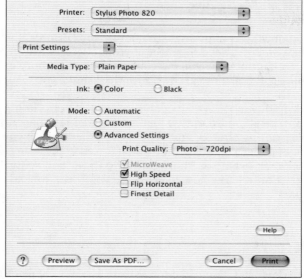

Figure 8-6:
Select
photo-
quality print
options
in the
expanded
Mac OS X
Print
window.

Figure 8-7:
The Print
option
resides in
Organize
mode.

... click Print.   With the Organize mode button selected...

Printer and Presets

The Printer drop-down box allows you to choose your printer. If you have only one printer, you don't need to select anything here. However, if you are using more than one printer, or you have access to one or more network printers, use this drop-down menu to choose the printer you want to print to.

In the Presets drop-down box, you can choose the type of printing that you want to perform. The standard option just means standard paper. However, because you are printing photos, you should click the drop-down menu and choose the type of paper you are printing on. (For example, you can choose Photo on Photo Paper — Fine or Photo on Matte Paper and so forth.) This setting just helps iPhoto know how to calibrate your print job, so you'll get the best results.

Style options

In the Style drop-down list, you can choose from a variety of printing styles: Standard Prints, Contact Sheet (a sheet of thumbnail images), Full Page, Greeting Card, N-Up, or Sampler. The box beneath the Style drop-down list has a variety of options that change depending on which Style option you select. I discuss all these various options in the upcoming sections.

Standard Prints

The default option in the Style drop-down box is set to Standard Prints, as you can see in Figure 8-8. Using the size drop-down menu below the Style drop-down list, you can choose to print the photo as a 2 x 3, 4 x 6, a 5 x 7, or an 8 x 10 image. Just choose the size that you want and then click the Print button.

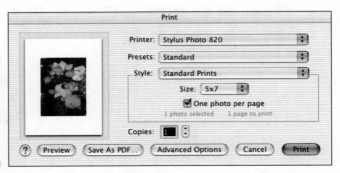

Figure 8-8:
Use the Standard Prints style to choose a print size.

Before printing a 5 x 7 or an 8 x 10, however, keep in mind that print quality always comes back to resolution. If the photo that you want to print doesn't have a high enough resolution, the print quality won't be very good. Fortunately, iPhoto can detect when a photo doesn't have a high enough resolution to print the size that you want. In this case, a yellow triangle with an exclamation point appears in the upper-right corner of the photo area, shown in Figure 8-9. Keep in mind that the yellow triangle is just a warning. It doesn't keep you from printing — it's just there to let you know that quality may be low.

Yellow exclamation icon

Figure 8-9:
The yellow warning triangle tells you that the photo resolution is too low for the size photo you want to print.

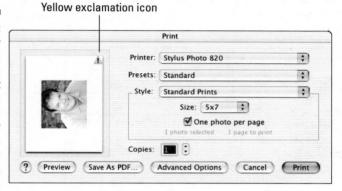

From the Standard Prints option, you can also choose to print multiple photos per page. Just choose the size that you want and then deselect the One Photo Per Page check box, as shown in Figure 8-10, and iPhoto will fit as many pictures on each page as possible. Of course, the reality here is that you can print two 4 x 6 prints per page, two 5 x 7 prints per page, or one 8 x 10.

Figure 8-10:
You can print multiple photos per page.

Contact Sheet

To print a sheet of small images, click the Style drop-down menu and then choose Contact Sheet. Move the Across slider bar to adjust the size of the images that you want to print. As you move the Across slider to the right, the number in the box to the right of the slider increases. This number denotes how many columns of photos will fit across the page. For example, as you can see in Figure 8-11, I move the slider bar to print six copies of the same photo across each line on one page. Although the photos won't adhere to standard photo sizes when I do this, you can still cut them out and pass them around to friends or relatives, for example. You can move the Across slider bar to the far right and make the pictures quite small, even to the point where they are basically the size of thumbnails.

Figure 8-11:
Use the
Contact
Sheet
feature to
print small
contact
prints on
one page.

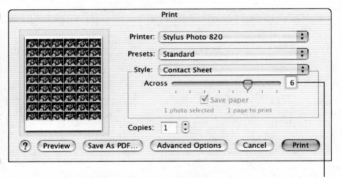

This indicates how many columns of photos print across the page.

You should keep in mind a few important concepts regarding contact sheets:

✔ If you select one photo to print and use the Contact Sheet option, the same photo is repeated over and over on the contact sheet, as shown in Figure 8-11.

✔ If you select several photos to print, the photos are all placed on the contact sheet. Use the Across slider bar to adjust their printing size.

✔ You can also select an entire roll or an album to be printed using the Contact Sheet feature. (Just select the roll in the Viewer pane or the Album in the Source pane and click the Print button.)

✔ If you don't select any photos, the Contact sheet will show everything in the current photo album or the Photo Library, depending on what's selected in the Source pane.

As you work with the Contact Sheet option, notice the Save Paper check box directly beneath the Across bar. If you select this check box, vertical photos are rotated 90 degrees so they fit more snugly with other horizontal photos, thus saving paper. This makes them easier to cut out, but less convenient for viewing because any portrait photos are displayed sideways.

Full Page

The Full Page option allows you to print a photo using the entire sheet of photo paper. You can use the Margins slider bar to adjust the margins around the photo. Just move the Margins slider bar to the left to decrease the margin or to the right to increase the margin and then simply click the Print button. Keep in mind that when you use Full Page, only one photo can fit on each page, and the resolution of the photo that you want to print must be high or you'll see a lot of jagged lines and other problems.

Greeting Card

The Greeting Card option positions your photo on the printed page so that the page can be folded to create a greeting card. When you choose Greeting Card from the Style drop-down menu, you see Style radio buttons to create a single-fold card or a double-fold card, shown in Figure 8-12. A single fold card creates one vertical fold, whereas a double-fold card uses one vertical fold and one horizontal fold.

Figure 8-12: The Greeting Card option allows you to create a single-fold or double-fold greeting card.

Keep in mind that office supply and discount stores sell greeting card paper, which will give you much better results than ordinary photo paper when trying to create greeting cards.

N-Up

The N-Up option (which stands for "number up") is a simple template designed for printing a single photo or even a group of photos. When you choose the N-Up style, you can determine the number of photos that you want to print on a single page. You can print between 1 and 16 copies of the same photo on a single page, all sized accordingly. For example, in Figure 8-13, I am printing all 95 of my Christmas photos. In order to save paper but still get decent sized prints, I have chosen to print 9 photos per page, which will require11 pages to complete the block of 95 photos.

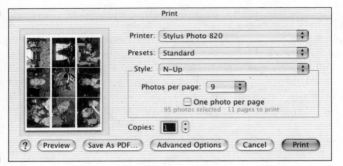

Figure 8-13: N-Up is a template that allows you to easily print photos and conserve paper.

Keep in mind that N-Up is simply a template to help you get the number of photos you want on a single page, thus saving you paper and giving you the size photos you want. However, keep in mind that the photos printed this way will not conform to standard frame sizes, such as 4 x 6.

Sampler

The Sampler option gives you two templates where you can print a combination of photos at different sizes, or a single photo at different sizes. Simply choose Sampler from the Style drop-down menu. In the Template drop-down menu that appears, shown in Figure 8-14, choose 1 or 2. Template 1 gives you one large photo and two small ones, whereas Template 2 gives you one larger photo and up to five small photos.

Keep in mind that the templates do not print the photos to standard frame sizes, such as 4 x 6 or 5 x 7. So, if you want to frame the photos, make sure you use the Standard Prints Style option instead of the Sampler.

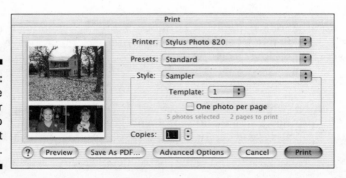

Figure 8-14: Use the Sampler templates to get different size prints.

One thing that iPhoto doesn't do

One aggravating thing that iPhoto doesn't do is give you more control over print arrangement per sheet of paper. For example, there is no way in iPhoto to print a standard 5 x 7 *and* two 4 x 6 prints on a single sheet of paper — even though they will fit. iPhoto doesn't give you a template you can use to select these standard photo size combinations. I hate to use the "w" word here, but Windows XP does give you this option through a printing wizard, so I expect to see this limitation of iPhoto fixed in the near future.

Other printing options

Aside from the standard Style options, you should take note of a few other options on the Print dialog, as explained in the following sections.

Previewing before you print

If you want to see how the printed photos will lay out on the page before you click the Print button, just click the Preview button. This formats the pictures as a PDF file and then opens Adobe Acrobat Reader to display the print job. This feature is really helpful when you're printing multiple pages at the same time because the Print window only displays one page to you. Another great feature of Preview is that you see the full resolution of the photo. In other words, this feature allows you to see how the picture will look when you print it.

Save As PDF

If you click the Save As PDF button, you can save the current print job as a PDF file. This feature can be really helpful if you want to share the job with other users over a network or via e-mail. Because PDF is a standard format that any computer using Adobe Acrobat Reader can use, this is a great way to share photos quickly. You can put an entire album on a contact sheet, save it as a PDF, and then e-mail it to someone for review.

Advanced Options

Clicking the Advanced Options button gives you a shortcut to the standard Mac Print window that I explore earlier in this chapter. You can configure the printer for photo printing here, make multiple copies, and so forth.

Choosing the paper size

iPhoto's print feature assumes that you're using 8½ x 11 paper (standard letter-size paper). Of course, you may be using something different, but you may have noticed that iPhoto's Print window doesn't give you the option to make a paper selection. That's okay because you can choose the Paper size that you're using by choosing File⇨Page Setup. Use the Paper Size drop-down menu to choose the paper size that you want to use. You can even specify your own size, such as 4 x 6, 5 x 7 and so forth.

Ordering Prints Online

Although printing photos directly from your Mac's printer is a cool way to get hard copies of your photos, you can also order prints online. You can do this quickly and easily directly from within iPhoto, thanks to an arrangement between Apple and Kodak. In order to use this feature, you need an active Internet connection. iPhoto allows you to directly connect with a Kodak online interface from which you can order the prints that you want. You pay for those prints online, and in a few days, you get the prints in the mail from Kodak. At the time of this writing, 4 x 6 prints are around 49 cents each, and an 8 x 10 costs only $3.99. You can even order a 20 x 30 poster for about $20. Of course, you'll have to pay shipping charges, and possibly sales tax, depending on where you live. Overall, though, the process is quick, easy, and painless. Just follow these steps:

1. **After making sure that your computer is connected to the Internet, select the photo(s) that you want to order prints of in the iPhoto Viewer.**

2. **In the Organize pane click the Order Prints button, shown in Figure 8-15.**

Figure 8-15: Start the photo order process in Organize mode.

3. **iPhoto connects to the Internet and accesses the Kodak processing center.**

   If a connection to the Internet can't be made, you'll see a message telling you so. Check your Internet connection or wait and try later.

4. Click the Enable 1-Click Ordering button and enter the required information.

You'll need to enter your name, credit card number, mailing address, and other information. You'll also need an Apple ID, which is your e-mail address. The good news is that you only have to enter all this information once because the Kodak Web site will remember who you are from now on.

5. In the Order Prints window that appears, shown in Figure 8-16, each picture appears that you originally selected for print ordering.

Use the provided boxes to enter the quantity and size of the prints that you want. If you see a yellow exclamation point next to certain sizes, the resolution may be too low to print the photo at that size. You can still order it if you want, but the warning just lets you know that the photo may not look great when it is printed. As you make your selections, the order total is calculated.

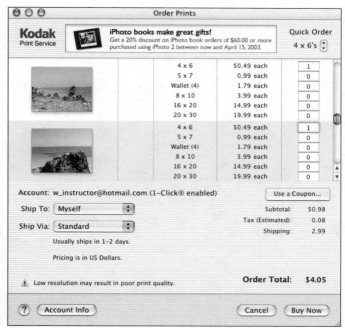

Figure 8-16:
Make your
order
selections
here.

6. When you're done, click the Buy Now button.

You'll see a message telling you that a confirmation will be sent to you via e-mail.

Of course, Kodak isn't the only online processing center available. A number of additional services may work better for your needs than Kodak, but iPhoto doesn't provide a direct way to use these. However, all you have to do is drag the photos that you want to send to an online photo center to your desktop and then use Internet Explorer or Safari to upload them to the online photo center of your choice. Most online photo centers offer a few simple steps for uploading your pictures and selecting the prints that you want. Check out these popular and reputable online photo centers for details.

- ✔ www.snapfish.com
- ✔ www.photo-lab.net
- ✔ www.fotki.com

Chapter 9

Using Electronic Photos

*O*ne of the great advantages of digital photos is that you can use them in ways you could never use print photos. In the past, you took your roll of film to the developer who printed your pictures for a fee. That was cool — and still is — but if you wanted to share those photos in any way, you had to order more prints, mail them out . . . you know the drill.

Enter the digital camera, which creates photos that are digital files that can reside on and be used on any up-to-date computer. Suddenly, you don't need to have multiple prints made — you can simply e-mail photos to friends and family or post them on the Web.

Need to store your digital photos for posterity? No problem — because your photos are electronic, you can create multiple copies and store them on CDs, disks, or even on the Internet if you like.

The best thing about electronic photos is that you have so many choices of what you can do with them — and iPhoto is here to help you. In this chapter, I give you a look at the features iPhoto provides for using your photos electronically, and I also give you a quick peek at a few options you can find on the Internet, outside of iPhoto.

E-Mailing Photos

E-mailing photos to friends and family is one of the great joys of digital photography — and one of the biggest sources of pain and aggravation. Why, you may ask? It all comes down to a little word called *bandwidth*. When you send a photo, your e-mail program has to break the photo down into little pieces that are sent over the Internet to the recipient's mailbox at his (or her) Internet Service Provider. When the recipient connects to the Internet and begins downloading the e-mail from his Internet Service Provider, all those pieces are reassembled in the photo you see before you.

That's all cool, but the problem occurs when a photo's file size is too big. For example, say that I have a 3.2 megapixel camera. I'm trying to capture a great photo of my kids that I can print as an 8 x 10, so I set the camera to capture a high-resolution JPEG file of the kids. No problem: I take the shot, import it to iPhoto, and print it. But what if I'm so happy with the photo that I decide to e-mail it to my mom? I send it to her, but I don't think about the file size, which is 3 megabytes (abbreviated as MB) in size. My mom uses a dialup account with a modem that downloads only 56 kilobytes per second, which means that downloading my 3MB photo will take 20 minutes, or longer. If there is a lot of line traffic and noise, it may not download at all. In fact, many users have a mailbox limit of 5MB, so if I send a couple of photos, I will flood her mailbox and keep her from getting any other mail.

Whew! It can all get very confusing and frustrating, If the only people you communicate with have broadband service (DSL, cable, or satellite), you can be a little more flexible, but if you want to e-mail photos to friends and family members who have dialup modems, you need to reduce the size of those photos so that these folks can reasonably download the photos in a few minutes rather than a few hours.

By the way, in case you are wondering, 1000 kilobytes (1000K) equals 1 megabyte (1MB).

Say, in my scenario, that Mom wants a high-quality photo so she can print an 8 x 10 of the kids as well. She'll need that high-quality, high-size image if she's planning to print an 8 x 10. That's no crime, but the problem is sending that photo through e-mail. Because Mom has a dialup account, she can only get 56K per second, which is going to take awhile with my 3MB file. In this case, I simply tell Mom what she is getting into and send it along, or I can be a good son and simply print and send her a copy via snail mail.

Of course, if Mom doesn't want to print the 8 x 10, I have no reason to send her a file this big. The computer monitor can't display resolution this high, and if she only wants to print a smaller photo, such as a 4 x 6, she doesn't need all that resolution. Once again, your photo decisions all come back to file size, resolution, and what exactly you want to do with the photos.

The good news is that iPhoto has already thought about all this for you. Using iPhoto, you can easily choose a size that you want so you know exactly what you are sending via e-mail and how large the photo is in terms of kilobytes or megabytes.

Of course, to be able to e-mail photos, you have to have an e-mail account set up with your Internet Service Provider (ISP), and you need to have Mail configured and ready to go. iPhoto 2 can also work with Microsoft Entourage, Eudora, and AOL. If you are stumped about configuring your e-mail client, see the Apple Help for instructions on configuring Mail, check the instructions your ISP gave you, or check out *Mac OS X All-in-One Desk Reference For Dummies,* by Mark Chambers, published by Wiley Publishing, Inc.

Before you try to e-mail photos to friends and family, you need to make sure iPhoto knows which mail program you are using. Because iPhoto can work with Mail, Entourage, AOL, or Eudora, you'll need to make sure iPhoto is set to use the e-mail program you want. Simply click iPhoto⇨Preferences. Using the Mail drop-down menu, choose the e-mail program you want to use.

Sending e-mail

After your e-mail program is configured and ready to roll and you have used iPhoto preferences to select the e-mail program you are using, you can easily attach a photo to a message and choose the size for the photo you want by following these steps:

1. **In the iPhoto Source pane, click Photo Library or the album that contains the photo you want to e-mail.**

2. **In the Viewer, select the photo that you want to e-mail.**

3. **Click the Email button that appears in the Organize pane, as shown in Figure 9-1.**

   The Mail Photo dialog appears.

4. **In the Mail Photo box that appears, as shown in Figure 9-2, use the drop-down menu to choose the size that you want. You have the following options:**

   • **Small (240 x 320):** If your recipient only wants to see the photo on the screen and not print it, you can use this small size. Most photos sent using the Small feature will be 100 K or less, which makes for easy downloading no matter what kind of connection the recipient has. However, a photo this small will not have enough resolution to print well.

   • **Medium (640 x 480):** Using this size, your recipient will be able to open and easily see the detail in the photo on the screen and print a small print of the photo. This setting keeps the file size generally to under 150K, so the photo is still small enough to travel the Internet without much trouble.

- **Large (1280 x 960):** This option is good enough for your recipient to print a 4 x 6 print from the photo. The photo will also fill most of the computer screen when viewing. This option keeps the photo to about 450 K or less, so download time will take a little longer than the Medium selection. For printing, though, this option is your best shot.

- **Full Size (Full Quality):** This option emails your photo in the size it currently is. However, your photo will be converted to a JPEG file automatically, so if the photo is a TIFF file, you'll see that the Estimated Size is still smaller than what you may have imagined. (A JPEG file is a compressed file that can more easily be sent over the Internet than an uncompressed file.)

5. **If you want to include the titles and comments you created in iPhoto, just keep the Titles and Comments check boxes selected. If not, clear them.**

6. **Click Compose.**

    The photo is processed and converted to a JPEG format (if it isn't a JPEG already).

Select a photo in the Viewer.

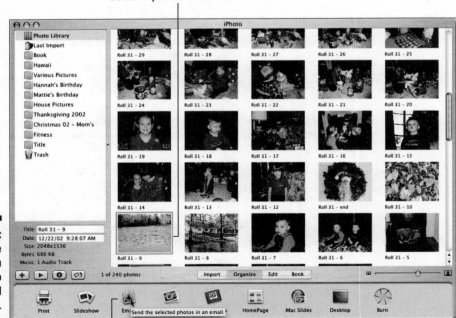

Figure 9-1:
Select the photo you want to e-mail and click Mail.

Click to send the selected photo.

Figure 9-2:
Use the Size
drop-down
menu to
choose the
size of the
photo.

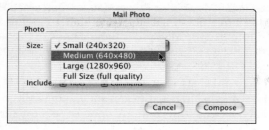

7. **The e-mail program launches, and a new e-mail message appears with the photo inserted.**

8. **Simply enter the recipient's e-mail address, type a subject in the subject area (iPhoto will put the name of the photo as the subject, but you can change it), and type any text that you want in the body of the message.**

9. **When you are done, click Send.**

If you do need to send high-quality photos, make sure that you send them one at a time. Do not select multiple photos and send them in the same e-mail message if the photos are large (450K or higher). You can find information about the size of your photos by selecting the photo in Organize mode, and then checking out the Bytes information displayed below the Source pane.

You may have noticed a few issues and limitations of the iPhoto Mail feature:

✔ **You can send photos in the JPEG format only.** Any photo you select is converted to JPEG before it is placed in your e-mail message. This helps ensure that file sizes stay as small as possible. However, what if you want to mail a TIFF or Photoshop file to a friend? You can do this, but you can't do it from iPhoto. Instead, simply open an empty mail message, and then open iPhoto. Click on the photo that you want to send in the Viewer and drag it to the e-mail message. It will be exported to your e-mail message in its original format. However, be sure to carefully consider the file size before doing this — some TIFF and Photoshop files can be as large as 10MB!

✔ **iPhoto only works with Mac OS X Mail, Eudora, Entourage, or AOL.** However, what if you use another e-mail program? That's no crime, but iPhoto will not work with it, no matter what you have selected in your OS X Preferences. You can try one of two work-arounds:

• You can export photos that you want to mail out of iPhoto. Using the Export feature, you can also scale the photos and choose a file type. Then you can simply drag the photos into your e-mail message from whatever program you are using. See the upcoming "Exporting photos" section for more information.

- Or, if you are using Mailsmith, PowerMail, or QuickMail Pro, you can download a free utility called iPhoto Mailer Patcher, which will make iPhoto use the Mail program you choose in System Preferences. You can download the utility from `homepage.mac.com/jacksim/software`.

✔ **Cropped photos may not scale well.** When you e-mail photos, iPhoto scales them to the size you choose. However, if you have cropped the photo without using the Constrain feature, don't expect the photos to come out to a standard size. In other words, iPhoto will scale them as best it can based on how you cropped the photos. If you want to make sure that the photos are printable in standard size when your e-mail recipient gets them, choose the original file in the Photo Library and click File➪Revert to Original. Then, recrop the photo using the Constrain feature. See Chapter 6 for step-by-step instructions on cropping photos.

Exporting photos

Now, maybe the iPhoto way of sending photos in e-mail messages doesn't work for you. Maybe you want to have more control over the photos, send your photos with a different mail application other than the e-mail clients supported by iPhoto, or compress a bunch of them to send all at once. Maybe you just want a good way to export photos and scale them so you can store them on a CD. No matter what your need, iPhoto doesn't leave you stuck: You can easily export photos, select a size you want, and scale them down if you like. Here's how:

1. **In the iPhoto Source pane, click the Photo Library or click an album to locate the photo(s) you want to export.**

2. **Click the photo you want to export.**

   To export multiple photos, hold down the ⌘ key as you click all the photos you want to export.

3. **File➪Export.**

4. **The Export Images window appears, as shown in Figure 9-3.**

   If the File Export tab is not already selected, click the tab to select it.

5. **From the Format box, choose to export your file in the JPG, TIFF, or PNG format.**

   If you want to export some other type of file types from iPhoto, you need to drag them out of iPhoto to a folder or your desktop in order to export them instead of using the Export command. You then have to scale them as needed in another graphics program.

6. **In the Name area, select either the Use Filename or Use Title radio buttons to determine how your exported file will be named.**

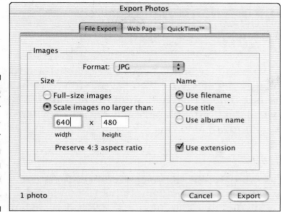

Figure 9-3:
Make your selections for exporting an image from the File Export tab.

7. **Under Size, select either the Full-Size Images radio button or the Scale Images No Larger Than radio button and enter a desired size, such as 640 x 480, in the Width and Height boxes.**

8. **When you've adjusted all the settings in this dialog, click Export.**

9. **In the dialog that appears, enter a filename and choose a location (such as your Desktop) where the file should be saved; click the Save button.**

Posting Your Photos on the Web

E-mailing a bunch of photos around to friends and family can be a difficult task. If you have 20 vacation pictures that you want to show to friends and relatives around the country, you *can* e-mail them a few at a time, but a better way is simply to post your photos on the Web. Then, your friends and family can simply access your Web site and see your photos any time they like.

Before you skip this section, thinking that you don't know enough to create a Web page, keep reading for a moment. iPhoto and a collection of Web services called .Mac bring the power of the Web right to your fingers. You don't need to know anything about creating Web pages at all — iPhoto and .Mac can do it for you! If you want a little more complexity, you can also use Web page creation features at .Mac, or if you are a Web pro yourself, you can even export your photos as Web pages and then manually upload them to your own Web site.

Regardless of your level of experience, one of these solutions is right for you — and it's a great way to share pictures!

Sharing your photos on the Web with iPhoto

Apple created a cool Web site called Mac.com that enables you to do all kinds of things with your Mac. You can create Web pages, store photos, get an e-mail address, share files, and a bunch of other fun and interesting things. To create Web pages by using iPhoto, you must have a .Mac account that will allow you to use the features of Mac.com.

Getting a .Mac account

So, how do you get a membership? Getting a membership is really easy, and best of all, you get a free 60-day trial membership. (If you like the free trial, you can sign up for a full membership for $99.95 a year.) To sign up for the free trial membership, just follow these steps.

1. **Make sure that you have an active Internet connection and click System Preferences in the Dock, or click Apple⇨System Preferences.**

2. **In System Preferences, as shown in Figure 9-4, click the Internet icon found in the Internet & Network section.**

3. **On the .Mac tab of the Internet dialog that appears, as shown in Figure 9-5, click the Sign Up button.**

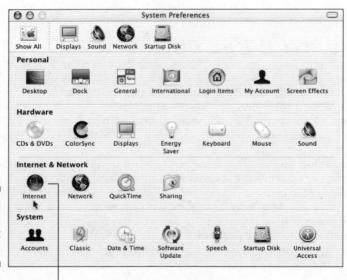

Figure 9-4: Click the Internet icon.

Click to begin signing up for a .Mac account.

Your Internet browser opens and takes you to the Apple .Mac Signup page, as shown in Figure 9-6. This page explains what you get with your free trial membership and how it differs from a paid membership.

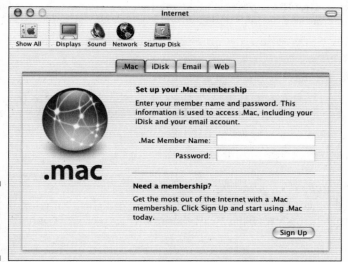

Figure 9-5:
Click the
Sign Up
button.

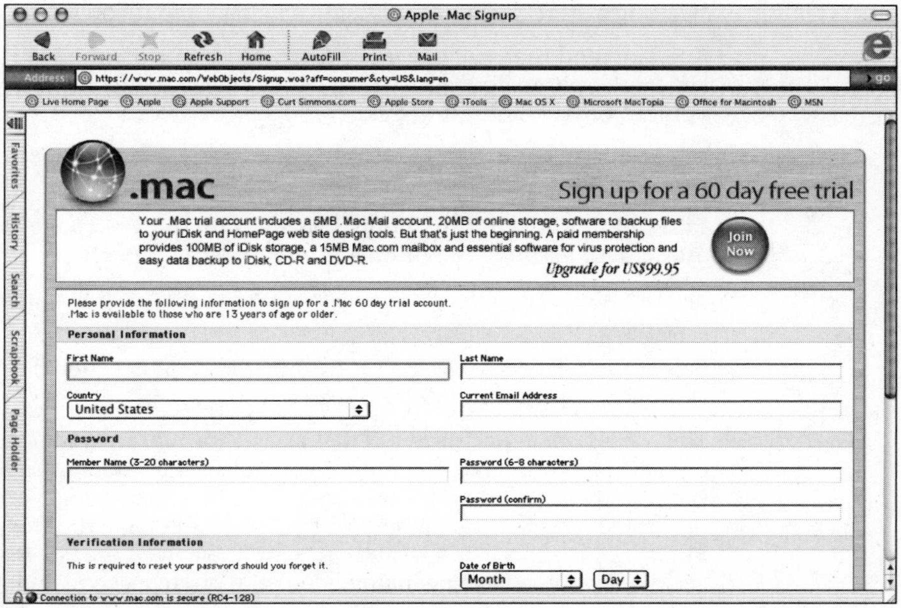

Figure 9-6:
Enter
sign-up
information.

4. **Enter the information requested on the Web page and click Continue at the bottom of the page when you're done.**

   After the account is created, you see a page that asks you to print your account information. This page contains your username and password, so you should keep it for future reference. You also see your Mac.com e-mail address, which you can begin using right away.

5. **After you've printed your account information, you are free to close the browser.**

   You now have a Mac.com account!

6. **Return to the .Mac pane of Internet System Preferences (refer to Figure 9-5); enter your .Mac Member Name and your Password.**

   You are now ready to begin using your .Mac account.

7. **Close System Preferences.**

Creating your Web page by using iPhoto

The great news is that a Web page where you can show off your photos in iPhoto is just a few clicks away. Before trying to create your Web page, however . . .

   ✔ Make sure that you have an active Internet connection.

   ✔ Make sure that you have set up a .Mac account — see the section "Getting a .Mac account," earlier in this chapter, if you haven't.

   ✔ Keep in mind that you can store up to 48 photos on one Web page (the size of the photos doesn't matter). If you need to store more than this, you can create multiple pages.

When you're ready, just follow these steps:

1. **In iPhoto, organize the photos you want on the Web page into an album and arrange the photos in the order you prefer.**

   See Chapter 4 to find out more about photo albums if you need more information.

2. **Select the album by clicking it in the Source pane; then click the HomePage button in the Organize pane.**

   You see a Connecting progress dialog, as shown in Figure 9-7, as iPhoto connects to your .Mac account. (If you didn't enter your .Mac Member Name and password on the .Mac tab of the Internet dialog, you'll be prompted to enter your .Mac Member Name and password for .Mac.) The Publish HomePage window appears, as shown in Figure 9-8. As you can see, your photos have been uploaded ; the photos also include their titles.

Click the HomePage icon.

Figure 9-7:
Click the
HomePage
icon and
wait for the
connection.

Click the HomePage icon.

3. **Click any of the buttons near the bottom of the window (refer to Figure 9-8) to select a framing option for your photos.**

   Click a different button to change the frame, or click the button on the far left to remove frames.

4. **To edit the captions you see on-screen beneath each photo, just click on the caption and retype the new text. You can also click the title and subtitle to change them as well.**

   Note that you have a 40-character limit on the captions you create for the photos.

5. **After you enter your captions, Control-click each caption and choose Spelling⇨Check Spelling to check each caption's spelling.**

   You can also select Speech⇨Start Speaking to have your captions read back to you — this helps you find captions that are poorly worded or awkward.

6. **After you are happy with your HomePage, just click the Publish button.**

   The connection is made, and the photos are transferred, as shown in Figure 9-9. Your photos are scaled to 800 x 600 so that they can more easily be displayed in a Web browser.

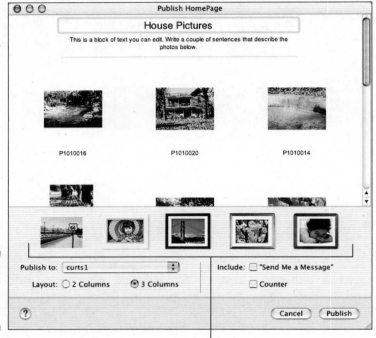

Figure 9-8:
The Publish
HomePage
window.

Select your frame options here.

7. **After the page is uploaded, you see a message, as shown in Figure 9-10, confirming that the page has been published and giving the URL that anyone can use to access the page.**

Be sure to note the HomePage address (the URL). It is case sensitive, so make sure that you type it correctly when you share it with friends and family. Your .Mac address will always be in the form of `http://hompage.mac.com/yourusername/PhotoAlbumX.html`, where X is the HomePage number, such as 1, 2, 3, or 4. Any pages you upload after your initial HomePage will simply jump to the next page number.

8. **On the confirmation message, click Visit Page Now to see your page.**

This opens your default browser so you can see your HomePage come to life. Your HomePage should look something like the one shown in Figure 9-11.

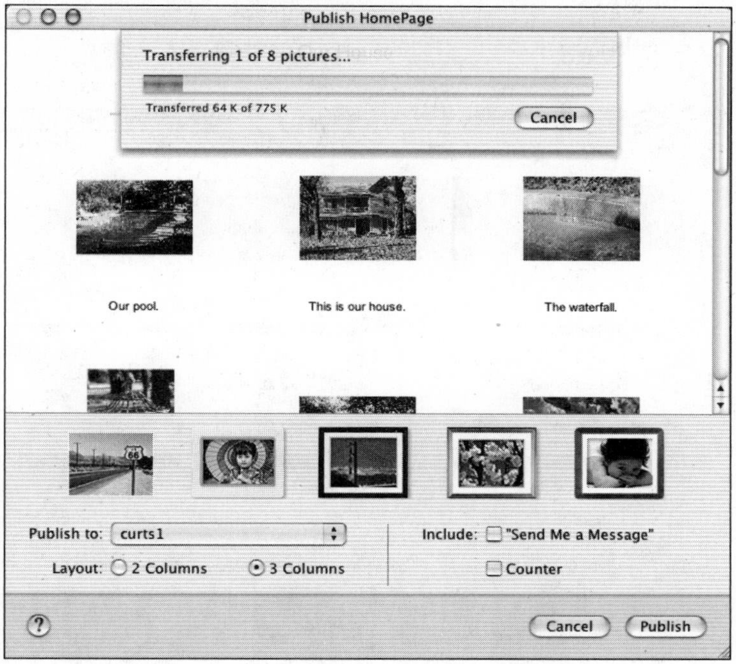

Figure 9-9:
Click
Publish to
upload your
HomePage.

Figure 9-10:
The address
of your new
HomePage.

While at your HomePage, you can click an image to see a slide-show version of the page, shown in Figure 9-12, or you can just click the Start Slideshow button (refer to Figure 9-11). In Figure 9-12, notice the arrow buttons at the bottom of the window that enable you to move forward and backward through the photos.

Click to start a slide show.

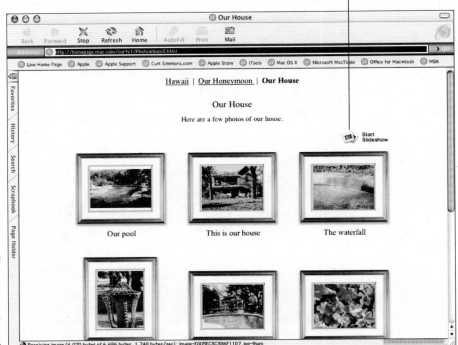

Figure 9-11:
Here's
what a
HomePage
looks like.

Figure 9-12:
You can
view the
photos at
your Web
page as a
slide show.

Editing your Web page

Time to face the facts — no matter how much proofing you do or how carefully you arrange your photos, they may not look the way that you want them to look when you publish them. Perhaps you made a mistake, or maybe you just want to change the order in which they appear. Regardless, .Mac doesn't leave you out in the cold. You can simply access your .Mac account and edit your HomePage, and here's how to do it:

1. **Connect to the Internet, open your browser, and access** www.mac.com.

2. **On the .Mac home page that appears, click the HomePage button at the top of the window.**

3. **If you are prompted to log in, enter your .Mac account username and password.**

4. **In the HomePage window that appears, as shown in Figure 9-13, select the page you want to edit in the Pages list and then click the Edit button.**

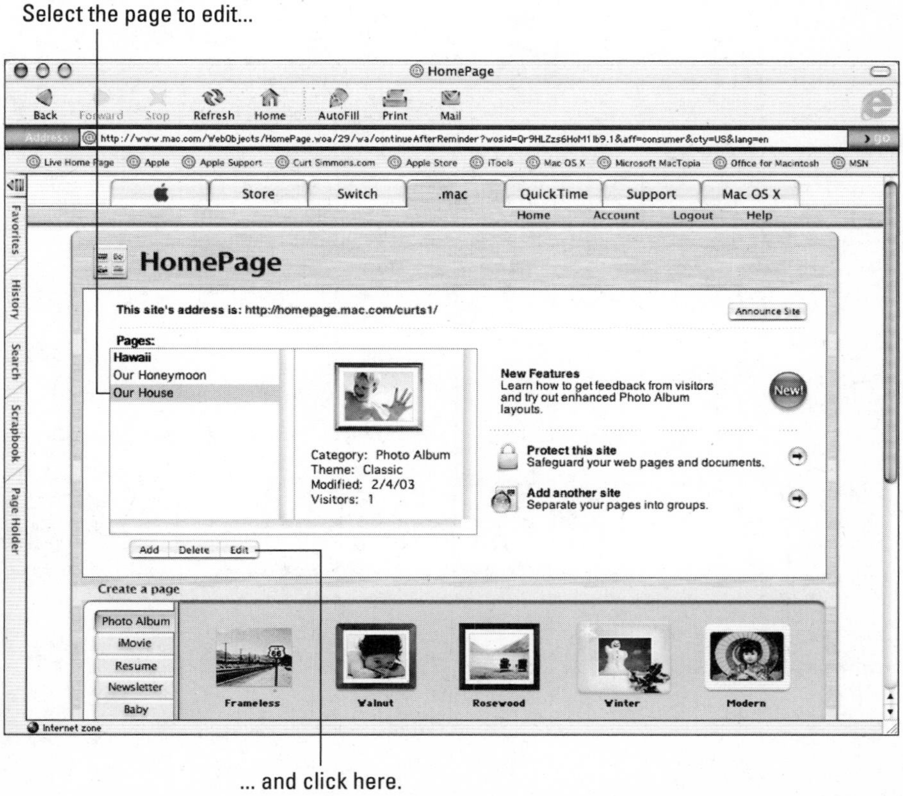

Select the page to edit...

Figure 9-13: Select the page you want to edit, and then click Edit.

... and click here.

5. **An Edit window appears where you can remove photos, change the captions, or make any other changes that you may want to make.**

As you can see in Figure 9-14, you can edit the captions by simply clicking in the dialogs and retyping. If you want to remove a photo, clear the Show check box that appears on the photo. Also, note that in the upper-right corner, you can change the column layout and theme as well.

6. **When you're done, click the Publish button (shown in Figure 9-14) to save your edits.**

Another way to fix a page (especially one that you intend to seriously over-haul) is to simply delete the page and then go back to iPhoto, re-create the page, and upload it. (To delete a HomePage, simply follow Steps 1-4 in the preceding step list, except click Delete instead of Edit in Step 4.) However, one issue to keep in mind is that *photos* are not deleted from Mac.com, even when you delete the page. The photos are stored your iDisk Pictures folder, so you'll have to go there to delete the photos if your storage space starts to run out. I explain how in the "Working with iDisk" section, later in this chapter.

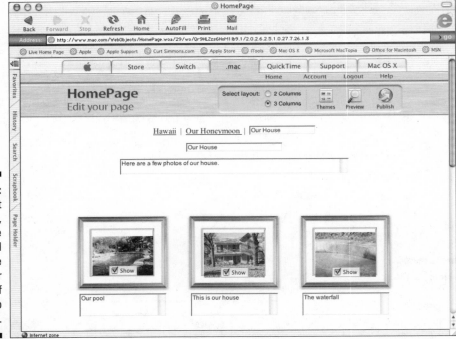

Figure 9-14:
You can edit captions, remove photos, and change the layout or theme of your Web page.

Creating a Web page at .Mac

Sure, iPhoto is a great and easy way to publish photos to .Mac. However, if you want more control, more flexibility, and more options, you can simply bypass iPhoto and go directly to .Mac to create your HomePages. After you play around with the options there, you'll probably find them more flexible and useful — without having to know any HTML or anything else about Web pages at all.

When you create a Web page at .Mac, you do everything through your Web browser and actually create the page on their site, rather than assembling it on your Mac and uploading it. As such, creating the HomePage can be little bit tedious and slow if you are using a dialup connection, but the ease of use and the results are well worth it.

The first thing you have to do is take a look at uploading your photos to your iDisk account. iDisk is basically a storage area on .Mac that you are given when you sign up for your .Mac account. You are given 20MB of storage space with the free trial membership, but if you want more, you can purchase full membership. A full membership will give you 100MB of storage space.

Working with iDisk

If you have a .Mac account, you get iDisk along with it. If you open System Preferences and click the Internet icon, you see how much space you are currently using in your iDisk account, as shown on the iDisk tab in Figure 9-15.

Figure 9-15: Use the iDisk tab to see how much storage space you have.

A word about public folder access

As you may notice in Figure 9-15, your iDisk is protected by Read-Only access. This means that people can see what is in your iDisk Public folder, but they can't change what is there. However, if you want a way to trade files and photos with someone, you can allow it by selecting the Read-Write radio button. This way, someone can see what is in your folder, copy it, and upload files to you as well. Although this easy way to trade files without the hassle of e-mailing them works great, keep in mind that any files uploaded to your Public folder will also count toward your megabyte limit.

You can also configure the iDisk tab to require users to enter a password to access your public folders. Just select the Use a Password to Protect Your Public Folder check box option to enable it, and you are prompted to enter and confirm the password you want to use. Then, just e-mail the password to those whom you want to allow to access your folder. You can return to this tab to change the password at any time if necessary.

So, how do you access your iDisk folders? In the Finder, just click Go⇨iDisk. This connects you to `idisk.mac.com`. You see a folder named after your .Mac username that contains several subfolders, as you can see in Figure 9-16, including the Public Folder where you can share files with other people. To get familiar with iDisk, it's a good idea to read the About Your iDisk file.

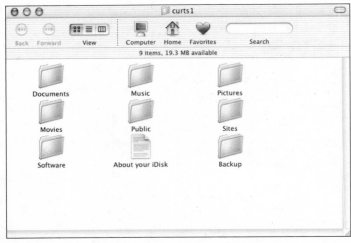

Figure 9-16:
Your iDisk folder.

To upload your photos, just drag the ones you want out of iPhoto and to the Pictures folder. They will be copied over the Internet to your Pictures folder so you can use them when you create your Web pages at .Mac. You can upload multiple photos by ⌘-clicking them in iPhoto and dragging the group to the Pictures folder. You may want to open the Pictures folder and create additional subfolders within it to keep your photos organized.

Before you start copying your photos, however, consider using the File⇨Export command in iPhoto to export them, rather than just dragging them to the Pictures folder. Why? When you export photos, you can scale them to a smaller size, thus reducing their file size. This will save you room on iDisk, and your Web page will work faster for your visitors who are trying to download all those photos.

Creating your Web page

Now that you have photos in iDisk, you are ready to start creating your Web page. Just return to www.mac.com, click HomePage, and sign in if necessary. This takes you to the same window you used to edit your existing HomePage (refer to Figure 9-13).

Instead of editing, however, you are free to create new pages. Click the Add button to add a new page. The HomePage options appear, as shown in Figure 9-17.

Figure 9-17: Choose the page you want to create and the template you want.

You can choose from the following kinds of pages:

- ✔ **Photo Album:** This option allows you to create a photo album page, just like the photo albums you create within iPhoto.

- ✔ **iMovie:** If you have exported a slide show from iPhoto to QuickTime, or created a movie in iMovie that has been exported to QuickTime, you can upload your movie to your iDisk Movies folder and show the movie on the Web.

- ✔ **Newsletter:** The option here provides you with templates to create a newsletter that Web surfers can access and read. Choose from the cool themes provided to create a really nice-looking newsletter!

- ✔ **Baby:** New baby in the house? Use the themes here to show off your baby pictures to the world.

- ✔ **Education:** Create a school events newsletter, school album, résumé, play tickets, homework page, and more!

- ✔ **Invite:** Create a cool invitation, and then just send the folks you're inviting to your event the page link.

- ✔ **File Sharing:** If you are sharing files in your Public folder, create a page showing what is available to be downloaded.

- ✔ **Site Menu:** This option shows you standard theme options, such as Graphite, Modern, Brushed Metal, and Western.

After you have decided on the kind of page you want, just click the tab, then choose from the list of templates. The template appears before you, ready for your input and customization.

What you then do depends on the kind of page you choose to create and what photos or movies you decide to upload. The following steps for creating a page with iMovie are an example for you to follow, but all templates basically work in the same manner. The main thing is to get familiar with the buttons and controls available to you in each template. In this example, I have created a slide show in iPhoto and then exported it as a QuickTime movie (see Chapter 11 to find out how). This is how I created the slide show:

1. **Make sure your Internet connection is active, and then open iDisk by clicking Go⇨iDisk in the Finder.**

   When iDisk opens, you see your folders, including a Movies folder.

2. **Open the Movies folder.**

3. **Drag the movie to the Movies folder.**

4. **After the upload is complete, open a browser and go to** www.mac.com.

5. **At .Mac, click the HomePage icon at the top of the page.**

6. **On the HomePage, click the Add button.**

7. **In the list of pages that appear, choose the iMovie tab, and then click a template that you like from the choices that appear to the right of the iMovie tab.**

    The template that you chose appears. I chose the Drive-in Movie template (as shown in Figure 9-18) for this example.

8. **Click the Edit button that appears in the upper-right portion of the window.**

    When you click Edit, a Choose button appears on the movie screen on the template.

9. **Click Choose.**

    The iDisk Image Library opens, as shown in Figure 9-19.

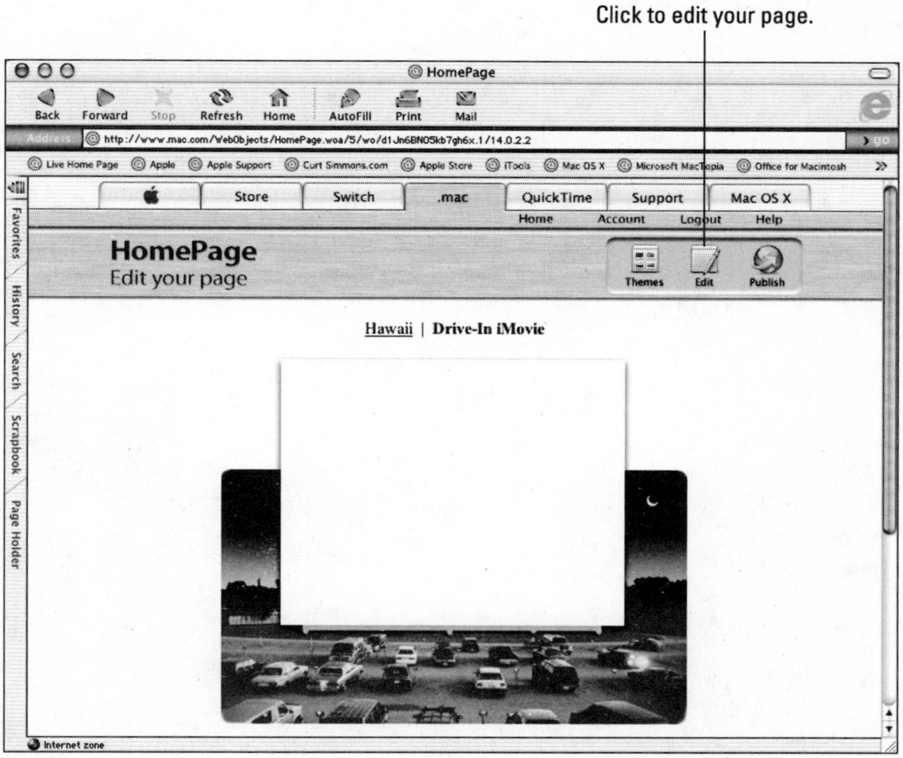

Click to edit your page.

Figure 9-18: The template that you chose appears.

10. **Browse to the Movies folder, choose the movie you uploaded, and click the Choose button.**

    Your movie is now loaded into the page.

11. **Next, edit the available titles and captions as desired.**

    Scroll around on the template to see the text boxes that you can edit. Just click in the box and type the text you want.

12. **When you are satisfied, just click the Preview button to see how everything looks.**

    The Preview button appears in the upper-right corner of the page and is shown in Figure 9-20.

13. **If you are satisfied with the preview, click Publish (refer to Figure 9-20).**

14. **If you decide to make changes to the page later, simply return to the main HomePage window, select the page, and click the Edit button.**

    See the "Editing your Web page" section earlier in this chapter for more information.

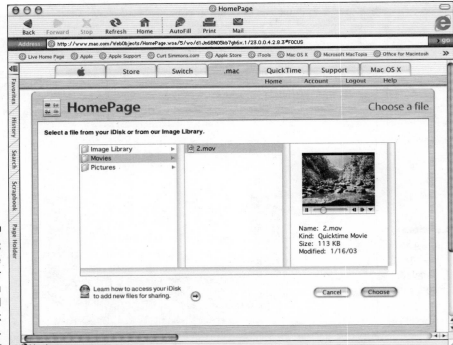

Figure 9-19:
Select the movie or picture you want and click Choose.

Click to preview.

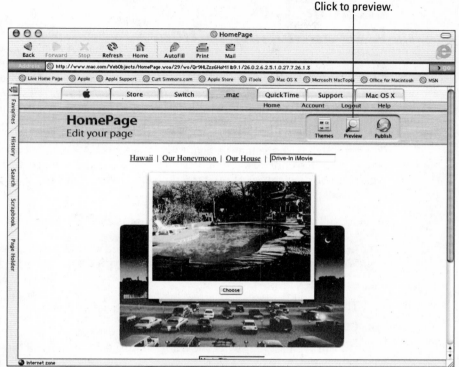

Figure 9-20:
Click the
Preview
button to
see your
creation.

Obviously, each template works a little differently, but the same basic controls apply to all. By using these templates, you can create some really cool Web pages without knowing a single thing about programming. Just create your pages and send the page addresses to your friends. They will be enamored and impressed with your skills!

Before you leave .Mac, let me point out one other item you may want. If you go to www.mac.com and click the HomePage icon to get to your HomePage, you'll see a Protect This Site button (refer to Figure 9-13). This option allows you to create a password for your site so that only people you know can access the site. After clicking the Protect This Site button, simply enter a password, select the On check box, and click Apply Changes. Now, anyone who wants to view your site will have to enter a password, instead of your site being free for all the world to see. Just be sure to share the password with all your friends when you give them the address of your page.

Creating Web pages with Web authoring software

All right, say you're a snazzy Web site owner with your own Web site. You use some Web site authoring tool, such as Adobe GoLive or Macromedia Dreamweaver (or even FrontPage if you are also using Windows). No matter: iPhoto can help you at least a bit if you want to upload a bunch of pictures to create thumbnails that your visitors can click on.

I'll admit, this isn't the most elegant way to create a Web page (you won't get all the graphics controls you may want), but if you need to create a quick Web page of 30 vacation photos to add to your site, you can't beat it for ease and speed.

To do so, all you have to do is export the photos as a Web page, and here's how:

1. **In iPhoto, select the film roll or album that you want to export as a Web page (or select individual photos if you like).**

2. **Click File⇨Export.**

   The Export Images dialog appears.

3. **Click the Web Page tab.**

4. **On the Web Page tab, as shown in Figure 9-21, enter the information requested.**

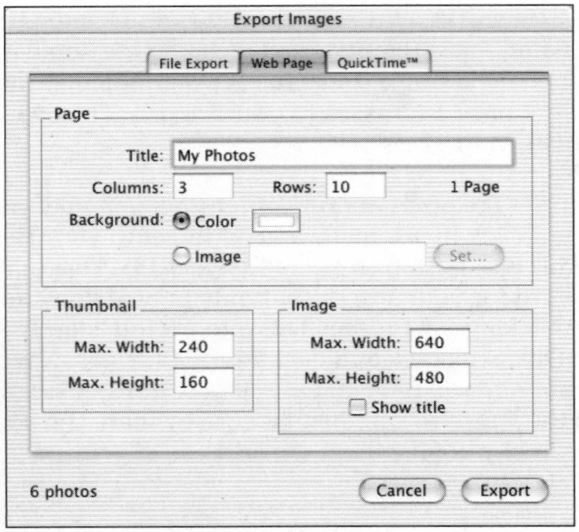

Figure 9-21: Exporting images as a Web page.

You have the following options:

- **Title:** Type a desired title for the Web page.

- **Column and Rows:** You can use the boxes to enter the number of columns and the number of rows you want displayed on each page. This feature basically organizes how the page with the thumbnails of your photos will look. Keep in mind that the more columns and rows you use, the more crowded the page will be. For this reason, the default of 3 columns and 10 rows often works best.

- **Background:** If you want to use an image for the background, select the Image radio button, and then click the Set button to browse for the image you want. Alternatively, you can specify a background color by selecting the Color radio button, and then clicking the color box. The Colors dialog appears, shown in Figure 9-22. Click the color you want with your mouse pointer, and then close the dialog.

Figure 9-22:
Choose the color by clicking on the wheel.

- **Thumbnail:** The default thumbnail size is 240 x 180. You can increase or decrease that value to adjust the size of the photo thumbnails. You can also choose to include the title of the photo and any comments you have placed on the photo.

- **Image:** When a user clicks on a thumbnail, the image appears in the Web browser. Use the Image max width and height to specify the size of the image. The default setting is 640 x 480, which is generally a good size for browser display. You can also include the title and comments on the actual image by selecting the check boxes.

5. **When you're done, click Export.**

6. **Choose a folder to save the files in and click OK.**

After you are done, you'll end up with an Index.html file and folders containing your pages, images, and thumbnail files on your desktop (or in whatever location you choose to save the files in). You can double-click the Index.html file to see the page in any browser. At this point, follow the directions for your particular Web authoring software to upload all the files to your Web site.

Other Free Web Options

Of course, iPhoto and .Mac give you lots of cool options for e-mailing and posting photos and slide shows on the Web; however, you are not limited to iPhoto's offerings. You can always export photos out of iPhoto (by using the Export option so you can scale them and choose the JPEG format) and then upload them to any number of Web sites that offer you free storage and free online photo albums. Then, all you have to do is send your friends and relatives the links. Check out these popular sites to get started:

- www.webshots.com
- www.ofoto.com
- www.imagestation.com
- www.photoisland.com
- www.picturetrail.com

Part V
Fun iPhoto Projects

The 5th Wave   By Rich Tennant

©RICHTENNANT

"Ooo-wait! That's perfect for the clinic's home page. Just stretch it out a little further... little more..."

In this part . . .

*i*Photo is great fun, and in this part, I take a look at some fun projects you can do with your photos. In Chapter 10, you find out how to create an iPhoto book, which you can order from Apple and have shipped right to your door. In Chapter 11, you discover the iPhoto slide show. See how to make the slide show, use your own music, and even how to export it to QuickTime. In Chapter 12, you can go beyond iPhoto to iMovie and see how you can combine your photos and movie clips to create a custom movie. In Chapter 13, you see how you can use iDVD to burn your slide shows and movies to a DVD so you watch them on any standard DVD player. Finally, in Chapter 14, you see how to use desktop pictures, make your own screen effect, and use helpful plug-ins.

Chapter 10

The iPhoto Book

*O*ne disadvantage of digital photos is that viewing them at your leisure, rather than in front of a computer, is difficult. Sure, you can print out the photos and put them in a standard photo album, but most of us want something more — to use our best digital pictures in a cool and new way.

Enter the iPhoto book, which is a hardcover book of a collection of your photos. You can custom-create your own book with a title, captions, and layouts of your choosing. And after your book design is finished, you upload the book to the friendly folks at Apple and pay a fee for the printing, and in a few weeks, your book arrives at your doorstep.

At first glance, this product may seem like a novelty, but stop and think for a movement. Remember that this book is a hardcover book, beautifully produced, of your photos. It's a great keepsake of

- ✔ A child's first birthday
- ✔ The trip of a lifetime
- ✔ A retirement party
- ✔ A wedding
- ✔ Your kid's first soccer game
- ✔ A small catalog of your products or services
- ✔ A yearbook
- ✔ Anything else that's really worth remembering

An iPhoto book makes a wonderful gift, too. Do you go to Mom's every year for Christmas? Use your digital camera to take a bunch of family photos and then use iPhoto to create and order a book for her — she'll love it.

In the rest of this chapter, I walk you through creating an iPhoto book. Creating an iPhoto book is easy, but I do point out a few pitfalls to avoid along the way.

What You Get from an iPhoto Book

If you're a seasoned skeptic, the first thing that you probably want to know is what you're going to get when you order an iPhoto book. I don't blame you. Before I first ordered an iPhoto book, I wanted to know what I would really get before I parted with my hard-earned money.

I can safely say that you can relax. The iPhoto book is high quality, looks great, and is something that you'll be proud of. When you order an iPhoto book, you get a real, hardback, 9-x-11-inch book from a real printer — not something that's been weakly bound together or printed on cheap paper. Here's what makes it such high quality:

- ✔ The book is linen covered and comes to you in a slipcover.

- ✔ Your photos and captions are printed on glossy, acid-free paper, so your photos look great and will last a long time.

- ✔ The book is printed on single-sided pages, and you can customize how those pages look.

Are you almost sold? Sure, but what about the price? The book costs $30 for ten pages (the minimum page count). Each additional page is $3 (a maximum of 50 pages). At first glance, that may seem kind of steep, but remember that the book is a hardcover that contains photographic pages — and it's custom built for you. In terms of a gift or keepsake to remember a special event or day, it's really pretty inexpensive. And payment is easy, too. After you create your book in iPhoto (and when you're happy with it), you upload it to Apple and pay the book fee.

If you're thinking that you can find a printer on the Internet for less, you might be right. But before you go surfing for your own printer, remember that iPhoto is integrated with Apple's ordering system, so you don't have to worry about whether the printer can use the same type of file format that you're using for your photos. And you have the peace of mind of going with a reputable company. Of course, Apple isn't in the book printing business; Apple outsources that job to a vendor, but you can rest easy that you'll actually receive your book and that you'll get it in a timely manner. You may want someone else to print your book (and that's no crime), but if you want to have it printed easily and without any worries, I'd stick with Apple.

Getting Your Photos Ready for the Book

The first task when creating an iPhoto book is to decide what pictures you want to include. This task is usually harder than you may first think because if you're like me, you want to put more pictures in the book than you can afford.

An iPhoto book can have a few pictures on a single page, one picture per page, or any combination (which usually looks best). The iPhoto book feature even allows you to produce a catalog or yearbook, which uses small pictures on each page. Sure, you can get a lot of pictures into your book this way, but the results don't look as good. The best book usually contains some pages with one large picture, some pages with two pictures, and occasionally some pages with three pictures.

When planning your book, take a hard look at your pictures and do a little culling. Of course, your book can be over the 10-page/$30 minimum, but remember that each additional page costs you $3. That can quickly add up, so think about your budget as you move forward.

When you start to sift through your pictures and choose the ones that you want to use, keep these points in mind:

- ✔ **You may love all your pictures, but they're probably not all book-worthy.** Try to be your own best critic and choose only those photos that really look great. If your photos are of people, which they probably are, try to choose only the photos that are flattering to those people.

  These photos will be printed for all time in your book, so you want the people in the book to look good forever.

- ✔ **Photos that have a lot of clutter don't work well.** Figure 10-1 shows my girls and me opening Christmas presents. I love this photo, but note the clutter in the picture and that my youngest daughter isn't even looking at the camera. This is a good one for a print or a slideshow, but it won't be the best one in a photo book. Again, save yourself some real estate and choose only the best photos for the book.

- ✔ **Don't use problem photos or be sure to edit them first.** Look at every picture very carefully before you include it in your iPhoto book. Use iPhoto's Edit mode to fix problems with brightness, contrast, or red eyes first. See Chapter 6 to discover more about fixing photos.

✔ **Avoid using black-and-white photos.** Although black-and-white photos look great as prints, the book printing process isn't that friendly to them, and they usually don't turn out that great in an iPhoto book.

Figure 10-1:
Although
I love this
photo, it
isn't the
best choice
for an
iPhoto book.

When you start culling your photos down to the ones that you want to use, create a digital album to keep the photos in. You can create your book only from an album in iPhoto, so click the Create a New Album button and drag the photos from the Photo Library to the new album. (See Chapter 4 if you need more details on how to create and add pictures to an album.)

After you select the photos that you want to use in your book in the album, drag them around in the album to create a preliminary order for the book. This will become the order in which the photos appear on the book pages. You can adjust this later while you're assembling the book, but you should get at least a preliminary order established in the album first. This will make designing your book easier. In particular, be sure that the photo that you want to appear on the cover of your book is the first picture in the album: That's one thing that iPhoto doesn't let you change later.

In fact, I'll go so far as to say that you can save yourself a lot of headaches and aggravation if you spend time in your album getting the order of the photos right. You *can* organize photos while you are working on the book, but it can be tricky and frustrating, so I recommend that you spend some time in the album getting the photos in order before you move forward.

Sizing your photos correctly

After your selected photos are in order, take a look at a couple of important issues concerning your photos, the first of which is size. Because iPhoto has photo templates hidden under each page, iPhoto has a limited number of ways that it can organize photos on a page. In doing so, iPhoto makes an assumption that your photos follow the standard 4:3 aspect ratio. Most digital cameras automatically shoot at the 4:3 aspect ratio, so iPhoto's templates are designed to hold photos at this ratio. If your photos aren't at this ratio, they won't lay out correctly on the page, especially if you have more than one photo on a page. Some photos will be too short, leaving a big white gap on the page, and some may even run off the page altogether.

So, how do you know if your photos are in the 4:3 aspect ratio? If you shot them with a digital camera, they probably are, but you can check them by dividing the width (in pixels) by the height (in pixels). If the value you get is 1.333 for a horizontal photo or .75 for a vertical photo, the aspect ratio is good to go.

If you haven't cropped any of your photos, and if you haven't changed your camera settings so that it no longer shoots at a 4:3 aspect ratio, you're probably in good shape. Even if you have done something to modify the 4:3 ratio, don't worry. You can use iPhoto to recrop the photos so that they fit neatly on iPhoto's book pages. Here's how:

1. **If you've previously cropped the photo, select the photo in your Viewer and then choose File➪Revert to Original.**

   This takes your photo back to its original appearance before you edited it.

2. **Select the photo in the Viewer and then click the Edit button to switch to Edit mode.**

3. **In Edit mode, use the sliders to adjust the Brightness/Contrast, the Red Eye feature to correct red eye if necessary, and the Enhance and Retouch tools to fix any other problems if necessary.**

   See Chapter 6 for more detailed instructions on editing photos.

4. **In the Constrain drop-down menu, shown in Figure 10-2, choose 4 x 3 (Book, DVD).**

   When you crop the photo, this option will constrain the photo to the 4:3 aspect ratio that you need for the book. If you want a photo to be cropped as a portrait, choose the 4 x 3 (Portrait) option on the Constrain drop-down menu.

5. **With your mouse pointer, click and drag to create the crop box on the photo as desired, as shown in Figure 10-3.**

Figure 10-2:
Choose the
4 x 3 (Book,
DVD)
constrain
option to
recrop
photos.

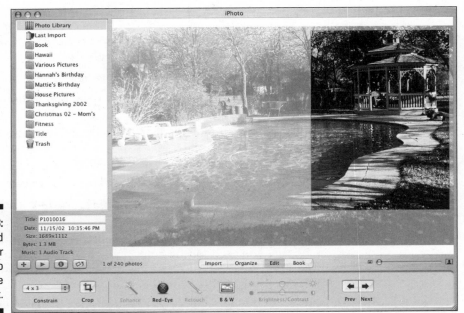

Figure 10-3:
Click and
drag your
mouse to
create the
crop box.

6. **Click the Crop button (as shown in Figure 10-2) to crop the photo.**

7. **Repeat these steps on your other photos as necessary to make sure that they're cropped with the 4:3 aspect ratio.**

Making sure that your photos are the right resolution

After your photos are sized and cropped correctly, you should think about one additional issue: resolution. Keep in mind that your photos will be printed, and the book printer can only work with what you send. If you use low-resolution photos, they won't print well and won't look good in your book.

To help you weed out low-resolution images in your book, iPhoto alerts you to them by displaying a yellow warning triangle on low-resolution photos when you use them in Book mode, as you can see in Figure 10-4. If you try to order a book with low-resolution photos, you will receive another warning before you place the order. The yellow triangle is just a warning — you are still free to use the photo in the book. The reality is, however, that your photos won't look good in the book without high enough resolution.

The yellow warning icon indicates a low-resolution photo.

Figure 10-4: Low-resolution photos trigger a yellow warning triangle when you go into Book mode.

If you see the yellow warning icon on your favorite photo, here are some remedies that you can try:

✔ **Move the photo within the book.** Adjust the location of the low-resolution photo onto a page with other photos (read the next section to discover how). This will decrease the size of the photo and hopefully solve the resolution problem. If the yellow triangle disappears, you know that you're safe.

✔ **Use an uncropped version.** If you've cropped the photo, try going back to the album and reverting to the original. This may give you enough extra pixels to solve the problem.

✔ **Delete it or keep it as is.** If all else fails, you'll have to remove the photo from the book or keep it and hope for the best.

Assembling Your Book

After you have all your pictures stored in an album and you've made sure that they all meet the 4:3 aspect ratio, you're ready to move into Book mode and begin the task of assembling your book.

To go into Book mode, simply select your album in the Source pane and then click the Book mode button. After you're in Book mode, you see the interface shown in Figure 10-5.

The interface enables you to put your photos in order, choose a theme to control layout and fonts, and enter titles and captions for your photos. The following sections show you how to work with each portion of the interface so that you can assemble your book quickly and easily.

Choosing a theme for your book

The first thing that you need to do to start assembling your book is to choose a theme. The Theme drop-down menu, shown in Figure 10-6, allows you to choose one of six different themes. The themes determine how your book will look when it's laid out. The following sections give you a quick overview of each theme.

Choose your theme carefully. After you've chosen a theme, you can change it later, but doing so will change your text fonts and even the layout and arrangement of the book. Choosing a theme first and sticking with it is best to avoid potential aggravations and frustrations.

The selected book page is displayed here.   Caption

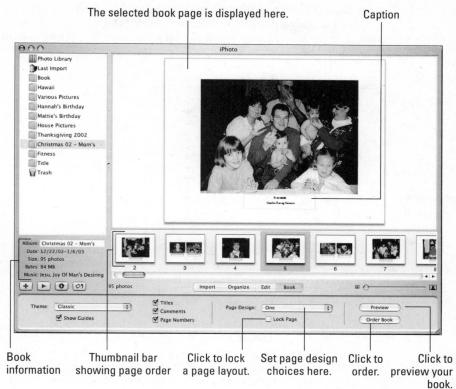

Figure 10-5:
In Book
mode, you
set the
options for
your iPhoto
book.

Book   Thumbnail bar   Click to lock   Set page design   Click to   Click to
information   showing page order   a page layout.   choices here.   order.   preview your
                                                                                     book.

Figure 10-6:
Choose a
theme from
its drop-
down menu.

Select your theme.

Catalog

The Catalog theme makes your book basically look like a catalog. Your pictures are aligned in rows with text boxes in which you can type information about each picture. You can choose to display eight pictures on a page (as shown in Figure 10-7), four pictures per page, or one picture per page. You can choose the number of pictures per page individually. In other words, each page doesn't have to have the same number of photos: You can mix and match. (I show you how later in the section, "Organizing photos on pages.") Note that the fewer photos you put on each page, the larger the photos will be in the book.

The Catalog theme also features the Introduction page, where you can place a bunch of text with no photos. Of course, this theme can be used to produce an actual catalog of products, but it can also be used to produce a directory of people. If you just have smaller photos and want to make the best use of real estate with an iPhoto book that looks like a typical photo album, this choice works well, too.

Classic

The Classic option provides a standard design in which you can display up to four pictures on a page. Each page allows you put a title and a caption with each photo, but you don't have much room for text, as you can see in Figure 10-8. This design maximizes the use of photos and minimizes text. The book is neat, clean, and simple.

Picture Book

A Picture Book theme is, well, a picture book. As you can see in Figure 10-9, no text or titles are allowed. The Picture Book theme uses minimal margins, so a photo that takes up one page stretches farther and fills the page more. In many cases, you'll want to choose a theme that allows you to enter text and captions around the picture. However, if your photos are self-explanatory, consider this option to make the best use of space. With the Picture Book theme, you can create pages that contain one, two, three, or four pictures.

Figure 10-8:
The Classic theme combines photos and text.

Figure 10-9:
The Picture Book theme doesn't use text or captions.

Portfolio

The Portfolio theme is a combination of the Catalog and Picture Book themes. Basically, this theme maximizes space, allowing you to insert titles and captions, as you can see in Figure 10-10. This theme works well for the same reasons that you might use a catalog, but the photos are larger (with a maximum number of four per page). Notice that the roll number/title will show up on the title caption. Don't worry: You can change it to whatever you want. See the "Inserting Titles and Captions" section later in this chapter for more information.

Story Book

The Story Book theme is a fun theme that displays photos at an angle, with a horizontal text box to balance things out. As you can see in Figure 10-11, if a page has more than one photo, the photos overlap. This design provides for an interesting coffee-table book, and it works great for books of birthday parties, vacations, or other fun times that you want to remember. You can display up to three photos per page.

Figure 10-11:
The Story Book theme displays images at an angle.

Year Book

The Year Book theme gives you rows of pictures with just enough caption room for a person's name and a little bit of additional information, as you can see in Figure 10-12. The Year Book theme, naturally, is great for yearbooks, directories, and other reference information. You can fit up to 32 photos on each page.

Figure 10-12:
The Year
Book theme
provides
room for lots
of small
photos and
captions.

Creating your cover page

After you select your theme, you're ready to begin working on your pages.
When you select your album and click the Book mode button, iPhoto assumes
that the first photo in your album should be used as the cover page. The *cover
page* is what appears on the front of your book's cover — not the first page in
the book. When you receive your groovy book, this cover page will appear on
the linen-bound cover, complete with whatever title you type in.

The photo that you want to use on the cover must be the first photo in the
album. Although you can move pages around on the thumbnail bar when in
Book mode, iPhoto is fussy about the cover page, so you need to place the
cover page first in the album before switching to Book mode.

To reorder photos in your album, just click the Organize button to go back to
Organize mode, and then select your album in the Source pane. Drag the
photo you want to use as the cover photo so that it is first in your album.

After you have put the cover page first in the album, switch to Book mode
and select the cover page on the thumbnail bar. The image appears in the
Viewer, with two small text boxes beneath it. Type your title in the provided
text boxes. Notice that you can have a main title and a subtitle, as shown in
Figure 10-13.

Note the guidelines around the text boxes in Figure 10-13. If you can't see
them, select the Show Guides check box under the Theme selection menu.
You can type text on the page template only where iPhoto allows you to, so
the Show Guides check box option turns on the borders (they're blue) that
show you where the boxes are. Rest easy, though: The blue boxes don't
appear when your book is printed.

iPhoto

Christmas 2002

Figure 10-13:
The cover
page
appears on
the book's
front cover.

Blue guides   Type a subtitle here.   Type your title here.

Organizing your pages

After you create your cover page, you're now ready to begin assembling the
actual pages of the book. When you pick your theme, iPhoto makes an initial
stab at trying to organize the book for you. However, you can change the

---

What should I use for the cover photo?

While you're organizing your book, take a few
moments to carefully consider your cover photo.
Remember that the cover photo will be printed
on the outside of the book with the title that you
enter, so you want to make absolutely sure that
you're happy with the results. After all, this is the
first thing that a viewer will see when he picks
up your book. Keep the following suggestions in
mind when choosing your cover photo:

✓ **Use a simple photo.** Very busy, jumbled
photos often don't work well on the cover.
You want the cover photo to be something
that a viewer can look at quickly without a
lot of thought or study.

✓ **Try to keep the photo to just one or two subjects.** A photo of 1 or 2 people is much more
dramatic than one with 15. Of course, a 15-
person photo may be best for your book, but
it will require more scrutinizing from the
viewer, which generally isn't what you want
for the cover.

✓ **Use a photo that sums up the entire theme
of the whole book.** As you can see in Figure
10-13, because I'm designing a Christmas
memories book, I chose a photo of a wreath
that hangs on my mom's porch as the cover
graphic. In other words, a great photo will
tell someone what the book is about, even
if the title isn't read.

layout as you see fit, according to what the theme allows you to do. The following sections explore what you can do and how to avoid potential pitfalls along the way.

Creating an Introduction page

iPhoto gives you the option to use an Introduction page, which is simply text that you enter. Generally, depending on the theme, the Introduction page contains two boxes: one for the book title and one big block where you type a few paragraphs of text (up to about 200 words). The Introduction page has no photos, and you don't even have to include an introduction at all if you don't want to. To create one, just click the Page Design drop-down list (refer to Figure 10-5), choose Introduction, and the page is inserted on the thumbnail bar right after your cover page. As you can see in Figure 10-14, boxes to type text in appear. The layout of this page will vary, of course, according to the theme that you chose.

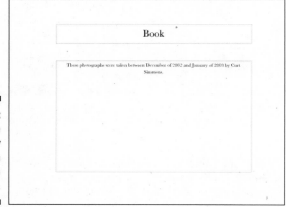

Book

These photographs were taken between December of 2002 and January of 2003 by Curt Simmons.

Figure 10-14:
You can use a text-only Introduction page, which is optional.

If you want to use an Introduction page, select it at this point in your book creation so that it's inserted on your thumbnail bar. You don't have to type the text right now — you can return to that later if you like.

The introduction page, even though it doesn't contain any photos, still counts as one of your total pages when the book price is calculated.

Moving pages around

After you choose your theme and create your cover and Introduction page, organize the rest of your book. Hopefully, you did most of your organizing in Organize mode in the album, which you'll find easier to work with because you're controlling the actual order of the *photos* — not the order of the *pages* — which is what you do in Book mode.

In other words, use the album to organize the photos in the order you want them to display in the book, and then use Book mode to determine how many photos are displayed on each page. For example, say you are creating a year-book for a civic club you belong to. Because you probably want the photos to run in alphabetical order, organize the photos in alphabetical order in your album. Then, in Book mode, simply determine how many photos you want displayed on each page. iPhoto doesn't reorganize the photos — it just lays them out on the pages in the order they are placed in the album.

You must get into your brain how iPhoto sees your book. If you look on the thumbnail bar, you see each page in your book, numbered according to how iPhoto will organize it. For example, in Figure 10-15, you see the cover page (which is first), the Introduction page (the first real page of the book), and then each page thereafter. iPhoto reads your book pages in a left-to-right format, just as you read. What you see on the thumbnail bar is exactly how the book will look when it's printed and bound.

Figure 10-15:
The thumbnail toolbar shows you the order of your book.

The key point here is that if you haven't organized your pictures the way you want them to appear in the book, go back to Organize mode and drag them around in the album until the order is right. iPhoto is very forgiving, adjusting the book automatically to any organizational changes that you make in the album.

However, you can also directly move pages around within Book mode. For example, suppose that I have a few pages with one photo per page and I decide to move one of the pages around. No problem: Just drag the page to its new location on the thumbnail bar, shown in Figure 10-16. If you go back to Organize mode and look at your album, you'll see that the change is made there, too.

The moral of the story is simple. Any change that you make in Organize mode (in the album) affects the order of the book. Any change that you make in Book mode affects the order in the album. The two items stay in sync at all times; they're not mutually exclusive.

Figure 10-16:
Reorder pages by dragging and dropping photos on the thumbnail bar.

Organizing photos on pages

Along with moving pages around as needed, you can also organize photos on the pages. If you want each page to have only one photo, your task is rather easy. If you want two or more photos on each page, you have to make some decisions about what photos should be grouped together.

As a general rule, grouped pages should follow one theme or idea. In other words, photos on the same page should be related to each other in some way or at least be similar. Of course, this is just my suggestion, and you must make the ultimate decisions about what works for your pictures. Just keep in mind that grouped pictures on a page tend to look better if they function as a group.

What happens when you group several pictures on a page? Keep in mind that iPhoto has already tried to organize your pages for you, depending on the theme that you select. When you change the number of pictures on a page, it has a trickle-down effect. Take a look at Figure 10-17. As you can see on the top image, page 2 has one photo, page 3 has one photo, and page 4 has two photos. iPhoto groups your images at random on different pages, keeping the order your specified in the album.

Suppose that I want page 2 to have two photos on it. I simply select page 2 on the thumbnail bar, and then from the Page Design drop-down menu, I choose Two. Now look at the bottom image of Figure 10-17. As you can see, page 2 now has two photos, one of the original photos from page 4 has now become page 3, and page 4 has pulled the photo from page 5 (not shown), and so on. In other words, changing the layout on one page affects all other pages after it.

I really want to reemphasize organizing your photos in the album first so that you need to make only minor adjustments in Book mode. Book mode doesn't allow you to drag and drop photos to new locations — only pages!

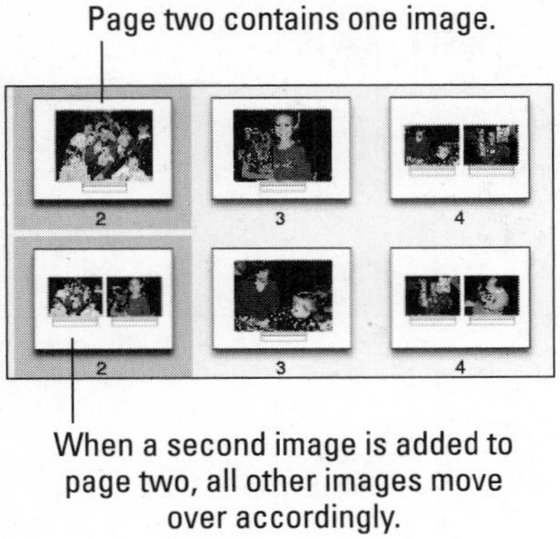

Page two contains one image.

Figure 10-17:
A change on
one page
affects all
other pages
after it.

When a second image is added to
page two, all other images move
over accordingly.

You can, however, easily rearrange photos on an individual page. For example, say you have three photos on a page, and you decide that you want the bottom photo to fit at the top of the page. No problem: Just select the page on the thumbnail bar. The page appears in the Viewer. In the Viewer, just drag the photos around on the page to reorganize them. Note that you can't change their positioning on the page (because pages are actually templates), but you can change which photo goes where.

So how can you get the layout that you want? One helpful feature is the iPhoto lock feature, which allows you to lock a page so that it can't be changed. For example, take a look at Figure 10-18.

Figure 10-18:
An unlocked
page can be
changed.

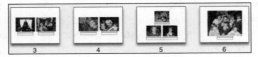

If I want to make sure that page 4 doesn't change, I can lock it so that no additional changes to the book affect this page. To do so, I simply select page 4 on the thumbnail bar and then select the Lock Page check box (located beneath the Page Design menu). When I do so, a little padlock icon appears under the page on the bar, as you can see in Figure 10-19.

Figure 10-19:
Lock a page
to prevent
changes.

The padlock icon indicates a locked page.

Now suppose that I want to change page 3 so that it has three photos instead of two. I select page 3, click the Page Design drop-down menu, and then choose Three. As you can see in the before (top) and after (bottom) shots in Figure 10-20, the original page 5 photo is bumped up to page 3 and the next photo in line (what was page 6) now becomes page 5. Because I locked page 4, it retains its location, and the other photos just flow around it.

The layout page three changes from two photos...

Figure 10-20:
A locked
page isn't
affected by
a new page
flow.

... to three.   The locked page is unaffected.

The lock feature is great to use, but there's one problem: After you lock a page and then reorganize pages, iPhoto expects you to keep that page locked. If you unlock it, iPhoto may rearrange the book around to accommodate the newly unlocked page, screwing up everything that you've done! After you lock a page, try to keep it locked. Also, if you decide to change themes in the middle of this process, all locked pages are automatically unlocked, so be careful!

If all this seems maddening, well, it is a little. However, here's the primary trick to keep in mind. When you make changes to a page, photos are shuffled from right to left. The trick is to simply work on your book from left to right. This way, each change that you make to a page won't be affected by the change that you make to the next one in the page list.

Mixing it up

When you're thinking about the page layout, stop and think about your overall book. Sure, you can mix single-photo pages, two-photo pages, and so on in a book, and this approach looks fine. However, while you're organizing everything, keep in mind that your book will look better if you place single-photo pages next to multi-photo pages. In other words, don't put all your single-photo pages together and all your multi-photo pages together. Mix them around to make your book look more interesting.

Inserting titles and captions

After you complete your layout, the hard part is finished. All you need to do now is add titles and comments, apply page numbers, and format them to suit yourself. This part is rather easy (unless you're suffering from severe writer's block).

Creating your titles and captions is relatively simple. Basically, you just enter the title and any caption text that you want in the provided boxes on each page. Remember: If the boxes aren't showing up on your screen, select the Show Guides check box under the Themes drop-down menu in Book mode. By default, the title of the photo is whatever it is in the album, but you can change it by just clicking the title text and then retyping your new title. The location of the title and text is determined by your theme, and you can't change it. If you entered any information in the Comments box for the photo, that information appears in the caption box. Again, just edit it as you like. (See Chapter 5 to find out more about adding titles and comments to photos in the iPhoto Library or an album.)

Notice in the lower portion of the Book mode interface that you have three check boxes labeled Titles, Comments, and Page Numbers, as shown in Figure 10-21. If your theme provides these features (which all themes do except Picture Book), you'll see the title, comments, and page numbers on each page. However, you don't have to use them. If you don't want to see titles for your pages, just clear the Titles check box. The same is true with Comments and Page Numbers. Keep in mind that clearing these check boxes affects all pages in your book — not just the selected page.

These check boxes, however, don't work on the Story Book theme. In other words, the check boxes allow you to remove titles and comments from a theme, but they can't be used to add titles and comments to the Story Book theme, which doesn't allow them in the first place.

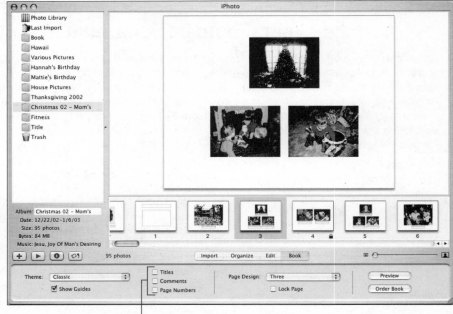

Figure 10-21:
Clear these
check boxes
to remove
an item from
your book.

Clear to remove these features from your book.

iPhoto only gives you so much room to add text. Basically, after you fill the text box, you're out of luck. If you enter too much text, a yellow warning triangle appears, as shown in Figure 10-22. If this happens, edit your text until it fits within the provided box. Otherwise, it won't come back from the printer intact.

Figure 10-22:
Your caption
must stay
within the
provided
text boxes.

Edit your iPhoto book carefully!

Be careful before finalizing your order! Nothing is worse than ordering a $30 book and finding out when you get it that you misspelled a word or have a sentence that doesn't make sense! Fortunately, you can check your spelling on each page using Apple's dictionary, although the process is a bit cumbersome.

To access the dictionary, select any text box and then choose Edit⇨Spelling⇨Spelling. The standard spelling dialog appears, which queries you about questionable words. Note the Check Spelling as You Type menu selection on the Edit⇨Spelling submenu. This option sounds great, but it's a bit of a pain: You have to turn this feature on in each new text box because it doesn't work continuously as you move through your book.

Of course, spelling isn't the only editorial problem your text may suffer. All the words in the following sentence *Two bee ore knot too bee* are spelled correctly, but nobody would know what the heck you were talking about if you put it in your book! You need to read very carefully to make sure that your text is correct. I strongly recommend having someone else read your titles and captions as a backup because editing your own text is often difficult. Also, you can have your Mac read your text aloud to you, which will help you find mistakes. Just Control-click a text box, and from the submenu that appears, choose Speech⇨Start Speaking. Listen to your Mac's computerized voice to make sure everything sounds just right.

By default, each theme in iPhoto gives you a preselected font that's used for title and captions, depending on the theme that you select. You can make two changes here:

- ✔ **The font and font size.** To change the font, choose Edit⇨Font⇨Show Fonts. This opens the Fonts dialog. Simply select the font you want and the size. Remember: The change that you make affects all pages in your book. You can't individually change pages or words.

- ✔ **The color of the font.** If you Control-click some text or a word, a submenu appears from which you can choose Font⇨Show Colors. If you choose this option, a color wheel appears from which you can change the color of the text by clicking the desired color. Of course, think carefully before doing this because black text usually looks best in an iPhoto book.

Also, note that changing the color occurs in a field-by-field basis: It doesn't affect other text fields for the photo, any other photos, or any other pages. To change all the font colors in a book, you will have to manually edit every text field.

Previewing Your Book

When you believe that your book is perfect, preview it. In Book mode, click the Preview button, found in the lower-right portion of the interface, and a new window appears that shows you exactly what your book will look like, as you can see in Figure 10-23. Use the arrow buttons in the upper-left corner to move through your book. Clear the Show Guides check box to remove the blue box borders around your text. If you see a problem, you can edit your text directly in Preview mode. If you have a layout problem, go back to Book mode, make your changes, and preview the book again.

You can also print your book as a way to preview it. Sometimes you can find errors on a printed page that you just don't catch onscreen. Just return to Book mode and choose File⇨Print. You can also save a copy of your book as a PDF file, which you can then easily e-mail to someone else who can proofread your book for you, if you happen to be grammar-challenged. Choose File⇨Print and then click the Save as PDF button. (PDF is a standard file format that can be read on any computer that has Adobe Acrobat Reader, which is available for free download from www.adobe.com.)

Use these arrows to page through your book.

Uncheck this box to hide guides.

Figure 10-23: Preview allows you to see how your book will look after it is printed.

If you send a PDF file via e-mail, keep in mind that your PDF may be several megabytes in size, depending on the number of pictures included in your book. See Chapter 9 for more about e-mailing large files.

Ordering Your Book

The glorious day finally arrives! Your book is finished, you've edited it, you've previewed it carefully, and you're ready to send it across the Internet to Apple to be printed and sent to you. As a last check, make sure that your book is at least 10 pages long and no longer than the maximum length of 50 pages. (If your book is less than 10 pages long, you'll get a book with blank pages at the end.) If you order more than 50 pages, all the pages after 50 are truncated.

Also, keep in mind that if you have yellow warning triangles on any photos due to low resolution, you'll be warned about them again during ordering. You can still order your book with the photos, but don't be surprised if the low-resolution photos don't look that great when you get the book.

When you're ready to order, just do the following:

1. **Connect to the Internet.**

2. **In Book mode, click the Order Book button, shown in the lower-right corner of Figure 10-24.**

   iPhoto converts your book to a format that's better for Internet transmission. Be patient: This may take a few minutes. At the end of this process, an Order Book window appears, shown in Figure 10-25.

3. **Before you can complete your iPhoto book order, you must enable 1-Click Ordering, so click the Enable 1-Click Ordering button.**

   The 1-Click Account window appears, shown in Figure 10-26.

4. **If you have an Apple ID and password, enter it here, click Sign in, and go on to step 6. If you don't have an Apple ID, click the Create New Apple ID button.**

   You probably have an Apple ID and password if you have ever purchased anything online from Apple.

5. **If you choose to set up a new account, you'll see the Create an Apple ID window shown in Figure 10-27. Enter the requested information and click Continue.**

   You'll also be asked to enter credit card information, shipping information, and so forth.

   When you're done setting up 1-Click Ordering, you'll return to the Order Book window (refer to Figure 10-25).

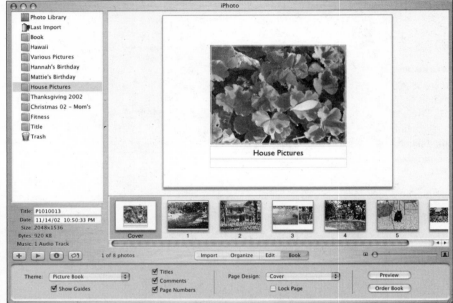

Figure 10-24:
Begin your
order
process by
clicking the
Order Book
button.

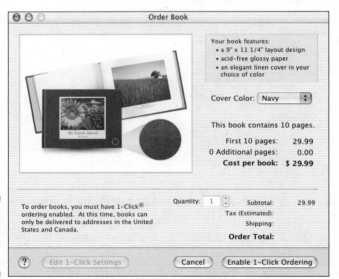

Figure 10-25:
The Order
Book
window.

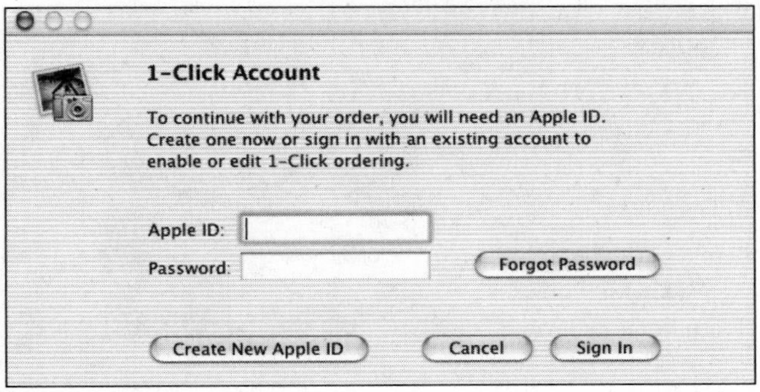

Figure 10-26:
Enter your
1-click
Account
information.

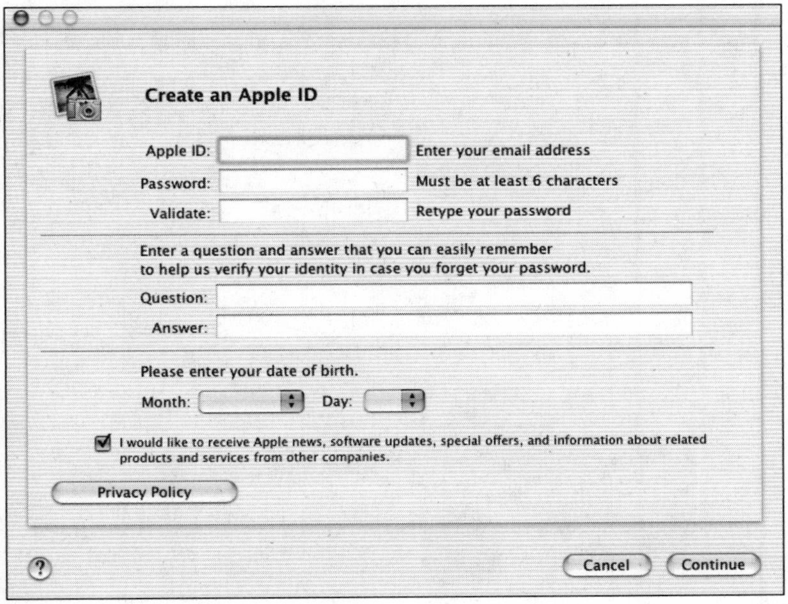

Figure 10-27:
Create an
Apple ID
and
password
here.

6. **Use the Cover Color drop-down list to select the cover color for your book.**

7. **Use the Quantity field to select how many copies of the book you want to order.**

8. **Choose shipping information, shown in Figure 10-28.**

   You can choose Standard or Express shipping.

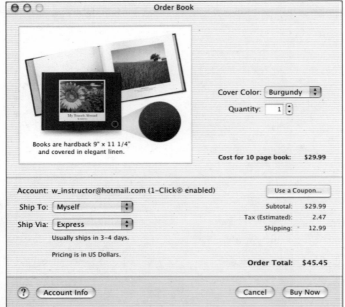

○ ○ ○   Order Book

Books are hardback 9" x 11 1/4"
and covered in elegant linen.

Cover Color: [Burgundy ▲▼]

Quantity: [1]▲▼

Cost for 10 page book: $29.99

Account: w_instructor@hotmail.com (1–Click® enabled)   [Use a Coupon...]

Ship To: [Myself ▲▼]   Subtotal: $29.99
                                            Tax (Estimated):   2.47
Ship Via: [Express ▲▼]   Shipping: 12.99
          Usually ships in 3–4 days.

          Pricing is in US Dollars.

                                            Order Total: $45.45

(?) (Account Info)   (Cancel) (Buy Now)

Figure 10-28:
Choose the
cover color,
quantity, and
shipping
method.

You'll see your total cost at the bottom of the page. When you're done,
just click the Buy Now button. All you have to do now is sit back and
wait for your book to arrive in the mail!

Chapter 11

Making a Slide Show

*O*ne of the best ways to show a collection of pictures is with a slide show. In the past, if you wanted to make a slide show out of your pictures, you had to haul your negatives down to a film processing center, have slides made, buy or rent a slide projector and screen, and then pray for a dark enough room to show them properly. Additionally, you had to cue the music yourself on a stereo and hope that everything came out all right in the end.

Enter the digital age: a time when slide shows can easily be created on computers with any number of applications and can be shown on a computer or even on a large screen using a liquid-crystal diode (LCD) projector. Slide shows are certainly nothing new in the computing world, but iPhoto makes them really easy. You can assemble the slides, put them to music, and watch the show on your Mac directly from iPhoto, or export the whole thing in the QuickTime format. With a QuickTime file, you can watch the slide show in QuickTime, e-mail it to friends and family, or (if you have a DVD burner) even burn the slide show onto a DVD and watch it on your TV. (See Chapter 13 for details on using your DVD burner with iPhoto.)

Making a slide show in iPhoto is a real snap, and in this chapter, I show you how.

Grasping the Fundamentals of a Good Slide Show

Slide shows are simply collections of pictures that you display in a certain order. You can play music as a background for the slides; or if you're showing your slides to a group of people, you may narrate while the slides progress. There are no hard-and-fast rules for creating a slide show, but if you're going to go to the trouble of creating one, keep a few concepts in mind while you work. After all, you want your slide show to be the best that it can be.

Show a progression of events

Slide shows generally work best if the slides portray some kind of progression of events. For example, say you take a trip to the Grand Canyon, return home with 50 photos, and decide to create a slide show of your vacation. Your best bet is to organize the slide show chronologically. In other words, start with a shot of your family loading the car for the trip, move to any interesting slides that you took along with way (hey — that giant ball of twine was worth the 200-mile detour), and then to shots of the Grand Canyon, and so forth. When you assemble the slides in a progression of events, your viewers feel like they went with you and experienced the highlights of your trip. (Well, maybe not all the whining emanating from the back seat, but you get the idea.)

However, a progression of events doesn't always work with a collection of slides. For example, if you go on a hiking tour in the mountains, all your slides are probably nature scenes. In this case, a progression of events may not work that well because you need to diversify the photos. In the next section, I tell you how.

Diversify your slide show photos

In a slide show, diversifying your photos is important. By *diversify*, I mean not showing similar photos one after the other. Take a family reunion, for example. You put the photos in chronological order to give a clear overview of the entire event but conclude with a number of posed family shots in a row. Your best bet is to mix those photos up a bit. Show some posed shots mixed with the casual shots that you took. This diversifies your slide show and makes the transition from one photo the next more interesting.

The same concept holds true if you have a bunch of nature photos. If a natural progression from one photo to the next doesn't seem to make sense, diversify them. Don't show two pictures of a mountain in a row — mix the pictures up a bit to create more interest and texture in your slide show.

Watch out for duplicates

When you take a bunch of pictures at a single event, you may end up with pictures that are very similar. Avoid the temptation to put every picture in the slide show; consider removing some pictures that are very similar to others. Displaying some pictures that are similar is okay, but as a general rule, you want each picture to be a separate statement. If too many pictures seem to have a duplicate feel, the slide show quickly becomes uninteresting.

Edit or delete poor shots

Unfortunately, not every picture that you take is great. Sometimes the lighting or quality is simply not good, or the picture just doesn't come out right. Your human subjects may have their eyes closed or have a strange expression. Where you can, edit the pictures using iPhoto to make them better, but don't put bad pictures in your slide show. If you can't fix the picture and make it better, get rid of it. (See Chapter 6 for more tips on editing with iPhoto.)

Use music that matches the mood

Using iPhoto, you can easily add music to your slide show by importing your own or using the canned tunes that come with iPhoto. However, before you get creative with music, think about the overall tone of the slide show. If the slide show is about a family vacation to Walt Disney World, you may want peppy, happy sounding music. If you're showing a family reunion with a lot of people photos, consider something soft and classical. If your slide show uses a lot of nature photos, classical music also works well. When you think about music for your slide shows, remember the mood of the event when you took the pictures. Festive photos and vacations often work well with upbeat music, whereas family holidays and such are often nicer with classical music. Think of the overall tone and feel of the slide show and then search for music to match that mood.

Keep your narration to the point

If you're displaying your slide show for a group of people and narrating it live, spend some time preparing what you want to say and time the photo transitions in the slide show to give you enough time to talk. You can manually control the movement of the slide show with iPhoto, but you may find that cumbersome. If you want to narrate, consider writing a script and rehearsing in advance so that your slide show presentation comes off without a hitch.

Another tip to remember is to keep the narration to the point. I once watched an hour-long slide show at a church. The slide show contained about 30 slides, so every slide had about 2 minutes of narration. At first, the slide show was interesting, but after a time, the narration dragged and the gaps between picture transitions were too long. In short, the audience began to lose interest. Giving some details and relating some experiences is fine but make sure that you show enough pictures to balance the narration. If you keep that in mind, plan carefully, and follow the other tips given throughout this section, you're sure to get and hold your audience's attention.

Assembling Your Pictures

To create your slide show, first gather the pictures that you want and then assemble them in the order that you want. You should take a few actions to prepare your photos for the slide show, and the following sections explore them for you.

Check the size of your photos

Before you start assembling those pictures for your slide show, think about quality and size for a moment. As you probably well know, all pictures aren't created of equal size. This can become a problem when you create a slide show because those images are displayed on your Mac in full-screen mode. This means that iPhoto will stretch or shrink the photos to fit the size of your screen.

In order for your Mac to display those images correctly, without having to stretch them to fit, your pictures need to match up to your Mac's screen settings, at least generally. In other words, if your screen resolution is set to 1024 x 768, your photos need to be at least this big so that your Mac doesn't have to stretch them. If your screen is set to 800 x 600, your pictures need to be at least this size in order for no stretching to occur. So what's the big deal about stretching? Stretching causes jagged lines and sometimes graininess.

How do you know whether your pictures will look good on the Mac? Simply check your monitor resolution against the size of your pictures. Here's how:

1. **Choose Apple⇨System Preferences.**

   This brings up the System Preferences window.

2. **In the Hardware section of the System Preferences window, click the Displays icon to bring up the Displays window.**

   The Displays window should open to the Display tab by default. If it doesn't, click this tab to select it.

3. **The Resolutions box (shown in Figure 11-1) in the Display tab shows you the current screen resolution.**

   As you can see in Figure 11-1, my display resolution is 1024 x 768. In order for my photos to display correctly in the slide show, they need to be at least this size.

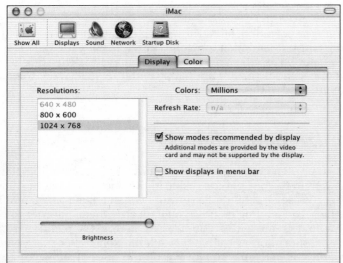

Figure 11-1:
Check your display resolution in System Preferences.

4. **Close the Displays window and, back in iPhoto, select the first picture that you want to use in your slide show.**

   In the lower-left of the iPhoto interface, take note of the size of the photo. The size should exceed your display resolution in order to display correctly in screen mode.

    If you don't see the size, click the Show Information about Selected Photos button.

5. **Click through the rest of the photos and check their sizes.**

So what do you do if you have photos that you want to use that don't adhere to the display resolution size? You can try one of these three basic work-arounds:

✔ **Change your display resolution to a lower value, such as 800 x 600.** This will, or course, affect the quality of everything on your screen because lower resolutions don't look as good. However, note that iPhoto does not support a resolution of 800 x 600 on some monitors, so you'll need to check your System Preferences to see if this is even an option.

✔ **Export the photos into another image editing program, such as Photoshop Elements.** Create a black background the size of your display resolution and then paste the photo onto the background. Save the new photo file and import it back to iPhoto. Now when the picture is displayed in the slide show, it will retain its original size, but you'll see the black background around it.

✔ **Export the slide show.** You can specify a lower display resolution when you export and then simply play the slide show with QuickTime Player. See the "Exporting Your Slide Show to QuickTime" section later in this chapter for details.

Resolution *is* important in slide shows, but it may not be the end-all-be-all either. You can still use smaller resolution photos in your slide show, but they simply may not be as crisp and clear as you may like. The trick is to do some experimenting, and if you are not happy with the quality, try some of the tricks I mentioned in this section.

Organize your photos

The next step when creating your slide show is to organize the pictures that you want in it. Your photos reside in the Photo Library, in a film roll, or possibly across several film rolls (or not even in a film roll, depending on your settings), depending on how you imported them. In order to create the slide show, first create a new album and then drag the pictures from the desired film roll(s)/library to that new album. Remember that you can't rearrange photos in the Photo Library; iPhoto doesn't allow you to drag them around, so in order to organize the photos, you'll need to get them into an album. (I cover how to create albums in detail in Chapter 4.)

After you have the photos that you want in an album, simply click them and drag them around in the Viewer until you have them in the order that you want, as shown in Figure 11-2.

If you can't see all your photos in the Viewer, remember to use the Magnifier slider bar to reduce the size of the photos in the Viewer so that you can more easily work with them.

Figure 11-2: Drag photos around to organize them in the order you want for the slide show.

Edit the photos if necessary

After your slide show photos are organized, take a good look at them. Use iPhoto's Magnifier slider bar (to the lower right of the Viewer) to make the photos larger and then carefully look at each one. Make sure that your photos are of good quality, look for red-eye, and see whether any should be cropped.

If you need to fix any of the photos, simply select a photo, click the Edit button to go into Edit mode, and make any needed edits. Click the Organize button to go back to Organize mode, select the next photo, and repeat. If you need help with editing photos, see Chapter 6.

Here is a word of warning concerning cropping: When you crop photos, you often change their size to something nonstandard. In other words, your Mac can't display the photo in full-screen mode and maintain the ratio of width to height *(aspect ratio)* on your cropped photo because the photo would be distorted. In this case, iPhoto will fill in the empty areas with a black background, as you can see in the photo in Figure 11-3. That may not be any big deal to you, but just keep this point in mind before you crop a photo.

Figure 11-3:
Cropped
photos may
display with
black
borders to
keep the
aspect ratio
correct.

Fix the transition speed and repeat option

When you play your slide show, iPhoto displays each photo for two seconds by default before transitioning to the next one. Also by default, iPhoto repeats the slide show endlessly until you press any key on your keyboard, which stops it. However, you can change both of these settings.

Select the album you will be viewing as a slide show. This automatically opens Organize mode. In the Organize pane at the bottom of the iPhoto interface, click the Slideshow button. This opens the Slideshow Settings window, shown in Figure 11-4. You can see the transition rate in the Play Each Slide for *xx* Seconds box. You can set this rate up to 30 seconds per slide. As a general rule, five seconds per slide is plenty, especially if the slide show will be set to music. If you'll be narrating your slide show, you can override the automatic transition and manually control it, which I show you how to do in the "Playing Your Slide Show" section later in this chapter. You can also speed the slide show up or slow it down while it is playing using the Up and Down arrows on your keyboard.

To prevent the slide show from running in an endless loop, just deselect the Repeat Slide Show check box. If you want to randomize your photos while the slide show is playing (which you don't if you have organized them in an album), select the Display Photos in Random Order check box.

Figure 11-4:
Change the
transition
and repeat
options in
Slideshow
Settings.

Adding Music

If you want to have music playing while you run the slide show, you can choose between the default choices provided by iPhoto and music directly from iTunes. iPhoto gives you two classical selections by default: *Minuet in G* and *Jesu, Joy of Man's Desiring*. If you prefer, of course, you can have no music at all.

If you want to use your own music, iPhoto can read anything stored in your iTunes library, which is a new feature in iPhoto 2. You can also choose to use a playlist from iTunes as well.

TIP

If you need detailed information on working with iTunes, check out *Mac OS X All-in-One Desk Reference For Dummies*, by Mark Chambers, published by Wiley Publishing, Inc.

After you're ready to make a music selection, just follow these steps:

1. **In Organize mode, click the Slideshow button on the Organize pane.**

2. **In the Slideshow Settings window, shown in Figure 11-5, select the Music check box, and then use the drop-down menu to choose Sample Music, iTunes Library, Top 25 Most Played (in iTunes), or My Playlist.**

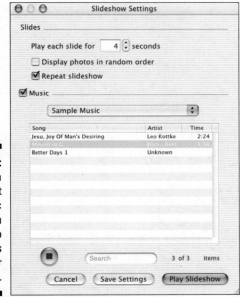

Figure 11-5:
Select a
default
music
option in
iPhoto
Preferences
or use your
own.

3. **Select the song that you want to use in your slide show from the list of songs that appears in the Song box.**

   For example, if you choose iTunes Library on the drop-down menu, you see all the songs currently in your iTunes Library.

4. **To hear the song you have selected, click the Play button.**

5. **When you are happy with your selection, click the Save Settings button.**

   You can return to the Slideshow Settings box at any time and choose a different song if you like. Just remember to save your settings again if you make a change.

Two slide show aggravations

When you set up your slide show, you may notice two basic iPhoto slide show limitations. The first concerns music. When you use a music file, the file is played over and over throughout the duration of your slide show. In other words, you can't use multiple songs during a slide show. Second, when your slide show ends, the music abruptly stops. You can't fit the timing of a slide show to the length of the music, unless you try to do so manually by calculating the number of seconds that each slide is displayed to come up with the length of music (ugh!). You can fit the slide show to music if you create the slide show in iMovie or iDVD, however. See Chapters 12 and 13 to find out more about using iPhoto with these applications. Also, if you have QuickTime Player Pro, you can create a sound file that is a combination of multiple songs and then import it into iTunes, where you can use it as your slide show music selection.

The second limitation is the transition. iPhoto gives you a nice, smooth transition from one picture to the next, but you can't change it — you're stuck with the default transition. By comparison, if you create a slide show in iMovie, you can select any number of transitions to use, but if you create a slide show in iDVD, you can't use a transition at all. These problems aren't that big of a deal, but they are aggravations that I hope to see changed in later versions of iPhoto.

Playing Your Slide Show

You can play your iPhoto slide show automatically or manually. Automatic playback is a bit easier, but manual playback gives you more control, especially if your slide show has narration. In the next section, I discuss the ins and outs of both methods.

Automatic playback

If you prefer, you can play your slide show back automatically on-screen without any additional preparation. Playing a slide show this way shows your pictures in full-screen mode, complete with default transitions and the music that you selected in Slideshow Settings (if you selected any). (See the previous section, "Adding Music" for more on selecting music for your slide show.)

 Select the album that you want to see by clicking it in the Source pane and then clicking the Play Slide Show button found just below the Source pane. If you have a photo in the album selected in the Viewer, iPhoto starts playing the slide show from that point and moves forward. This feature is a great way to see how things look while you create your slide show. The music starts at the beginning, regardless of which photo you start the slide show with.

Another way to automatically play your slide show is to select the album that you want to play by clicking it in the Source pane, and then clicking the Slideshow button on the Organize pane. This once again opens the Slideshow Settings box. Just click the Play Slide Show button to play it.

Either way you get these, your slide show plays gently and easily without any help from you.

To pause the automatic playback of your slide show at any time, press the space bar. To resume playing the slide show, press the space bar again. Note, however, that pausing the slide show only pauses the pictures: It doesn't pause any music that is playing with the slide show.

Manual playback

What if you want to control the slide show on the screen instead of having iPhoto automatically play it for you? If you're narrating the slide show, you'll probably want to do so. The good news is that you can manually run the slide show easily. Just start the slide show by clicking the Play Slide Show button and then use the left- and right-arrow keys on your keyboard to move forward or backward. However, note that after you press one of the arrow keys, iPhoto turns off automatic advancement, so you'll have to manually move through the rest of the slide show as desired, or iPhoto will leave you stuck on one photo. If you want to go back to automatic advancement after you press an arrow key, press the space bar, and iPhoto takes over again.

Exporting Your Slide Show to QuickTime

Playing the slide show on a Mac is great, but you may want to use the slide show on another computer or simply prefer to run the slide show in QuickTime Player rather than iPhoto. No problem: You can export the slide show as a QuickTime movie. Any computer that has QuickTime Player can play the slide show, including Windows computers.

Before you get export happy, you need to do two things:

  ✔ **Check for errors.** Preview the slide show and make sure that you have everything just right. After you export it, you can't edit the exported file to fix mistakes (unless you purchase QuickTime Player Pro). You'll have to go back into iPhoto, edit your slide show, and then export it again as a new file.

✔ **Think about file size.** When you export your slide show, you get a QuickTime movie that may be anywhere from several hundred kilobytes to several megabytes in size. If you're going to e-mail that slide show to friends, you need to think about file size. If you have a bunch of slides, you may need to reduce the overall slide show to make it shorter — and if you're using music, consider using MP3. AIFF and WAV files are much, much larger than MP3, so if you're going to e-mail the slide show to other people, convert the sound track to MP3 to reduce the overall size of the movie because this will make a big reduction in file size. iTunes can easily convert your music files to MP3 format. Of course, if you're burning the slide show to a DVD or you're not e-mailing it to anyone, you don't really have to worry. One other action that you can take is to reduce the overall size of images so that they're displayed in a smaller window on the viewer's screen. I show you how to do that later in this section.

After you resolve these issues, you're ready to export your slide show. Select the album that holds the slide show and then choose File⇨Export. Also note that you can export a subset of an album by simply selecting the photos that you want to export, rather than exporting the entire slide show.

On the Export Images window that appears, click the QuickTime tab, shown in Figure 11-6. You see three different areas where you must select options before exporting your movie.

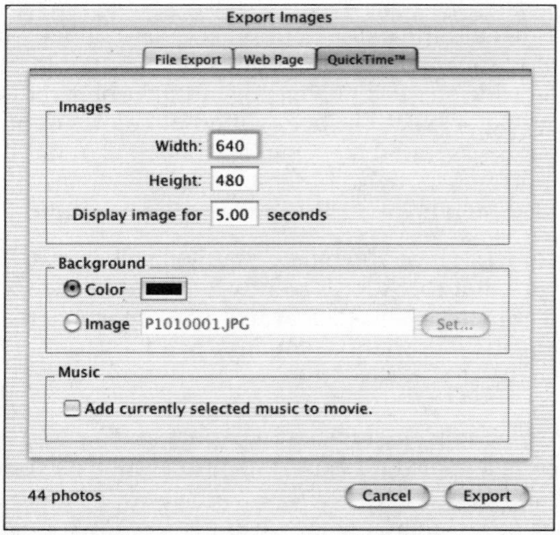

Figure 11-6: QuickTime Export.

QuickTime Player Pro or iPhoto?

iPhoto gives you a quick and easy way to create slide shows, but you'll find more flexibility and more control using QuickTime Player Pro. With QuickTime Player Pro, you can assemble slide shows, save them, go back and edit them, and use different music tracks within the same slide show. Your Mac is equipped with QuickTime Player, but in order to get QuickTime Player Pro, you'll need to upgrade, which will cost you about $30. To upgrade, open Macintosh HD⇨ Applications⇨QuickTime Player. A box appears asking if you want to upgrade to the Pro version. Choose to do so and follow the instructions that appear. Before you pay your hard-earned money to upgrade, however, check out iMovie: You can do the some of the same things there and export to QuickTime as well. See Chapter 12 to discover more about iMovie's capabilities.

- ✔ **Images:** The default size for your images is 640 x 480, displayed for the number of seconds that you originally chose in iPhoto Preferences. To lower the width and height values for smaller file sizes (and thus easier e-mailing), you can do that here. Reducing the size to, say, 320 x 240 scales the photos down, but your viewers will see the QuickTime movie in a smaller window. This defines the width and height of the QuickTime movie you are creating. If you're not worried about file size and you want to see the movie in full-screen mode, change the settings to 1024 x 768. Again, however, you'll need to keep these numbers small if you intend to e-mail the slide show.

- ✔ **Background:** By default, the export option is to use a background color of black. This color appears around pictures that cannot fit on the entire window when the slide show is playing. Select the Color radio button and then click the Color box to select a different color, or you can also use an image for a background by selecting the Image radio button and clicking the Set button to browse for an image. Keep in mind, though, your background should be neutral and not a distraction to your photos.

- ✔ **Music:** If you want to include the music that you selected in Slideshow Settings, make sure that the Add Currently Selected Music to Movie check box is selected here. If not, clear it. If you are worried about e-mailing the slide show to friends, you may need to cut the music in order to keep the file size lower.

After you make your selections, just click the Export button. You'll be prompted to give the file a name and export location (such as your desktop). Make your selection and then click Save. The slide show is exported, and in a moment, you see your new QuickTime movie appear, ready to be played in any QuickTime Player.

Chapter 12

Using iPhoto with iMovie 3

In This Chapter
▶ Importing movies and pictures
▶ Editing photos and clips
▶ Assembling your movie
▶ Working with transitions, titles, and effects
▶ Exporting movies

*J*ust as iPhoto gives you a fun and cool way to create slide shows with your pictures, Mac OS X also gives you another application for creating slide shows and movies: iMovie 3. Just imagine a program that allows you to import digital data and photos, create movies and slide shows, and control the audio as well. You can even use narration! If this sounds too good to be true, it's not. iMovie 3 is a great application, and you can use it to take your photos and movies to the next level.

So, why talk about a video-editing application such as iMovie in an iPhoto book? The answer is simple: Although iPhoto gives you a quick and easy way to create effective slide shows, it doesn't give you as much flexibility as you may want. To really customize slide shows and make them what you want them to be, you need to use iMovie. iMovie gives you total control over transitions, title pages, effects, and audio. Additionally, you can connect your digital video camcorder to iMovie and import your movies into iMovie, just like you import your digital pictures in iPhoto. You can then mix video and pictures if you like and create your own professional-looking movies. If your Mac has iDVD and a SuperDrive, you can also burn your movie to a DVD and watch it on your DVD player. You can find out more about iDVD in Chapter 13.

Before I begin, let me offer a disclaimer. Because this is an iPhoto book, I primarily focus on creating photo slide shows in iMovie. Entire books have been written just on iMovie, so I can't possibly cover everything in this chapter. However, if you get bitten by the iMovie bug and can't wait to find out more, check out *iMovie For Dummies* by Todd Stauffer (published by Wiley Publishing, Inc.), which offers all kinds of cool tips and tricks.

Getting to Know iMovie 3

iMovie 3 is a free application that you can download from Apple, or you can purchase it as a part of the iLife CD, also from Apple. You may be using iMovie 1 or 2, in which case, you need to upgrade by downloading the new version for free from www.apple.com/imovie. You can find out which version of iMovie you are using by opening iMovie (you'll find it in the Dock or in your Applications folder) and clicking iMovie⇨About iMovie.

Before you upgrade or purchase iMovie, you should make sure that your Mac can handle the demands of iMovie. The odds are good, however, that if you can run iPhoto without any problems, iMovie will work just fine. To be on the safe side, make sure your Mac meets the following requirements:

- A 300 MHz processor on any Mac Power G3 or G4.
- OS X.
- 256 MB or RAM or greater recommended. (If your Mac is limping along when you run iPhoto, iMovie will probably give it an even harder time.)
- 2 GB of free disk space.
- QuickTime 6.
- A Mac with a FireWire port (if you only want to work with photos in iMovie, you don't need the FireWire port).

If you already have iMovie and are ready to move forward, first check out www.apple.com/imovie and download the current plug-in packs. The plug-in packs contain additional enhancements and features, such as transition effects that you can use in your movies. Simply download the plug-in packs, and then double-click on the ReadMe file. Follow the installation instructions that appear.

After you have iMovie installed, take a couple of minutes to get familiar with its basic interface. Like iPhoto, iMovie contains some specific interface portions, so you'll probably feel at home with iMovie very quickly.

You can open iMovie by clicking the iMovie icon in the Dock, shown in Figure 12-1, or you can open it from your applications folder.

Either way, the iMovie interface opens, shown in Figure 12-2.

Figure 12-1:
The iMovie icon in the Dock.

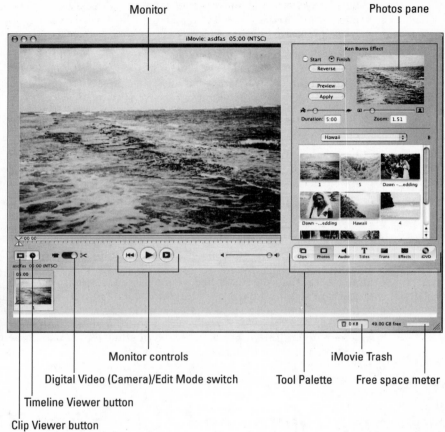

Monitor

Photos pane

Figure 12-2:
The iMovie
3 interface.

Monitor controls

Digital Video (Camera)/Edit Mode switch

Timeline Viewer button

Clip Viewer button

iMovie Trash

Tool Palette   Free space meter

Here are the main parts of the iMovie interface:

- **Monitor:** This TV-like area displays your film clips and photos. You watch your movie or slide show in this area as you assemble it.

- **Digital Video (Camera)/Edit Mode switch:** This switch is used to toggle between Digital Video (Camera) mode and Edit mode. Use Digital Video mode when you want to import digital video from your camcorder; use Edit mode when you are working on your film clips and pictures.

- **Monitor controls:** Use these controls to move backward and forward through your movie. The controls will look different, depending on if you are in import or edit mode.

- **Playhead:** This arrow shows you the location of your movie along the scrubber bar as the movie is playing.

- **Scrubber bar:** This bar represents the total duration of the selected clips. You can drag the Playhead along the scrubber bar to get to the point of interest in the video.

- **Clips/Photos pane:** The **Clips/Photos pane** holds all the film clips you import, and you can access your photos directly from iPhoto and see them on the Photos Pane. Just click the Clips button or Photos button in the Tool Palette to switch between the two panes.

- **Tool Palette:** Use these buttons to add transitions, titles, effects, and audio to your movies or slide shows.

- **Free space meter:** This meter shows you how much available storage space is on the Mac's hard drive and how much space your current movie is consuming.

- **iMovie Trash:** iMovie has its own Trash that holds portions of movies, clips, or photos that you decide to discard.

- **Clip Viewer/Timeline Viewers:** You can toggle between the Clip Viewer and the Timeline Viewer using the buttons directly under the Monitor.

At first glance, the iMovie 3 interface may seem a little intimidating, but don't worry. If you stop and think about it, iMovie 3 has three basic portions of its interface: a *Monitor* area so you can see what you are doing, a storage area called the *Clips pane,* where you keep all your film clips, and an assembly area where you put together your movie or slide show (also known as the *Viewers*). You find out how to use all these areas and much more in the rest of this chapter.

Importing Photos and Movies into iMovie

Without some photos or film clips, you can't do much with iMovie. In fact, you can't do anything at all. So, your first order of business is to get some photos or film clips into iMovie. Then, you can begin working on the movie you want to create. As a point of reference, iMovie considers video clips or slide shows "movies," so I'll use the term movie throughout this chapter.

You can import digital film clips, QuickTime movies, and you can directly use your iPhoto pictures within iMovie. The following sections show you how to import media into iMovie 3.

Importing digital video

iMovie 3 is designed to be a movie production studio. As such, its primary purpose is to work with digital video. As I mentioned, however, many photo

enthusiasts use iMovie 3 as a way to create slide shows because of the flexibility iMovie 3 brings to the table. But, no one can deny that iMovie 3 is primarily intended to be a movie-editing and production center.

With that said, I'll bet that those of you who have a digital camcorder have already experimented with iMovie, or you will shortly. So, how do you import digital video into iMovie? The process is amazingly simple, just like importing digital images from your camera to iPhoto. However, like iPhoto, you have to have the right camera — or camcorder, in this case.

iMovie 3 works with digital video camcorders only. It is not friendly to analog video recorders, even current models that use 8mm cassettes. In short, analog camcorders don't work with iMovie; you have to use a digital video camcorder. (If you have an analog camcorder and aren't planning to upgrade, or if you just have a lot of analog footage lying around from years gone by, check out the following section for some suggestions on getting around this limitation.)

To import to iMovie, your digital camcorder also has to have a FireWire connection. If you check out the back of your Mac, you can find a FireWire port. If you look on your digital camcorder, you should also find a FireWire port. (It will not look the same as the port on the back of your Mac: Like USB ports, one end of the connection is different from the other.)

Your camcorder may not call the FireWire port a FireWire port. It may call it an IEEE 1394 port or an i.LINK port. If you're uncertain, check your camcorder documentation to make sure you have a FireWire port. When you are sure you can connect to your Mac with a FireWire port, you are almost ready to begin importing video.

Before you begin the import process, you should pay attention to a couple of import settings. iMovie works with clips of video, which are imported to iMovie directly to the Clips pane. You can change this so that all clips are put on the Clip Viewer at the bottom of iMovie, but I suggest that you begin by having clips import to the Clips pane because this method is much easier.

Also, you can have iMovie automatically create clips based on scene breaks. Each time you stop and start your camcorder, a timestamp is used on the film. iMovie can detect this timestamp and create clips according to when you stopped and started the video, which gives you nice, clean clips that are easy to work with as you assemble your movie.

Both the scene break settings and import clip setting options can be set by choosing iMovie⇨Preferences. On the Import tab of the Preferences dialog that appears, shown in Figure 12-3, make sure that the Automatically Start New Clip at Scene Break check box and the Clips Pane radio button are selected. (They should already be selected by default.)

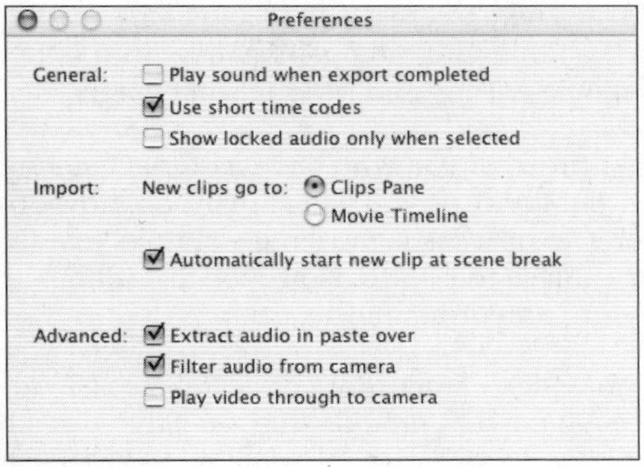

Figure 12-3:
Set Import
Preferences
here before
you begin
importing
video.

Preferences	
General:	☐ Play sound when export completed
	☑ Use short time codes
	☐ Show locked audio only when selected
Import:	New clips go to: ⦿ Clips Pane
	◯ Movie Timeline
	☑ Automatically start new clip at scene break
Advanced:	☑ Extract audio in paste over
	☑ Filter audio from camera
	☐ Play video through to camera

Now you are ready to import digital video from your camera to iMovie. Just
follow these steps:

1. **Connect your camcorder to your Mac using the FireWire cable that
came with your camcorder.**

2. **Start iMovie by clicking the icon in the dock.**

   The new project dialog appears, shown in Figure 12-4.

3. **Click the Create Project button.**

   In the box that appears, give the project a name and click OK.

Figure 12-4:
Click Create
Project to
create a
new movie
project file.

Welcome To iMovie
There is no project open. What would you like to do?

(Open Existing Project)   (Quit)   (Create Project)

4. **Turn on your camcorder.**

   iMovie detects the camcorder, and the Monitor window turns blue.
   iMovie automatically switches to Digital Video mode.

5. **Turn the camcorder to VCR or VTR mode in order to play back the
movie on the videotape.**

6. **Click the Import button that appears just below the Monitor window
in iMovie.**

My camcorder is connected, but iMovie doesn't see it

Generally, iMovie can detect most digital cam-corders. If you believe that you have the cam-corder connected correctly but iMovie doesn't seem to see it, take these troubleshooting steps:

- **Make sure the camcorder is correctly con-nected to the Mac.** Check the connections to make sure they are snug.

- **Turn the camcorder off and turn it back on.** If the camcorder was already turned on when you started iMovie, iMovie may not detect it.

- **Ensure that you are using the latest FireWire drivers.** Each new release of FireWire drivers fixes problems that occurred in earlier versions, so you may

need to download the latest update. Visit www.info.apple.com/support/ downloads.html and search for *Fire-Wire*. Then, download the latest driver ver-sions and install them on your Mac.

- **Check the brand of your camcorder.** Some JVC camcorders do not work with Macintosh because the FireWire circuitry is not compatible. Check the Apple compati-bility page at www.apple.com/imovie/ compatibility/camcorder.html.

- **Be aware of possible software conflicts.** For example, if you have installed EditDV, a professional digital video editor, you may not be able to use your camcorder with iMovie until you uninstall EditDV.

This will make your camera start playing the tape, and iMovie will begin importing it.

A new clip appears on the Clips pane, and iMovie records your video as it streams to the Mac over the FireWire cable. If you chose to allow iMovie to create new clips at scene changes, new clips appear as appro-priate. If there are no scene changes or you disabled this option, iMovie continues to record the movie as one clip. However, iMovie has a maxi-mum clip length of 9 minutes and 28 seconds (2GB). After this period of time has been reached, a new clip is automatically created.

7. **When you want to stop importing, just click the Stop button (which is the same button you used to Play the camera).**

Importing analog or existing digital video

As I mentioned earlier in this chapter, iMovie 3 doesn't work with any analog video. What that actually means is that you can't import analog video *directly* from an analog camera. However, if you are like me, you have miles of analog tape lying around that you would like to use in iMovie. That's no crime, and there are a few possible work-arounds that can solve this problem:

✔ **Check your brand of camcorder.** If you have a Sony digital camcorder, the Sony camcorder may be able to play analog tapes as well. If this is the case, the camcorder can digitize the movie and transfer it over to iMovie without any additional help from you. Just follow the steps in the previous section for importing video.

✔ **Connect your old analog camcorder to your digital camcorder and re-record your analog video onto digital video through the connection.** Then you simply use the new digital tape and import the film into iMovie. You need to check out your camcorders to see if you have compatible connections to join the two together.

✔ **Buy a digital video converter box.** You plug the box into your FireWire port, and then plug your analog camcorder into the box as well. You play the video, and the box converts the analog video to digital video that can be imported into iMovie. A converter box costs around $300, so this is not a cheap solution. Visit your favorite electronics store for details.

Finally, what if you have existing digital video on your Mac that you want to import into iMovie? You can do this as well, provided that the movie file is saved as a DV Stream. In iMovie, simply choose File⇨Import File, and then browse to the DV Stream file and click Import.

I want to import a QuickTime movie, but the movie file is grayed out

You can import QuickTime movies that you have created with iPhoto, or any QuickTime movies that you download from the Internet — sort of. If you tried to import a QuickTime movie using the File⇨Import File command, you probably noticed that all QuickTime movies are grayed out and you can't select them. This is because iMovie cannot import QuickTime movies directly. You have to resave them as a DV Stream, and to do that, you need QuickTime Player Pro.

The version of QuickTime Player that shipped with your Mac doesn't have this capability by default, so you need to upgrade to the professional version, QuickTime Player Pro, which costs about $30 and can be downloaded over the Internet.

To download QuickTime Player Pro, make sure your computer is connected to the Internet, and then choose Macintosh HD⇨Applications⇨QuickTime Player. A dialog appears prompting you to get QuickTime Player Pro. Click the Get QuickTime Pro Now button, and follow the instructions that appear. After you have upgraded, open your movie in QuickTime Player Pro, and then resave the movie as a DV stream. Now, you can import the movie into iMovie (whew!).

If you don't see the dialog asking you if you want to upgrade from QuickTime Player to QuickTime Player Pro, just open System Preferences by clicking the icon in the Dock. Click the QuickTime icon on the System Preferences dialog. Click the Connection tab, and then click the Registration button and follow the instructions that appear.

Using digital photos from iPhoto 2

Importing digital video into iMovie is a real snap, but for you photo lovers out there, using your iPhoto pictures with iMovie is even easier. iMovie 3 and iPhoto 2 are directly linked so that you don't actually have to import anything.

In the iMovie Tools Palette, just click the Photos button, and you'll suddenly see your entire Photo Library appear before your eyes, as shown in Figure 12-5. Click the drop-down menu and you'll see that you can access any of your albums, directly within iMovie!

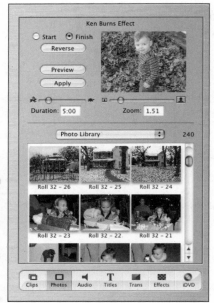

Figure 12-5:
Your Photo Library and albums directly appear in iMovie.

Importing photos that are not in iPhoto to iMovie

You may have some photos on your Mac that are not stored in iPhoto, but you want to use them in iMovie. In this case, you can manually import those photos into iMovie using the File⇨Import command. Simply browse to the photo and click the Open button to import it.

The major difference here is that iMovie sees your photo as just another movie clip and it will import it on to the Clips pane, not the Photos pane, which is reserved for iPhoto pictures only.

Of course, an easier work-around is to simply import any photos you want to use into iPhoto first, and then use iMovie to work with those photos, because iMovie is linked to your Photo Library. You may find this process easier and less confusing. See Chapter 3 to find out more about importing photos into iPhoto.

Editing Video Clips

After you import your video or photos into iPhoto, your next task is to edit your video clips as needed. You should spend a few minutes looking at them and deciding if you need to make some changes. For example, here are some of the changes you may want to make:

- **Split clips:** Sometimes, clips are too large to work with, or you may want to split a clip into several different pieces so that you can organize your movie differently.
- **Crop:** You can crop portions of video, just like you can a photo. The crop action allows you to specify the video that you want to keep.
- **Cut:** You can also cut portions of video from one clip and paste the cut portion into another clip if desired.

The good news is that these controls are easy to use. The bad news is they can be a bit confusing, depending on what you want to do, so the following sections examine each of these and explain how to edit your video.

Splitting a clip

Say you have imported a 60-second clip. As you watch the clip, you realize that you would like to split the clip into two different pieces so that you can organize the movie differently with other clips. iMovie gives you an easy way to split a clip. Just follow these steps:

Editing photos in iMovie

Because photos are static, you don't need to edit them within iMovie. However, if you need to make a few changes to some of your photos, such as adjusting the brightness and contrast of the photo, iMovie does give you the capability to make these changes, which you can find out more about in the "Exploring Effects" section in this chapter. But if you need to make substantial changes to photos, such as cropping or fixing red-eye, do them in iPhoto before using them in iMovie.

1. **In iMovie, select the clip that you want to edit by clicking it on the Clips pane.**

   The clip appears in the Monitor window.

2. **In the Monitor window, click and drag the Playhead arrow to the position on the scrubber bar where you want to split the clip, as shown in Figure 12-6.**

   You see the clip zip by in the Monitor as you move the Playhead around. When you find the location you want, simply release the Playhead.

3. **Choose Edit⇨Split Video Clip at Playhead.**

   The split clip now appears on the Clips pane.

Figure 12-6: Place the Playhead in the location of the clip where you want to split the clip.

The Playhead   The scrubber bar

You may have noticed that imported clips and photos have names that don't make sense to you. This is also true when you split a clip. You can rename any clip or photo by simply clicking its name in the Clips pane area and typing a new name.

Cropping a clip

Not all video footage is good footage. Sometimes, the footage is simply boring (like when you are waiting for your dog to do a trick), or perhaps you've accidentally filmed an empty wall for two minutes. Regardless, you can crop away portions from the beginning and end of video from a clip that you don't want to keep. The following steps show you how:

1. **In iMovie, select the clip that you want to edit by clicking it on the Clips pane.**

   The clip appears in the Monitor window.

2. **Aim your mouse pointer at the bars just under the scrubber bar, as shown in Figure 12-7, click, and begin dragging.**

   As you drag the two triangles, the area between them turns yellow on the scrubber bar. The area that has turned yellow is the area *that will be kept* when cropping occurs. In other words, you highlight the area you want to keep. Anything outside the highlighted area will be cropped away.

3. **Click Edit⇨Crop.**

   The cropped portions are placed in the iMovie Trash.

Figure 12-7: Move the triangles to select the area that you want to keep.

Anything outside these triangles will be cropped away.

Make a mistake? No problem, just choose Edit⇨Undo. In fact, you can undo up to ten steps back, so iMovie is very forgiving. If you need to undo all the changes you have made to a clip since the last time you saved the project, no problem: Just click Advanced⇨Restore Clip.

Cutting a portion of a clip

The cropping command cuts away the beginning and ending of a clip — anything you leave outside the protected yellow area. However, what if you want to cut a certain portion of the clip, or perhaps cut something out of the middle of the clip? In this case, you use the Cut command. The confusing thing about the Cut command is that the yellow area works in reverse. When you crop a clip, you cut away all nonyellow area. When you cut something from a clip, you highlight it in the same manner, but when you choose Edit⇨Cut or Edit⇨Clear, you cut away the portion of the video that is highlighted in yellow. As you can imagine, it is important that you keep the cropping and cutting functions straight in your mind, but if you make a mistake, just remember your good friend, the Edit⇨Undo command!

Working with Photos in iMovie

Working with your iPhoto pictures in iMovie is a breeze, and you'll find that mixing your photos with film clips, or just using your photos to create a cool slide show in iMovie is just as easy.

iMovie 3 automatically uses the Ken Burns effect. The Ken Burns effect, named for the filmmaker who pioneered it in films such as *The Civil War*, uses a pan-in and pan-out approach so that the photo looks as though it is moving. This is the same effect that you see on OS X screen effects when you use photos for the screen effect. It's rather cool and adds a great dimension to your photo.

So when you work with photos in iMovie, the only thing you need to do is determine how you want the Ken Burns effect to work and the amount of time (duration) that you want the effect to run. Adjusting these values is really easy, and here's how you do it:

1. **In iMovie, click the Photos button on the Tools Palette.**

2. **Browse through your Photo Library and locate the desired photo, or use the drop-down menu to choose one of your iPhoto albums.**

3. **Select the desired photo, and then select the Start radio button at the top of the pane.**

4. **Adjust the Zoom slider bar to fix the location of the photo where the Ken Burns effect will begin, shown in Figure 12-8.**

   The location you choose will be the start of the Ken Burns effect. You can start with the photo zoomed in or zoomed out — the decision is entirely yours.

Zoom slider

Figure 12-8: Move the Zoom slider bar to the location where you want the Ken Burns effect to begin.

5. **Select the Finish radio button, and then move the Zoom slider bar to the location where you want the Ken Burns effect to end.**

   Using steps 4 and 5, you have just created the zoom field that you will see in the final product.

6. **Click the Preview button to see the Ken Burns effect in action.**

   Repeat steps 4 and 5 to make any additional changes you want.

7. **Finally, use the Duration slider bar to adjust the amount of time that you want the Ken Burns effect to run.**

Did you notice the Reverse button? This option reverses your start and finish points that you have established for the Ken Burns effect. Use this option to simply reverse what you have already configured, without having to redo the settings.

After you are finished, your photo is now ready to be added to your movie, and I'll show you how to assemble your movie in the next section!

Assembling Your Movie

After your video clips are edited, you are ready to assemble your movie. Whether you are using video clips, photos, or both, assembly works in the same manner. You simply organize the clips or photos on the Clip Viewer in the order you want to view them in the movie you are making. The good news is that the organization is not permanent. You can move clips or photos around any number of times until you have them just right, and here's how you do it:

1. **In iPhoto, make sure the Clip Viewer is selected by clicking the Clip Viewer button.**

   The Clip Viewer button appears on the lower left side of the interface just under the Monitor, shown in Figure 12-9.

Figure 12-9:
Click the
Clip Viewer
button.

Clip Viewer button   Clip Viewer

2. **Drag the movie clips from the Clips pane to the Clip Viewer in the order that you want to view them.**

You can drag several film clips from the Clips pane at one time by holding down the Shift key and clicking and then dragging the items. You can drag clips back to the Clips pane or around to different places on the Clip Viewer as needed.

3. **To place photos on the Clip Viewer, open the Photos pane by clicking the Photos button on the Tool Palette.**

4. **Select the desired photo from your iPhoto library or album, adjust the Ken Burns effect as necessary (see the previous section), and click the Apply button.**

Your photo is automatically added to the Clip Viewer.

5. **Repeat this process to add more photos.**

You can also ⌘-click photos in the Photos pane and click Apply to add several of them at one time.

6. **After you are done, click the Play button on the Monitor to take a look at your movie so far, shown in Figure 12-10.**

This gives you your first look at the order of your clips. Again, make any desired changes until the order is just right.

Figure 12-10:
Photos are added to the Clip Viewer, which is your assembly area for your movie.

As you are adding photos or film clips to the Clip Viewer, the photos or film clips have to be rendered. This process takes a few moments, and you see a small red line above each photo or film click showing you the progress.

After you have organized your photos on the Clip Viewer as you like, you may decide that you want to edit the length of time that a photo is displayed in your movie. Remember that each photo is treated as a clip, and you can assign the duration of the photo as you like using the Duration slider bar on the Photos pane (see the previous section). By default, photos are displayed for about ten seconds, but you can change that on the Photos pane. If you already have the photo on the Clip Viewer, you can change the duration there too. The following steps show you how to change the duration a photo is displayed after the photo is on the Clip Viewer:

1. **In iMovie, select the Timeline Viewer.**

   The Timeline Viewer button looks like a clock and it appears just below the Monitor window. This turns your Clip Viewer into the Timeline Viewer.

2. **Select the photo you want to adjust.**

3. **Use the Duration slider bar underneath the Timeline Viewer to adjust the duration of the clip, shown in Figure 12-11.**

4. **Repeat steps 2 and 3 for each photo you want to edit.**

Figure 12-11:
In the Timeline Viewer, move the duration slider bar to change the amount of time the slide is displayed.

Duration slider

Adding Transitions

One of the great features of using iMovie to create slide shows instead of using iPhoto is the transition effects that iMovie gives you. (Besides the transitions that come with iMovie, you can download and install the additional vendor samples from www.apple.com/imovie.) The iMovie transitions give you more flexibility and control over the speed and mood of the transitions between each photo or film clip, and they are a real snap to use.

Before you start adding transitions, you should stop and think for a moment about your movie. Transition effects are very cool, but it's important that you think about the flow of your slide show or movie, instead of just using every effect possible. Some transitions are slow and soft, whereas others are faster and more aggressive. Additionally, you can control the speed of the transition, so think about the overall pace and mood of your movie. Also, think about any music that you want to play in the background (which I explain how to add in the section, "Working with Audio," later in this chapter). Ask yourself if the transitions enhance the overall theme and mood and if they work well with the music.

Also, before adding transitions, keep in mind these two pointers:

- **Transitions consume time on your clips.** For example, let's say that a photo displays for five seconds, but you have a two-second transition leading into that photo. The transition takes two of the five seconds, so the photo appears unhampered for only three seconds. Keep this in mind as you work because you may need to lengthen the duration of some clips.

- **A transition cannot be longer than the slide.** Because part of the slide's duration is taken by the transition, you can't use a three-second transition on a photo that has a duration set at two seconds. Again, watch your duration times and adjust them as necessary to accommodate your transition time.

To add transitions to your movie, just follow these steps:

1. **In iMovie, click the Trans button found on the Tools Palette, shown in Figure 12-12.**

2. **Select a photo or movie clip on the Clip Viewer, and then click one of the transitions.**

   An example of the transition appears in the small preview window in the in the Trans pane.

3. **To preview the transition in the Monitor, click the Preview button in the Trans pane.**

   The transition appears in the Monitor. You can see an example of the Warp transition in Figure 12-13.

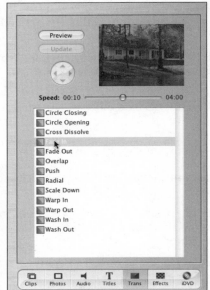

Figure 12-13:
Click
Preview to
see a
transition
previewed
in the
Monitor.

4. **Use the Speed slider bar (just below the preview window in the Trans pane) to adjust the speed of the transition so that the speed is appropriate for your movie.**

5. **When you are happy with the transition, simply click and drag the transition from the Trans pane to the Clip Viewer, as shown in Figure 12-14.**

6. **Place the transition between the desired clips, as shown in Figure 12-15.**

7. **Repeat this process to place additional transitions between other clips.**

   As you finish inserting transitions, your Clip Viewer will look like the example in Figure 12-16.

8. **When you are finished adding transitions, click anywhere in iMovie so that no clip is selected, and then click Play in the Monitor area to see what your movie looks like.**

9. **If you want to make any changes, do so now. To remove a transition, simply drag it off the Clip Viewer and drop it in iMovie Trash.**

Figure 12-14:
Drag the
transition
from the
Trans pane.

Figure 12-15:
Place the
transition
between the
desired
clips.

Figure 12-16:
Transitions
in the Clip
Viewer.

Creating Titles

Another cool feature of iMovie is titles. iMovie gives you several preconfig-
ured titles with motion that you can quickly and easily add to your movies.
You can add subtitle text, credits that scroll from the bottom of the screen to
the top, or a crawl that moves across the bottom of the screen from right to
left, like a weather update. All you have to do is customize those titles and
insert them where you want. In addition to the standard title features, you
can also superimpose text on any photo or clip in a number of cool and interesting ways.

I show you how to use these features, but after you get your feet wet, you'll
quickly discover that many different options are available to you. This is one
area of iMovie where you'll definitely want to spend some time experimenting
and having fun!

Creating a standard title

A standard title contains text on a black background. After you create the
title slide, you simply drag it to the Clip Viewer, where it becomes another
clip for all practical purposes. You can then adjust the time of the clip just as
you would any other. To create a standard title, follow these steps:

1. **Click the Titles button on the Tools Palette.**

2. **In the Titles pane that appears, shown in Figure 12-17, select a desired
   title effect from the list.**

   You can see a sample of the title effect in the display window at the top
   of the screen.

3. **Depending on the effect you chose, you might have to adjust the
   Speed and Pause by using the sliders below the preview window.**

   The Speed slider controls how fast the text moves across the screen (if
   you chose a title with motion). The Pause value determines how long the
   title pauses on the screen before disappearing.

4. **If you want to use a color for the title, click the colored box labeled
   Color to bring up a color palette, and then select a color for your text
   by clicking it in the palette.**

5. **If you want to use a black background for your title, select the Over
   Black check box.**

Figure 12-17:
Choose a
title from the
Titles pane.

6. **If you will be exporting the movie to a QuickTime format, select the QT Margins check box to make sure the lettering does not run off the screen.**

7. **Use the Font drop-down menu to choose a desired font and move the size slider bar to adjust the size of the wording.**

8. **Enter the desired text for the title in the provided spaces at the bottom.**

9. **When you are done, simply drag the title from the list of titles to the Clip Viewer and place it in the desired location.**

   It now appears on the Clip Viewer as an additional clip, as shown in Figure 12-18.

10. **Click the Play button in the Monitor to preview the title slide.**

By the way, you aren't limited to using titles just at the end or beginning of a movie. You can create additional titles and drag them wherever you want. For example, if you want to divide your movie into three sections, just create the different title slides you want and drag them to the appropriate locations on the Clip Viewer.

Figure 12-18:
The title
slide now
appears as
a clip.

You can make your own titles outside of iMovie. For example, you can use any graphics program to create a title slide containing text and graphics. Then simply save that title slide as a JPEG file and import it into iMovie. The title becomes another clip that you can add to your Clip Viewer!

Creating a superimposed title on a clip or photo

Although the black title or color title is nice, you can also superimpose a title on a photo or a movie clip. The process is basically the same, but you simply select the clip that you want to use and clear the Over Black check box. Then, select the title effect you want, adjust the Speed, Pause, Color, and Font settings as desired and type the text that you want. The text is displayed in the small window on top of the clip or photo, as shown in Figure 12-19.

When you are happy with the title, simply drag the title on *top* of the desired slide in the Clip Viewer. The title text then appears on the clip on the Clip Viewer.

Figure 12-19:
The title text
is displayed
over the
photo.

Text is displayed over the photo.

Running credits at the end of your movie

iMovie 3 provides a cool way to make your movie look even more professional by adding end credits. You know how it goes: The movie ends and the credits roll by. You can do the same with iMovie. If you look on the Titles pane, you can see a title option for Rolling Credits, or Rolling Centered Credits. By selecting this option, you can create an additional title slide that appears at the end of the movie (just select the Over Black check box and drag the slide to the Clip Viewer), or you can use a picture or video and have the credits roll over the clip. This kind of title slide works exactly the same as the others: Just put it at the end and enter all the text in the provided boxes. It's fun, fast, and simple, so check it out.

Other fun options

Aside from the basic title options you've explored, iMovie gives you some additional fun title options that you'll find on the Titles pane, or that you receive when you download the plug-in pack. I don't list them all here, but here are some of the more interesting ones:

✔ **Music Video:** This option places credits in the lower-left portion of the screen, à la MTV, as you can see in Figure 12-20. You can use these for real music videos that you create, or just for fun.

✔ **Scrolling Block:** This option allows you to place a scrolling block of text on the screen, which can be used in a number of situations. Use this option when you need more text than a standard title gives you space for.

✔ **Stripe Subtitle:** This option creates a stripe along the bottom of the page where you can put a subtitle. This option can add a professional-looking touch to your clips. This option looks great on interview tapes, where you want the name and title of the person to appear as they are speaking, or in a case where you have videotaped a speaker or a presentation.

✔ **Typewriter:** This is a cool effect that makes the text on the clip look as though it is being typed, one letter at a time.

Figure 12-20: The Music Video title adds some fun to your clips.

"My Flower Day"
Hannah and Mattie
Curt's Records

Exploring Effects

Aside from cool titles and transitions, iMovie 3 also provides you with some effects you can apply to clips and photos. Some of the effects are simply for fun, whereas others allow you to fix some common problems with clips and photos. If you click the Effects button on the Tools Palette, you see the Effects pane, shown in Figure 12-21.

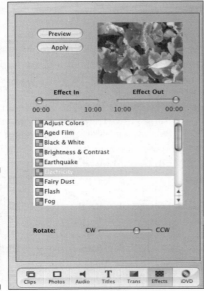

Figure 12-21:
Click the
Effects
button to
bring up the
Effects
pane.

As you can see, the Effects pane works just like the Trans and Titles options. You simply select the photo or film clip on the Clip Viewer, choose an effect, make adjustments to it as needed, and then apply the effect to any desired clip or photo by clicking the Apply button. As with transitions, you need to experiment with the Effect In and Effect Out settings to determine how the effect runs on the clip or photo and for what duration. You can only apply effects to clips or photos one at a time, and when you apply an effect, the clip or photo will be re-rendered on the Clip Viewer.

One effect I want to call your attention to is the Adjust Colors effect. This effect simply allows you to clean up a clip or photo by adjusting the hue shift, color, and lightness of the clip or photo. In short, this is a quick editing trick that makes a clip in need of some lighting work look better.

Other effects fix problems or create certain looks, such as Black and White, Sepia Tone, or even Soft Focus. Some effects are simply for fun, such as the Earthquake effect, which makes your photo or film clip appear to shake. Just spend some time playing around with these options and you'll probably find a few fun and helpful uses for them.

Working with Audio

Another big advantage of using iMovie 3 over iPhoto for creating slide shows is the audio feature. In iPhoto, you can use one music selection and play it in an endless loop until the slide show ends. With iMovie, you can use multiple songs, add narration, and even throw in a few sound effects here and there. If you are using movie clips, you can even override the movie's soundtrack with something else for a selected scene. In short, iMovie 3 gives you complete control over audio, which is a big plus when you are creating slide shows and movies. And like iPhoto, iMovie is also integrated with your iTunes library for easy access to any music you have stored there.

If you click the Audio button on the Tools Palette, you see the Audio pane, shown in Figure 12-22. The drop-down menu provides access to three different items:

- ✔ **iTunes Library:** Grab any song from your iTunes library. When this item is chosen on the drop-down menu, you see the iTunes library songs listed on the Audio pane where you can select them.

- ✔ **iMovie Sound Effects:** This option provides a broad listing of Skywalker Sound effects, including such items as birds, cold wind, chuckles, laughs, squeaky door, and so forth. You'll also find standard sound effects, such as an alarm, dog barking, rain, crickets, and so forth.

- ✔ **Audio CD:** You can insert any audio CD into the Mac's CD drive and access the songs directly from iMovie.

As you may notice in Figure 12-22, you also have the option to record narration by simply pressing the red record button and speaking into the Mac's microphone. Your narration starts recording at the Playhead point on the Timeline Viewer.

Before you can add audio to your movie, you have to switch to Timeline view by clicking the Timeline view button, found just below the iMovie Monitor. As you can see, iMovie 3 gives you different audio tracks that you can use to add audio to your movie. The dual track allows you to use two audio tracks at the same time: For example, you can use one for narration and one for music, as shown in Figure 12-23. You can even use music and narration in the same audio track if you want.

The following sections explain how to use all these features.

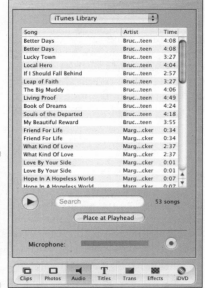

Figure 12-22:
Access
iTunes, a
CD, or use
prerecorded
sound
effects in
your movies.

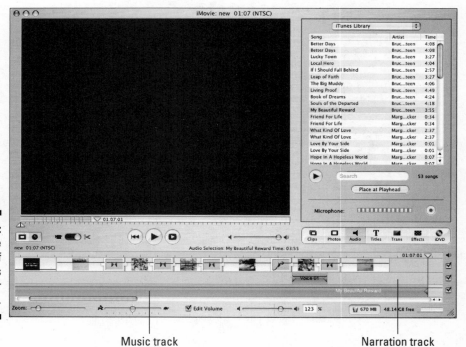

Figure 12-23:
You can use
a number of
soundtracks
on your
movie.

Music track   Narration track

Adding sound effects

The sound effects that appear on the Audio pane are readily available for you to use. Just drag the sound effect to an audio track in the desired Timeline location, as shown in Figure 12-24. You can then click the Play button on the Monitor to see your movie roll and hear the sound play where you have inserted it. You can then drag the sound effect around until it is in just the right location. Sound effects appear on the Timeline Viewer in a colored block.

Recording narration

You can also easily record narration (or additional sound effects) using your Mac's microphone. This feature allows you to watch the movie and record the narration directly on to the Timeline. Before you record narration, of course, you should spend some time practicing what you want to say, or maybe even writing a script.

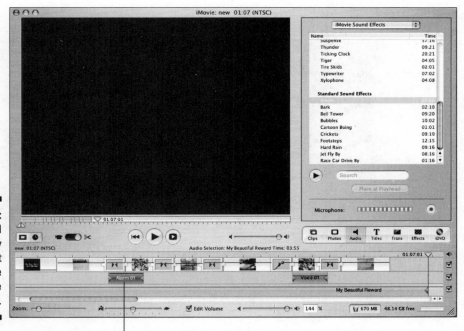

Figure 12-24: Add a sound effect by dragging it to the Timeline Viewer.

Sound effect on the Timeline Viewer

When you're ready, here's how you record your voice:

1. **On the Timeline Viewer, click and drag the Playhead to the desired position where you want your narration to begin.**

2. **In the Audio pane, click the Record button.**

3. **Begin speaking your narration.**

   The movie plays in the Monitor window as you record.

4. **When you are done, click the Record button again to stop recording.**

   You see that your voice appears as a new audio clip on the Timeline, as shown in Figure 12-25.

5. **Click Play on the Monitor to hear the narration and watch the movie roll.**

   You can adjust the location where the narration begins by simply dragging the audio clip on the Timeline. You can add as many audio clips to your movie as you like. If you are unhappy with an audio and want to redo it, just drag the old one to the iMovie Trash.

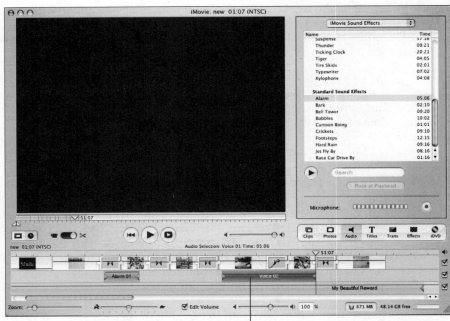

Figure 12-25: The narration track appears on the Timeline.

Narration track

Adding music tracks

iMovie can insert music tracks directly from your iTunes Library from the Audio pane in iMovie You can also simply record a track from an audio CD from the Audio pane. Here's how:

1. **In Timeline Viewer, position the Playhead where you want the music to start.**

2. **Insert the desired music CD in your Mac's drive.**

   The audio tracks from the CD appear on the Audio pane.

3. **Drag the desired track to the position you want on the Timeline Viewer.**

   The track is copied to the Timeline Viewer

4. **Click the Play button in the Monitor to see your movie played with the music you have added.**

Notice the Edit Volume check box at the bottom of the Timeline Viewer. Select the check box, and then use the volume slider bar to adjust the volume of the audio tracks as needed. This feature allows you to individually control the volume of overlapping tracks. For example, you can have music and narration running at the same time. Select each track and adjust the volume of each separately so that the music doesn't overwhelm your voice.

As you can probably imagine, you can get creative with all these features and produce a really cool and interesting audio track that backs up your movie or slide show. I suggest you spend some practicing with these features, and then let the creative wheels start turning.

Exporting Your Movie

After you have put everything together, made your adjustments, watched the movie, and decided you are satisfied, you are ready to do something with the movie. You may want to export it back to your camera where you can record it onto a tape, or you can export it to a QuickTime file so that you can watch on a computer. You may even want to create a new iDVD project with it so you can burn the movie onto a DVD. (See Chapter 13 for details on iDVD.)

Regardless of how you want to use your movie, exporting is easy:

✔ **To export your movie to a tape:** Connect your camcorder to the Mac's FireWire port and put a writeable tape in the camcorder. Turn your camcorder to VTR mode. In iMovie, choose File⇨Export Movie. The Export Movie dialog appears. Make sure the To Camera option is chosen in the Export drop-down menu, shown in Figure 12-26. Press the Record button on your camera, and then, in iMovie, click Export in the Export Movie dialog. Your camera then records your movie onto a tape.

Note that some camcorders require more than the default five seconds to start recording. If you notice that the beginning of your movie is getting cut off when you play it back, increase the value in the Wait *xx* Seconds for Camera to Get Ready box on the Export Movie dialog and try again.

✔ **To export your movie to QuickTime:** Choose File⇨Export Movie. The Export Movie dialog appears. In the Export drop-down menu, choose To QuickTime. Then, in the Formats drop-down menu, choose the format that you want, such as Web Movie, Small, Email movie, Small, or Full Quality. Click Export, and then choose a name and location for the saved file when prompted.

✔ **To create an iDVD project:** On the Tools Palette, click the iDVD button. The interface allows you to add your current movie as an iDVD chapter. You can then click the Create iDVD Project to create a new iDVD project in iDVD (you must be using iDVD 3 or later). See Chapter 13 for more details about iDVD 3.

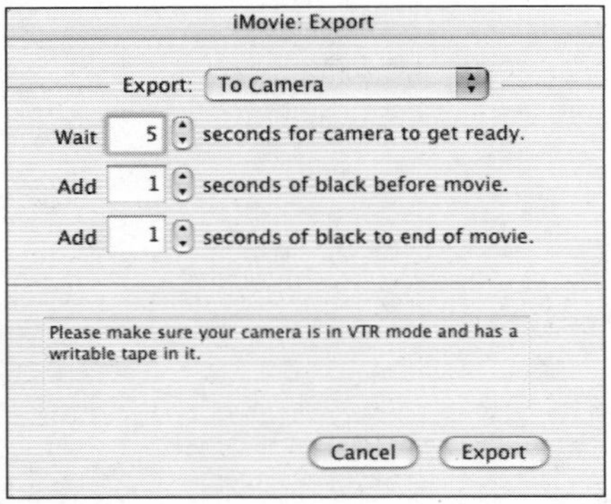

Figure 12-26:
Export your
movie.

iMovie: Export

Export: To Camera

Wait 5 seconds for camera to get ready.

Add 1 seconds of black before movie.

Add 1 seconds of black to end of movie.

Please make sure your camera is in VTR mode and has a writable tape in it.

Cancel   Export

Chapter 13

Creating a DVD Using iDVD 3

• •

In This Chapter

▶ Getting to know iDVD

▶ Using movies and slide shows

▶ Creating menus

▶ Using and customizing themes in iDVD

▶ Burning your DVD

• •

*U*sing iPhoto, you can easily create slide shows of your photos and set them to music. You can even mix those pictures with movies and title pages in iMovie, but after you're done creating these cool products, what then? Sure, you can watch your creations on your Mac, or send them to other QuickTime users so that they can watch them on their computers. However, you may want Grandma and Grandpa (who don't own a computer) to see them, or you may want to show your creations at a family gathering or some other event. You may also want to watch that slide show or movie on a standard DVD player.

OS X comes with software called iDVD. Using iDVD, you can easily create customized DVDs with menus and buttons. In fact, you can even use your photos from iPhoto and assemble a slide show directly within iDVD, or you can simply use the QuickTime slide show that you've already created. In this chapter, I show you how.

Note: To use iDVD, you'll need a Mac with a SuperDrive. If your Mac didn't come with one, you *can* take it to an authorized Apple technician to have one installed, but the cost is usually prohibitive. Third-party drives are not supported by iDVD. If your Mac has a SuperDrive, you're all set. If you've ever wanted to be in the movies, here's your chance.

Figuring Out What You Need to Burn a DVD

You need a few things in order to create a DVD on your Mac: iDVD, a SuperDrive DVD burner, and DVD-R discs. Obtaining iDVD is no problem. If you are using OS X and have a SuperDrive, you already have iDVD. You may see iDVD residing happily in the Dock, as shown in Figure 13-1. If not, just look in Macintosh HD⇨Applications to find iDVD.

This chapter focuses on using iDVD 3, the current version at the time of this writing. If you don't have iDVD3, you can purchase it as a part of the iLife package. It will cost you $49, and you can order it directly from Apple at www.apple.com/ilife. You must be using OS X version 10.1.5 or later to install iDVD 3.

Figure 13-1:
Click the
iDVD icon
that resides
in the Dock
to open
iDVD.

Lastly, you need DVD-R discs. The DVD-R discs work just like CD-R discs. They are writeable DVDs. You can order DVD-R discs directly from Apple from within iDVD, or buy them from an online retailer or at a local computer supply store. To order them from Apple, make sure you have an active Internet connection, open iDVD, and choose File⇨Shop For iDVD Products. This takes you to Apple's Web site, where you can buy a pack of DVD-R discs for about $5 each. However, you may consider shopping around. At the time of this writing, you can get a 10 pack of DVD-R Memorex discs from Amazon.com for $29, so definitely look around for the best deals.

Burning DVDs with iDVD

If you have used iPhoto, you'll find that the iDVD interface is rather similar and about as simple. Basically, you see a big preview window, shown in Figure 13-2, and a few navigation buttons.

Of course, behind those simple icons and menus are a number of powerful features that you can explore in this chapter.

So, what's the skinny on burning a DVD with iDVD? At first, the process seems terribly difficult, but after you get a handle on the basics, you'll be burning DVD after DVD in no time flat.

In a nutshell, you burn a DVD by following these steps:

1. **Plan the content of your DVD.**

   Before you start working with iDVD, decide what you want to put on the DVD. Your choices are photos or movies. Start out with a piece of paper and map out what you want to see and do with the DVD. After you burn a DVD, you can't erase and reburn it, but with a little planning, you can avoid wasting an expensive DVD-R. So spend a little time thinking ahead before you turn to iDVD.

2. **Create the files you want to use on the DVD.**

   Use iPhoto to create your slide show or iMovie to create a movie, or you can even use iDVD to create a slide show. (Refer to Chapter 11 for more on creating slide shows in iPhoto.)

3. **Use iDVD to assemble the files and create a menu that you'll use to navigate the DVD with your DVD player's remote control.**

4. **Burn the DVD to a disc.**

Sound easy? Basically, it is — and in the following sections, you find out just how to create your DVD.

Getting Your Pictures or Movies into iDVD

After you've planned your DVD and created the files that you want to appear on it, your next step is to get your pictures or movies into iDVD. The good news is that this is really easy. iDVD 3 is a part of Apple's iLife, and it is linked directly with iPhoto 2, iMovie 3, and iTunes. You can access your iPhoto Library, your iTunes Library, and movies from iMovie that you have prepared for iDVD from directly within iDVD. See Chapter 12 to find out more about iMovie.

If you have created a QuickTime movie using iMovie or a slide show using iPhoto, you can simply import those files into iDVD. iDVD can import slide shows and movies that are QuickTime files. You can easily create those QuickTime files using iPhoto or iMovie (see Chapters 11 and 12 to find out more about saving your slide show or movie in the QuickTime format). You can also assemble a slide show directly within iDVD.

Accessing photos, music, and movies from within iDVD

Because iDVD 3 is linked to iPhoto, iTunes, and iMovie, accessing your photos, music, and movies is easier than ever. In iDVD, just click the Customize button. A drawer pops out. You can click the Audio button to access your iTunes Library, the Photos button to access your iPhoto Library (shown in Figure 13-3), and the Movies button to access any movies you have prepared for use in iDVD.

Importing an existing slide show or movie

If you already have movies or slide shows that have been exported in the QuickTime format, all you have to do is import them into iDVD. One issue that confuses new users of iDVD is the initial interface. The preview screen may look like a sky, or it may look like a chalkboard or some other kind of graphic. These initial screens are basically blank templates for a menu page

that you also create. If you don't like what you see at the moment, don't worry. You can change it later. For the moment, as you are importing pictures or movies, just work with the default.

To import your existing slide show or movie, just open iDVD and import in one of the following ways:

- **Choose File⇨Import⇨Video.** Your slide show or movie is imported to the viewing area of iDVD.

- **Even easier, simply drag your slide show or movie file to the iDVD viewing area.** Either way, the movie appears as a button on the viewing area, as you can see in Figure 13-4. Note that, depending on the template iDVD is using, you may not see a picture appear on the button. Don't worry, though. Your movie or slide show has still been imported. Just double-click the button, and your file plays for you.

If you want to put more than one slide show or movie on a DVD, no problem: Just import the additional files. Each one appears on the title page in its own button.

There is a limit of six buttons per iDVD screen. If you want more than that, you can use a folder button where you can store additional movies or slide shows. See the "Organizing Your DVD with Folders" section later in this chapter.

Figure 13-3:
iMovie,
iTunes, and
iPhoto are
directly
linked with
iDVD 3.

Your movie button

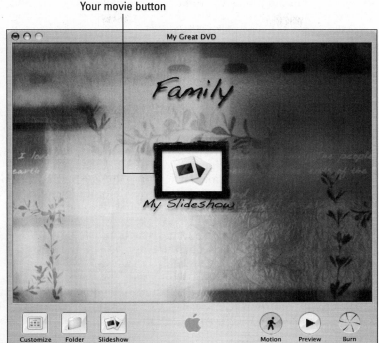

Figure 13-4:
Slide shows
and movies
appear in a
button in the
viewing
area.

Change your mind about something you've imported into iDVD? Just select
the slide show or movie on the iDVD interface and choose Edit⇨Cut. The
slide show or movie disappears in a cloud of smoke out of iDVD, but the slide
show or movie is not deleted from your hard drive: It remains safe in its original location on your Mac. You can also single-click the button you want to
eliminate and press the Delete key for the same result.

Creating a slide show within iDVD

If you don't want to create a slide show using iPhoto or iMovie, you can do
so using iDVD itself. You can also add background music, just as you would
when using iPhoto. The process is quick and easy, and you can even make
sure your photos fit to the music selection that you import. In other words,
you can have the slide show match the length of the background music.
Here's how you do it.

1. **In iDVD, click the Slideshow button.**

   This adds a Slideshow button to the iDVD theme on the Monitor window.

2. **Double-click the Slideshow button the Monitor.**

   This opens the My Slideshow window, shown in Figure 13-5.

3. **On the main iDVD interface window, click the Customize button.**

    This opens the drawer.

4. **Click the Photos button to open your iPhoto Library.**

5. **Locate the desired photos and begin dragging them to the My Slideshow window in the order you desire, shown in Figure 13-6.**

   The photos appear as thumbnails, shown in Figure 13-6. You can drag them around to change the order of the pictures for the slide show, and you can also use the Thumbnail drop-down menu at the bottom of the page to change the size of the thumbnails in the interface. You can have up to 99 photos in a single slide show.

6. **To add music to your slide show, click the Audio button on the drawer and locate the music file in your iTunes Library, shown in Figure 13-7.**

7. **Drag the desired song from the iTunes Library to the Audio well on the slideshow window, shown in Figure 13-8.**

   The song then appears in the Audio well.

   If the song you want to use isn't in your iTunes Library, choose File⇨ Import⇨Audio. Browse for the song you want and click Open. The song is automatically imported to the slide show well.

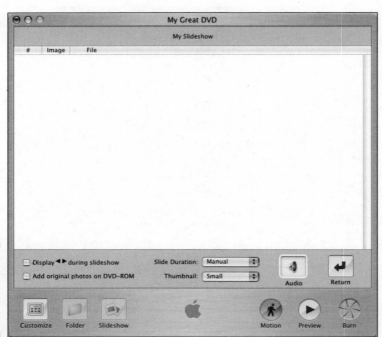

Figure 13-5:
The My Slideshow window appears.

Drag photos to the My Slideshow window.

Figure 13-6:
Drag the
photos to
the My
Slideshow
window.

Click to open your iTunes Library.

Figure 13-7:
Click the
Audio
button in the
drawer to
open your
iTunes
Library.

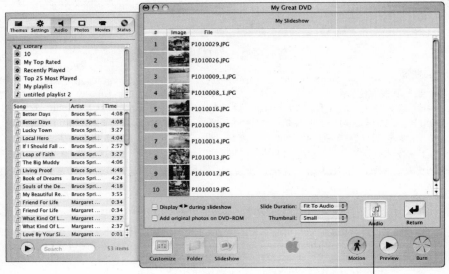

Figure 13-8:
Drag the
song to the
Audio well.

The Audio well

8. **Use the Slide Duration drop-down list to control how the slides advance.**

   As shown in Figure 13-9, you can choose Fit to Audio to fit the slide show to the audio file (in other words, the last slide ends when the music stops), or you can choose how many seconds you want each slide to be displayed. Notice the Manual option is grayed out. You can only use Manual advancement when you are not using a song with your slide show.

Figure 13-9:
Choose a
slide
duration.

1 second
3 seconds
5 seconds
10 seconds
✓ Fit To Audio
Manual

To display forward and backward arrows during the slide show, select the Display Arrows During Slideshow check box. You can then use the forward and backward buttons on your DVD remote to manually control the movement of the slide show.

Avoiding black space around your slide show pictures

If you have cropped any of your pictures, iDVD puts black space around the picture to fill in the leftover viewing area. If you are worried about each picture looking exactly the same in iDVD, your best bet is to keep each picture sized at 640 x 480 pixels. With this size, you can be sure the pictures fit evenly on a standard TV screen; therefore, iDVD will not have to put black space around the photo to make up the difference. This way, all your photos will look the same when you watch the DVD.

9. **When you're done, click the Return button.**

This takes you back to the main iDVD interface, where you can preview the slide show you just made by clicking the Preview button.

If you single-click the Slideshow button, a Slideshow slider bar appears, shown in Figure 13-10. This feature allows you to scroll through the photos in the slide show and choose the slide that you want displayed on the button. Just use the slider bar to locate the slide, and then simply click anywhere outside of the button. The photo will appear on the button.

Figure 13-10:
Use the slider bar to choose a photo for the button.

Organizing Your DVD with Folders

The folder option in iDVD is designed as an organizational tool. Say that you have three slide shows and three movie clips for a DVD about your family vacation. No problem: Your DVD menu will have six different menu selections by default — one for each item. However, using Folders, you can store the movies in one folder and the slide shows in another. This gives you two folders on your title page. Users then use the DVD remote to click the desired folder, revealing the movies or the slide shows. This works just like the menu options you see on the DVD of your favorite movie, where you can view extra features, such as interviews, trailers, and so forth. Folders give you a better way to organize your DVD if you have a bunch of stuff on it. You don't have to use folders, of course, but they are there if you need them.

Don't get too carried away with folders: Remember to keep the DVD interface easy for people to navigate. Too many folders and subfolders become more confusing than helpful, so try to keep things as simple as possible.

To use the folder option, just click the Folder button in iDVD, and a Folder icon appears in the viewing area. Just drag the items you want to put in the folder from the Photos or Movies panes on the drawer to the Folder icon.

Working with Title Pages

After you import the movies or slide shows into iDVD, you are now ready to make the title page you want. The *title page,* which is also called the *navigation page,* or *menu,* is the page that appears when you first put the DVD in the DVD player. The user then uses the DVD remote to select the slide show or movie they want to watch — just as you would with a regular DVD.

The cool thing about title pages in iDVD is that they are easy to make. You can use one of iDVD's preset themes as is, or customize a theme as you like. You can also change the menus that appear on your title page. You can explore the possibilities in this section.

Changing the title of your movies and slide shows

As I discussed earlier in the section, "Importing an existing slide show or movie," when you import your movies or slide shows into iDVD, each one gets its own button on the default title page. The titles of those slide shows or movies, however, may not be what you want for your final product. Keep

in mind that the people who play your DVD see everything on the title page, so you want the slide show or movie titles to be descriptive.

To change a title, just click the title of a slide show or movie button and type the title you want, as shown in Figure 13-11. The menu buttons are what users select with their remote controls in order to play the movies or slide shows. For this reason, an action title, such as Play Movie, often works best. If you have several movies on your DVD, be sure to name each one descriptively, such as Play Grand Canyon Movie and Play Yellowstone Movie.

Using themed title pages

iDVD gives you over 30 themed interfaces in 2 categories: New Themes and Old Themes (the old ones are brought over from iDVD 2), ranging from kid's pages to sports. You can see the themes by clicking the Customize button in the iDVD interface. A drawer appears. Click the Themes button and you'll see the theme thumbnails listed. Use the drop-down menu to toggle between the new themes and the old themes, as shown in Figure 13-12.

Figure 13-11:
Click the movie or Slideshow button titles and type a new title.

Figure 13-12:
You can
choose from
over 30
themes for
your DVD's
title page.

Notice that some of the themes have a Motion icon in their corner. This means that the themes feature some kind of music and motion. If you choose to use one of these themes, click the Motion button on the iDVD interface to see a preview of the motion.

Also notice that several of the themes have a box that says Drag Photos or Movies Here. This option allows you to display a photo on the title page or even have a movie running on the title page. Just click the Photos button or the Movies button on the drawer and drag the desired photo or movie file to the box, as shown in Figure 13-13.

To change a theme, simply double-click any theme on the Theme drawer. The theme in the viewer window changes. Notice that your current slide shows and movies are not removed or damaged. The fonts, colors, and buttons are simply adapted to the new theme. After you choose a theme, simply click the default title to type the main title you want.

Customizing title pages

The default themes may work well for you, but you can also customize those themes — at least somewhat. For example, you can lose the existing background image and use one of your own photos, you can change the music (on themes that use music), and you change the locations and fonts of titles.

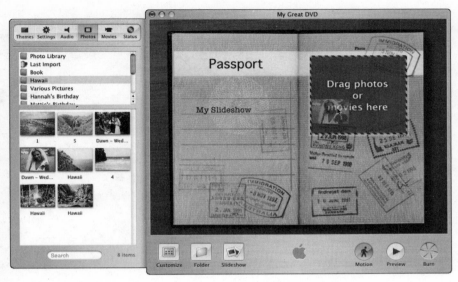

Figure 13-13:
You can
place a
photo or
movie on the
title page by
simply
dragging it
to the
provided
box.

To customize your title page, follow these steps:

1. **Click the Customize button on the iDVD interface.**

2. **Click the Themes button on the drawer, and then select the theme you want to customize.**

3. **Click the Settings button on the drawer.**

   The Settings pane, shown in Figure 13-14, enables you to change the Background, Title, and Button properties, among others.

4. **If you are using a motion theme, move the Motion Duration slider left or right to control how long the motion lasts.**

   The Motion Duration is set to a maximum of 30 seconds by default. Regardless of your setting here, the motion simply loops after it has finished its duration. If you like, you can change it to match up with your music. For example, if you decide to use a 15-second music clip, you can adjust the motion to 15 seconds so that the motion and the music loop naturally together.

5. **If you want to change the background image or movie that will appear on your title page, simply drag the picture or movie from the Photos or Movies pane to the Image/Movie well on the Settings pane.**

   Simply click the Photos or Movies pane, and then drag the movie or photo to the Settings button (don't release the photo or movie). This will change the window back to the Settings pane. Now drag and drop the photo or movie on the Image/Movie well. You can also drag and drop a custom audio clip to the Audio well from the Audio pane. If you don't

like the changes you made, just drag them back out of the wells to return to the originals.

6. **Move the Size slider to the left to reduce the point size of your title; move it right to increase the size.**

7. **In the Button section of the Settings pane, select the Free Position radio button in order to move the buttons around as desired (as opposed to having them aligned to an invisible grid).**

   If you want to keep the buttons aligned, you can leave the Snap to Grid radio button selected, and then use the Position menu to align the button to the left, right, or center. You can also click the From Theme button to select a different shape for your buttons, as shown in Figure 13-15.

8. **Use the Font, Color, and Size drop-down lists to make any desired changes to your buttons.**

9. **If you like the theme and think you'll want to use it again in the future, click the Save as Favorite button to save it.**

   A drop-down menu that enables you to save your new theme appears. If you don't want the changes applied to the original theme, make sure you clear the Replace Existing check box. This will allow you to save your new theme, but keep the original theme as it was before you changed the settings.

Before you consider your title page finished, you should check one additional item. Choose Advanced⇨Show TV Safe Area to see a box appear on your title page. The area inside the box, as shown in Figure 13-16, is a TV-safe area.

Figure 13-14:
The Settings pane.

Figure 13-15:
Select a
different
shape for
your
buttons.

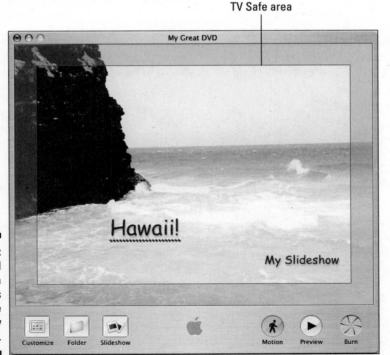

TV Safe area

Figure 13-16:
A shadowed
area
indicates
what is safe
for display
on a TV.

Anything outside the TV-safe area may not show up on the TV screen. This typically isn't a problem, but if you moved your buttons around close to the edge of your screen, you need to turn on this feature to make sure your buttons and title are within the TV-safe area. Because TV screens have different dimensions than computer monitors, some things may show up fine on the monitor, but be cut off on the TV screen. You don't want to burn a DVD-R and find out that some of your buttons are outside of the TV's viewing area!

Burning Your DVD

When you are satisfied with your title page and you've previewed everything on your DVD, you are ready to burn the DVD. Before you burn, make sure you have checked everything, including your spelling on the title page. You can't reburn a disc to fix a mistake, so check *everything* before you click that Burn button:

- ✔ **Check your menus.** Are they positioned in a pleasing way? Are they inside the TV Safe area?

- ✔ **Check your spelling on all menus and titles.** You would hate to burn a $5 DVD-R disk, only to discover that your title page says "Our Trip to Hawaiian."

- ✔ **Make sure you preview all slide shows and movies.** Are you happy with the way they look? You can't change them after the disk is burned (without burning a new disk).

When you are ready to burn the DVD, follow these steps:

1. **Insert a DVD-R disc into the SuperDrive.**

2. **Click the Motion button to make sure all motion on the title page is turned on.**

   If you don't, the motion won't work on the DVD.

3. **Click the Burn button.**

   The Burn button pulsates, letting you know it is ready.

4. **Click the Burn button again.**

   The burning process begins. Depending on the length of your DVD, some time may be required to burn it — even a few hours — so be patient. When you're done, iDVD ejects the disk automatically and asks if you want to burn another copy.

You're done! Head off to your DVD player and watch your new DVD!

Chapter 14

Other Fun iPhoto Features

*i*Photo is great fun. Whether you're editing photos, creating slide shows, making an iPhoto book, or anything else for that matter, the iPhoto software is easy, practical, and just plain enjoyable.

Aside from the standard tasks you can do with iPhoto, which you can explore throughout this book, I want to point out a few last-minute, fun ideas. These are easy tasks that can help you get a little more usefulness out of iPhoto.

In this chapter, you can take a look at using your photos as desktop pictures, creating your own screen effect, and using helpful plug-ins and scripts.

Using a Photo as Your Desktop Picture

Admit it — you love those cool desktop photos Mac OS X offers. They keep you feeling cozy and relaxed. However, you don't have to settle for the ones that come with Mac OS X: iPhoto allows you to customize your desktop photo by using one of your own. So your kids or pets (or your spouse) can romp across the screen, or you can see that beautiful photo of Mt. Everest you took last summer every time you use your computer. Regardless, you can set one of your photos as your desktop photo with just a selection and two clicks!

Before doing so, however, you need to adhere to a couple of rules if you want your photo to look really good. First, the photo you decide to use needs to be as large as your monitor's setting. Otherwise, OS X has to stretch your photo to fit, which causes you to lose some resolution and generally make the photo not look so great.

To do so, open System Preferences in the Dock, or choose Apple➪System Preferences to bring up the Preferences window. Click the Displays icon at the top and then check out the Display tab, shown in Figure 14-1. You can see your monitor's resolution in the Resolutions box. As you can see, my iMac is set to 1024 x 768, which means my photos need to be this size in order to display well.

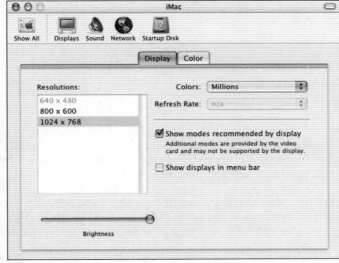

Figure 14-1:
Check out
the Display
tab in order
to find your
monitor's
resolution.

Now that you know your monitor's resolution, all you have to do is open iPhoto, select the photo you want to display, and then check out the size in the information area under the library and albums (if you don't see it, click the Show Information button). As long as the size of your photo is at least the size of your monitor resolution, you're in good shape. If your photo is smaller than your screen's resolution, you can still use the photo, but you may see jagged lines and other resolution problems when the photo is displayed on the screen.

The second issue you should keep in mind is cropping. Your monitor expects to use photos shot in a certain ratio, such as a 4:3, 3:2, and so forth. Vertical shots don't work well because the top or bottom of the shot usually gets chopped off. If you have cropped the photo you want to use, you may consider selecting it and choosing File➪Revert to Original. Then, recrop the photo using the Constrain feature to make sure it fits your display (in the Constrain menu, choose 1024x768 (Display), which is the second option). (To find out more about using the Constrain feature, see Chapter 6.)

Now you're ready to set your photo as the desktop background. Just select the photo you want in the Viewer, and then click the Desktop button found on the Organize pane (shown in Figure 14-2). Your photo immediately becomes your desktop photo for all to enjoy.

The good news is that you can change your picture over and over if you like. Just select a new photo in Organize mode and click the Desktop button to change it.

If at some point you want to go back to one of OS X's desktop photos, you can easily do that, too. Just open System Preferences by clicking it in the Dock, or choose Apple⇨System Preferences to bring up the Preferences window. Click the Desktop icon to bring up the Desktop window. In the Collection drop-down menu, choose Apple Background Images and click one of the thumb-nails to change the desktop to that image, as shown in Figure 14-3.

Figure 14-2:
Select the photo and click Desktop.

Click to switch to Organize mode.

Click to make the selected image your desktop background.

Figure 14-3:
Use the
Desktop
System
Preferences
to change
back to an
original
photo or
color.

Making Your Own Screen Effects

OS X's screen effects, formerly called *screen savers,* are pure entertainment. You can watch a graceful shuffle of images slowly fade in and fade out or slowly zoom in and out. In the past, screen savers helped protect computers from *screen burn,* a problem that occurred when an image remained unchanged on a monitor for too long. Monitors today are not susceptible to this problem, so screen effects are for pure enjoyment. After you enable a screen effect, the screen effect starts after a specified period of inactivity. You can stop the screen effect by moving your mouse or pressing any key on the keyboard.

As with the desktop picture option explored in the previous section, your screen effects work best if your photos have at least the same resolution as your monitor, such as 1024 x 768.

Creating a screen effect with your photos is really easy. Here's how:

1. **Organize the photos you want to use in the screen effect in an album in iPhoto, or simply select the photos you want to use in the Screen Effect by ⌘-clicking them.**

   See Chapter 4 if you need more information on how to organize an album.

2. **Click the Desktop button in the Organize pane.**

3. **In the Screen Effects dialog that appears, shown in Figure 14-4, click the drop-down menu to choose the album you want, if necessary, and then click the Screen Effects Preferences button.**

System Preferences opens and the Screen Effects tab appears. On the tab, shown in Figure 14-5, notice that Pictures Folder is selected, and you see a preview of your screen saver running in the Preview window.

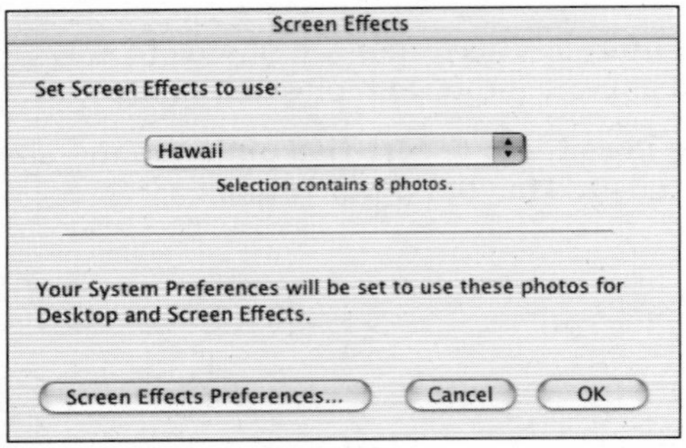

Figure 14-4: The Screen Effects dialog enables you to configure your own screen-saver effects.

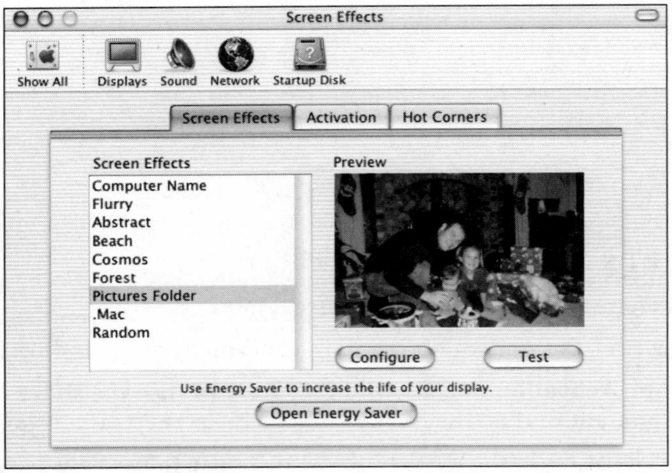

Figure 14-5: You see a preview of your screen saver on the Screen Effects tab.

4. **Click the Configure button to bring up the Configure dialog, shown in Figure 14-6.**

   As shown in Figure 14-6, you already have your folder selected, so you don't need to do anything in the upper portion of the window, but under Display Options, you see some features you may or may not want to use. They are

   • **Cross-fade between slides:** This option causes the photos to fade into one another, which looks nice.

- **Zoom back and forth:** When a photo is displayed, there is a soft zoom up and zoom back effect that makes the photo look like it is moving.

- **Crop slides to fit on screen:** Leave this option selected to make sure your photos display well.

- **Keep slides centered:** This forces the photos to stay centered, which they do anyway if they are full-sized photos.

- **Present slides in random order:** This option randomizes the order you originally created in your iPhoto album.

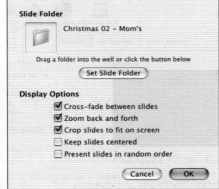

Figure 14-6:
You can set display options for your screen saver here.

5. **Click OK when you're done.**

   This returns you to the Screen Effects tab.

6. **Now click the Activation tab in the Screen Effects window.**

7. **On the Activation tab, shown in Figure 14-7, use the slider bar to set the amount of time that passes before the screen effect starts.**

   You can also use the radio buttons to choose to password protect your Mac so that your password has to be entered when waking the Mac from the screen effect.

8. **Click the Hot Corners tab.**

   On this tab, use the check boxes to enable hot corners, which are small areas in the four corners of your screen. When you move the mouse to a corner, the screen effect starts. If you don't want to use hot corners, just clear the check boxes.

9. **When you're done, close the Screen Effects window and click OK on the Screen Saver window.**

    This sets your screen saver.

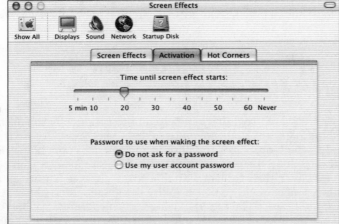

Figure 14-7:
Set the
duration and
password
options for
your screen
saver here.

Using Helpful Plug-Ins

A *plug-in* is an add-on software module, and you can use plug-ins with iPhoto. Obviously, iPhoto was designed to be a simple program that performs specific tasks. However, what if you really need iPhoto to perform some task that, well, it doesn't? In some cases, you can simply download a plug-in and extend iPhoto's capabilities.

A *plug-in*, then, is essentially a little piece of software that is designed to work with iPhoto so that you can do more with it. Plug-ins are generally free software programs that you can download, and if you visit www.version tracker.com/macosx and search for iPhoto, you end up with a list of useful little programs you can download and install.

It is important to note that these software modules are developed by individuals and are not guaranteed by Apple. Some of the plug-ins you'll find at Version Tracker work well — some not so well. So make sure you read the reviews posted by other users before you download and install the plug-in.

My best advice is to check out this list and download the plug-ins you need, but don't get in the habit of installing everything, because this may make

iPhoto more aggravating than helpful to use. So just try out the ones that you think you really need. The following sections point out some of the more helpful plug-ins that you'll find at version tracker.

New plug-ins are developed from time to time, so it's a good idea to check back at www.versiontracker.com periodically for new ones. Also, you can some-times find additional plug-ins simply by searching the Web for *iPhoto plug-ins*.

Better iPhoto Templates and BetterHTMLExport

Two simple freeware programs can help iPhoto produce better Web pages. As discussed in Chapter 9, you can choose File⇨Export and choose the Web page option, which organizes the photos you selected on a blank HTML page. You can then upload the pages to your own Web site using a Web site editing program. However, the problem with iPhoto's Web page feature is that it isn't very flexible. You can add some flexibility by downloading Better iPhoto Templates and BetterHTMLExport. Using these programs, you have the option to use additional templates and basically control the look of the Web page during the Export process.

File Dropper and File Dropper Eudora

File Dropper is a little utility that allows you to drag and drop any number of different files directly into a Mail message, and the Eudora version gives you the same feature with the Eudora mail program. The benefit for iPhoto is that you can drag and drop photos directly from iPhoto to the mail message with-out having to use the iPhoto Email feature. File Dropper allows you to resize the photos as well.

iPhoto Diet

Let's say you now have thousands of photos in your iPhoto library. That's a lot of data and a lot of data for iPhoto to manage. iPhoto Diet is a little pro-gram that scans your Photo Library and reduces its size by moving redun-dant photos to the trash. You also have the option of removing all the original copies of modified photos. Obviously, you want to think carefully before you delete original copies, but this program easily helps you do it if you want to shrink the size of your Photo Library a bit.

iPhoto Librarian and iPhoto Library Manager

These two programs allow you run multiple iPhoto Libraries and easily select the library that you want to use. For those of you who store thousands of photos, you may find that using multiple libraries is easier to manage and keep track of. With these easy tools, you can do just that.

Photo Fixer

This quick little utility can fix photos that iPhoto can't import. Basically, it converts images quickly to an iPhoto-friendly format.

Part VI
The Part of Tens

The 5th Wave   By Rich Tennant

"Remember, your Elvis should appear bald and slightly hunched.-- nice Big Foot, Brad.-- keep your two-headed animals in the shadows and your alien spacecrafts crisp and defined."

In this part . . .

Ah, the Part of Tens — that great place in every *For Dummies* book where you can get quick tips and information. In Chapter 15, check out ten tips for taking great photos. In Chapter 16, you can peruse ten quick iPhoto tips. In Chapter 17, read about ten output tips. Finally, in Chapter 18, take a look at ten common questions and answers.

Chapter 15

Ten Tips for Taking Great Digital Photos

*i*Photo is a great way to manage, store, and use your digital photos. Alas, however, iPhoto can't fix any old photo you import to it. Although iPhoto does give you some limited editing capabilities, it can't fix really problematic photos — I'm not sure that any photo software can — so in order to enjoy the photos you take, you should certainly learn some photography skills and techniques. For a quick reference, keep these ten important tips in mind.

Shoot at the Right Resolution

As I've mentioned a number of times throughout the book, resolution affects everything concerning your photos — their size, the quality, how well they print, and so on. *Resolution* refers to the number of pixels that are used to create the photo. The higher the pixel count, or the higher the resolution, the better the quality you get when you view them (especially when you print them). The quick lesson here is to shoot pictures at a high enough resolution to do what you want. You can't add more pixels later, so if you want to print

an 8 x 10, you have to shoot at a high enough resolution to get the good print quality you want (which is about 3.1 megapixels for an 8 x 10). See Chapters 8 and 9 to find out more about resolution for print and electronic output.

Think about Composition

Composition refers to the makeup of the picture. It includes the main subject(s), all other objects, and even the background. In other words, composition is what you see when you look through the lens of your camera. As a general rule, you should think of pictures in terms of subjects and objects. The subjects make up the main focus of the picture, while objects are there to complement the subject. This concept is especially true when photographing people. See the person or group as the subject, and then take a hard look at everything else in the picture — how do the objects complement or detract from the subject? The best pictures keep things simple and keep the main subjects as the focal points of the picture.

Think about Lighting

Lighting is a major factor when taking pictures, whether indoors or outdoors. Fortunately, most digital cameras come to you with a great flash system that can help with lighting problems. However, as a photographer, you should think carefully about lighting when you are planning to take pictures. All too often, digital photographers get a little lazy because they assume that they can adjust the lighting and contrast of the picture on the computer. Although you can do this to a certain extent, don't assume that iPhoto or any other photo-editing software can fix really bad shots due to lighting. Your best bet when taking photos is to take the best picture first and then do minor touch up with iPhoto.

So, what lighting should you use? The following two points are the best general advice I can give you:

- ✔ **For outdoor photography, the best light is overcast light.** Overcast light reduces shadows and creates warm tones, which are especially kind to human skin. Direct sunlight is rather harsh, so always think of overcast lighting when outdoors.

- ✔ **For indoor photography, use a well-lit room with natural light coming in.** Turn on all the lights in the room, including lamps. This generally gets you the best picture.

Avoid Red-Eye

Red-eye occurs when the flash from a camera reflects off the retina and retinal tissue in the back of the eye. The retina and blood vessels surrounding it reflect a red color, which bounces back to the camera, creating red-eye — that vampire look we all crave.

Red-eye is a common problem, and you can fix it easily with iPhoto, but you also try to avoid it in the first place. First, check your camera's documentation — you may have a red-eye reduction mode that will help solve the problem. If not, your best bet is to take pictures of people near windows where natural light is coming in. The more natural light that is available, the more the pupils of the eye constrict, keeping light out. Red-eye occurs because of the flash in a room that is too dark, so the simple solution is to find more light. This doesn't guarantee that you'll never see red-eye again, but it will help reduce the problem.

Red-eye can occur in shots taken outdoors as well, but you are unlikely to see it unless you try to take a picture of a person at dusk.

Shoot in the Correct Camera Mode

Many digital cameras these days come with a variety of shooting modes, such as action mode, portrait mode, landscape mode, and so on. It may seem like a no-brainer to say "shoot in the correct mode," but digital camera owners often become so excited by their digital cameras that they never really stop to discover how to use everything on the camera. Mastering the fine points of your camera is like programming the VCR — after all, how many of us really take the time to find out how to do it right? But with your camera, you really need to dig into the manual and learn how to do everything because you'll also discover how to take the best pictures with it when you do. So, shoot in the correct mode and find out what all your camera has to offer!

Remember That the Eyes Say It All

Most photographers, amateur and professional, spend a lot of time taking pictures of people. From the quick snapshots to staged poses, we love to have pictures of our friends and family members. When you are taking those pictures of people, focus your attention on the eyes of the subject. We tend

to focus on the smiles of people, but in truth, a person's eyes are the most compelling part of the face. When you are looking through the camera lens, take note of the eyes. Try to think of them as the center of your photo. When you do, you'll get great people pictures.

Take the Picture in Your Mind

If you are taking action shots of people, you don't have much time, if any, to plan the shot. However, if you are taking posed pictures of people, or perhaps a landscape shot, creating the picture in your mind before looking through the lens is a good idea. Try to envision what you want the picture to look like before you ever pick up your camera. In other words, create your own mental image, and then use your camera to shoot that mental image. This thought process will help you frame pictures and get really interesting shots. It's the "forethought" that counts!

When in Doubt, Zoom Out

One mistake that many photographers make is zooming in too closely on objects. Although getting close to your subject is great, you may end up with photos that are too close, in which case there is no way to fix the photo. A great feature of digital photography and iPhoto is the cropping feature, which allows you to cut away edges and portions of photos that you don't want. Because cropping is so easy, you should avoid taking photos that are too close-up — you can always crop them in iPhoto later, getting them to the level of closeness you desire. However, keep in mind that cropping can't fix everything. You want to crop photos slightly — not half of the photo. Doing so removes too many pixels, thus reducing the resolution of the photo and the size you can print. The key point here is to shoot your photo as close as possible, but leave yourself a little room for cropping work if necessary. See Chapter 6 to find out more about cropping.

Think in Terms of Circles

Photography research tells us that most people tend to look at photos in terms of a circle. Their eyes naturally focus on the main subject, and then they tend to move around the photo in a circle with their eyes, looking at everything else the photo holds. When you are taking pictures of groups of

people or even landscapes, think in terms of the circle. Look at the shot in the same way that others will probably look at it. This will often help you to make adjustments that make the photo better.

Watch the Background

Finally, watch your backgrounds. We often get so caught up in taking the picture of the subject that we forget to look at the background. What is behind the subject? Does the background help or hinder? Is the background too bright, too colorful, or just plain distracting? Be sure to look beyond the subject before you snap the picture.

Chapter 16

Ten Quick iPhoto Tips

*W*e can all use a few tips from time to time, even when working with great software like iPhoto. You'll find the tips in this chapter also scattered throughout the book, but I'm including my ten best tips right here in one place so you can easily find them. Apply these suggestions to your work and play with iPhoto to make your life easier and iPhoto more fun!

Back Up Your Photos

iPhoto is a great management software program. You simply import your photos and your Photo Library keeps track of them for you. Even if you change a photo, you can get the original back from the library by selecting the photo and choosing File⇨Revert to Original.

However, in the real world, bad things happen. Macs can have catastrophic failures just like any other piece of equipment out there. Your hard drive may crash, or because of something that happens, you have to completely wipe out the hard drive and reinstall OS X. So, your best bet is to always keep copies of your photos elsewhere, just in case things go bad. Whenever I import photos to iPhoto, I also copy all them to a CD so that I have them stored in a safe place away from my Mac — just in case. The cool thing about iPhoto 2 is that you can burn copies to a CD directly within iPhoto. Just select your Photo Library or the desired album you want to back up and click the Burn button found on the Organize pane. This feature then burns your photos directly to a CD or DVD for safekeeping!

Use Albums to Manage Photos

The photo library keeps all your photos safe and sound — you don't have to do anything with them at all if you don't want. However, working with your photos and keeping them organized is much easier if you use albums. With an album, you can combine different film rolls or photos from different rolls into one album. If you are creating a slide show, use albums to put the pictures in the order you like before you actually create the slide show. In fact, you can't even create an iPhoto book without first putting the photos you want in an album. So, keep in mind that an album is your friend: It's the best way to manage and work with photos in iPhoto.

Give Film Rolls and Photos Meaningful Names

Film rolls are labeled by date, according to when they are imported into iPhoto. Photos are often numbered by the roll number and the photo number, such as Roll 31 – 22. That's all great, but you can easily rename film rolls and photos by using a scheme that is more descriptive and helpful to you. As you import rolls, consider using a unified scheme, such as the date or event, so you can keep track of what you actually have. Believe me, those film rolls can add up; so over time, as soon as you import them, give all your pictures and film rolls names that are meaningful to you.

Watch Out for Those Yellow Exclamation Points

When you start to print photos or create an iPhoto book, some photos may have a yellow triangle with an exclamation point in the corner. Don't ignore these! The yellow triangle icon means that the photo doesn't have a high enough resolution to print well or look good in an iPhoto book at the size you are wanting. The yellow triangle doesn't keep you from printing or ordering your book, but it is a warning to you.

There are a couple of solutions. First of all, if you are using a scanned photo, you can try rescanning it at a higher resolution. (See your scanner documentation for details.) Otherwise, you can simply keep reducing the print or book

size of the photo until the triangle goes away. After it is gone, you can rest assured that you have enough resolution for the selected size so that the photo will print correctly.

Use Constrain When Cropping

When you crop a photo, use the Constrain feature that appears in Edit mode. The Constrain feature makes sure that the cropping adheres to some kind of standard print size, such as 4 x 3. If you freely crop the photo without using Constrain, you will probably not get a standard print size; thus the photo will not fit in a standard frame or paper photo album. If you have already cropped a photo that was not constrained, just select the photo, and then choose File⇨Revert to Original. Then use the original photo and recrop, using the Constrain feature.

Make Red-Eye Removal Quick

iPhoto's red-eye removal features works by removing red from the area you select with your mouse. Often, new users of iPhoto are afraid that removal will discolor skin and other areas of the eye, but it doesn't work this way. You don't have to try to box carefully around the eye — the removal tool won't change any other colors. So, don't spend a lot of time trying to create a careful box right around one eye — you can even make one big rectangular box to encompass both eyes so that you can remove the red-eye from both at the same time.

Choose Your Theme Before Creating the Book

The iPhoto book feature is really cool and easy to assemble. One caveat you need to remember, however, is that you need to choose a theme first, and *then* assemble the pages and text as you desire. Each theme has a different layout scheme, and different fonts are used on text. As such, if you change the theme in the middle of your layout process, all your text and photo arrangements will change as well. This may not be a big deal, but the odds are good that you'll have to go back and fix stuff. Make life easier on yourself and choose the theme before you do any work.

Remember That You Can Scale Images When Exporting

iPhoto gives you a great feature that allows you to scale photos when you export them. Sure, you can export a photo just by dragging it out of the Photo Library and dropping it on your desktop, but if you export using the File⇨Export command, you can choose to export the images in the format you want and scale the image to the size you want. For example, let's say you have a large TIFF file stored in iPhoto. You want to post the photo to a Web site. Because TIFF files don't work well on the Internet, you can use the export feature to export the photo as a JPEG and give the photo a standard size, such as 640 x 480. Remember that you can also export photos as Web pages or as QuickTime movies. Play around with the export features — they are your friends!

Choose Your Own Music When Creating Slide Shows

iPhoto includes some canned music that you can use with your slide shows, but you don't have to stop there. You can use anything in your iTunes library directly with iPhoto. In the Organize pane, just click the Slideshow icon to open Slideshow Settings. You see the songs from your iTunes library available for selection. This feature gives you more flexibility when creating your slide shows, and remember that you can export the slide show, along with the music, to the QuickTime format by using the File⇨Export feature.

Open Photos in Separate Windows

By default, iPhoto displays a large image of the photo in the main interface when you go into Edit mode. If you prefer, however, you can have each photo open in its own window in Edit mode. This feature gives you more flexibility, and you may find that editing photos this way is much easier. To have each photo open in its own window, choose iPhoto⇨Preferences, and change the Double-Clicking option to Opens in Separate Window.

Chapter 17

Ten Digital Photo Output Tips

The main purpose of taking any photo, of course, is to have some kind of output. Traditionally, that output has been prints of your pictures. You can have them enlarged, placed in a photo album, and make them available for all to see. With digital photography, however, you can also use electronic output to store photos, e-mail them to friends and family, or even post them on Web sites. All these options are great, but you should keep the following output tips in mind to make sure you get the best pictures possible.

Use the Right Resolution for the Job

As I've stated throughout this book, *resolution is everything*. Resolution affects the quality of your pictures and the print output, and it determines how big the picture is in terms of file size. In fact, I would say your number one output tip is to pay close attention to resolution — if the resolution is too low, your print quality won't be good. If your resolution is too high, the photo's size will be too large to e-mail to friends. As you are taking pictures, you'll need to spend some time thinking about how you want to use the photo — and then choose a resolution setting that is best for you. It is always best to shoot at a higher resolution than you need and then scale down from there. See Chapters 8 and 9 to learn about resolution.

Use iPhoto to Crop and Edit the Picture

iPhoto provides you with some limited editing tools, but the important ones that you are likely to use are provided for you. Namely, you can crop the photo, thus removing unwanted portions of it, and you can also adjust the brightness and contrast of the photo. You can also use the Enhance tool to fix color problems and the Retouch tool to remove small blemishes or spots. These simple-to-use tools will help you fix common lighting problems and remove portions of the photo that you simply don't need. Before generating either print or electronic output, run the photo through iPhoto's editing tools and fix those last minute problems. See Chapter 6 to find out about editing photos.

Use the Constrain Feature

Digital photos don't conform to standard printed photo sizes, such as 4 x 6, 5 x 7, 8 x 10 and so forth. If you want your photo to fit a standard print size, iPhoto's printing feature can help you, but you should also crop the picture by using the Constrain feature, which will make the photo a standard size that you select. The Constrain feature ensures that the photo will fit on precut photo paper for your printer, or that it doesn't get hacked to death when you send to an on-line printer service. See Chapter 6 to find out more about the Constrain feature.

Use Photo-Quality Paper

In order to print your photos, you'll need a good inkjet printer, a photo with enough resolution to print the size you want, and the right paper — namely, photo-quality paper. Photo-quality paper looks like typical photo paper that you get when you take pictures to be developed, and it produces great print results. You can't print quality pictures on regular copy paper, so invest in some good photo-quality paper — you'll find it any office supply store.

Remember Other Paper Options

You need photo-quality paper when you print photos, but keep in mind that other options are available to you. For example, you can buy that paper in precut sizes, such as 4 x 6 or 5 x 7. Also, you can buy card stock paper for printing greeting cards with your photos. The card stock typically provides

some kind of textured background and features premade creases for folding. Also, you can readily find T-shirt iron-on transfer paper. Just print your photo on this paper and iron it on a shirt — it's fun and cool!

Reduce the Photo's Size When E-Mailing

Say that you have taken a photo of your favorite pet. You shot the photo at 3.1 megapixels so you could print an 8 x 10. You love the photo and decide to e-mail it to a friend. Guess what? The photo, at that resolution, is probably way too big — possibly 3MB or more in size. If you want to e-mail photos, you need to reduce their size by cropping and also by saving the photo in a compressed file format, such as JPEG. See Chapter 9 to learn more about e-mailing photos.

Choose the Right File Format

iPhoto can work with a number of file formats for imported pictures. However, if you are using electronic output, you may need to resave those pictures in a universal file format, such as JPEG. Although you may shoot and save pictures in TIFF or some other file format, JPEG is the standard picture format used on the Internet, and is preferred for sending pictures via e-mail. See Chapter 9 to learn more about file formats.

Check the Photo's Size

Before e-mailing or printing a picture, you should check the photo's size and determine how the photo will print, or if the photo needs to be cropped before sending it over the Internet. For printing, the key word again is *resolution* — you can adjust the printed size of the photo with no loss in quality if the resolution is high enough. For e-mailing, just make sure that the photo is not too large. Crop it if you can in order to reduce transmission time.

Get Creative with Other Software

iPhoto gives you some basic editing tools, but it doesn't provide you with all the bells and whistles of other photo-editing software, such as Photoshop Elements or Paint Shop Pro. Using these tools, you can work with multiple

layers, change and edit backgrounds, add text and other graphics, and make use of a myriad of additional features. Use iPhoto to manage your pictures, but for serious image editing, you may consider purchasing another photo-editing software package. See Chapter 7 to learn more about editing beyond iPhoto.

Don't Forget to Back Up

Finally, your Mac is a stable operating system on which your data is safe, but this does not mean that catastrophic failures can't happen. To be safe, you should get in the habit of regularly backing up your iPhoto library to another location, such as a CD-ROM, so that your photos will be safe in the event that your Mac decides to die. See Chapter 4 to find out about backing up your photos.

Chapter 18

Ten Frequently Asked Questions

*T*he cool thing about iPhoto is that it's so easy to use that you aren't likely to run into many problems or questions along the way. Of course, as with any software, a few areas of iPhoto commonly cause some questions or confusion. So, in this chapter, I've organized ten of the most common questions that you may have about iPhoto, and I've given you the quick answers that you need.

Why Can't I Move Photos around in the Photo Library?

The Photo Library is basically a series of folders hidden beneath the iPhoto interface that holds your photos. When you import photos, different folders are used to hold the photos and keep everything organized. As such, you can't drag photos around in the Photo Library, and you can't move photos from one film roll to the next. If you want to organize photos for printing purposes, for a slide show or a book, or for any other reason, you simply need to create an album. You can drag photos from the Photo Library (even from different film rolls) to the new album, and then you can organize the photos in the album any way you like.

Can I Print Cropped Photos as Standard Sizes?

If you crop a photo freehand, you are likely changing the standard aspect ratio that digital cameras use when taking photos. As such, your photos may not print in standard print sizes, such as 4 x 6, 5 x 7, and so forth. To fix this problem, you need to revert to the original photo and then recrop the photo by using the Constrain feature so that your photo is constrained to the size you want to print. Just follow these steps:

1. **Open iPhoto and click the Photo Library in the left pane.**

2. **Locate the desired photo in the Library.**

3. **Select the photo and choose File⇨Revert to Original.**

   This action reverts the file to the way it was (when you originally imported it) by removing all cropping, red-eye adjustments, and anything else you may have done to the photo.

4. **Double-click the reverted photo.**

   This takes you to Edit mode.

5. **In Edit mode, use the Constrain menu to choose a standard print size (such as 5 x 7) that you want to constrain the photo to when you crop it.**

6. **Next, click and drag on the photo with your mouse pointer to create the crop box.**

   Notice that the Constrain feature keeps the crop box to the 4 x 6 format, as shown in Figure 18-1.

7. **Click the Crop button.**

   The photo is now cropped to the size that you selected and will print in that standard size.

How Can I Edit Each Photo in Its Own Window?

You can edit photos directly within the iPhoto interface, or you can have each photo open in its own window when you double-click it. To configure iPhoto so that it automatically opens each photo in its own window, choose iPhoto⇨Preferences. In the Preferences window, under Double-Clicking Photos Opens Them In, select the Separate Window radio button.

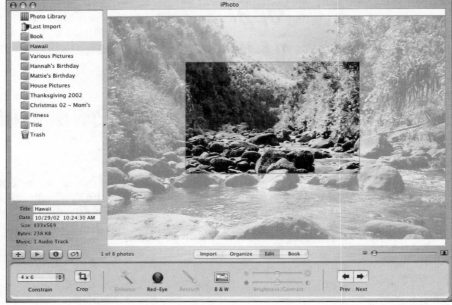

Figure 18-1:
The crop
box is
constrained
to the size
that you
chose.

Can I Control the Display Time of Each Photo during a Slide Show?

If you click the Slideshow button in Organize mode, you see a Slideshow Settings dialog box where you can determine the amount of time photos are displayed during a slide show, such as five seconds each. However, the value here applies to all slides in the show; you can't individually determine the amount of display time for each slide in iPhoto. If you need to set individual duration times for each photo, however, you can use iMovie to create the slide show. iMovie allows you to control the display time of each photo individually. See Chapter 12 to find out more about iMovie.

Can I Print Photos Even When a Yellow Triangle Appears?

A yellow triangle warning sign appears on photos when the resolution of the photo is too low to print well. The triangle appears when you try to print the photo or when you select it for an iPhoto book. The warning sign is just that — a warning. You are still free to print the photo or use it in your book, but iPhoto

is letting you know that the resolution is too low and you may not be happy with the quality you get. You can often fix this problem by reducing the print size for the photo (such as changing it from a 5 x 7 to a 4 x 6). After you have selected a more appropriate print size for that photo's resolution, the yellow triangle disappears.

How Can 1 Simultaneously Print Multiple Photos on Individual Pages?

iPhoto tries to help you save paper by combining prints on one page. For example, if you choose to print an entire album, the Print window appears, where you can select the 5 x 7 size. By default, iPhoto will print two 5 x 7 photos per page, but if you only want one photo printed per page, just select the One Photo Per Page check box, as shown in Figure 18-2.

Figure 18-2:
Select the
One Photo
Per Page
check box
to make
sure that
your photos
are printed
on separate
pages.

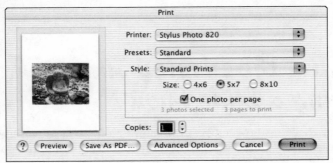

Can 1 View My Photo Library without Film Rolls?

Film rolls are used to help organize photos for your sake so that you can find them more easily. However, you can also easily view the entire Photo Library without seeing any film rolls — you just see photo after photo in the viewer. To stop using film rolls, first select the Photo Library. This puts you in Organize mode. Choose View⇨Film Rolls to turn off the feature.

Can I Change How Many Photos Appear on a Page of My iPhoto Book?

When you first began creating your book, you chose a theme. This theme makes some guesses about the number of photos that you want to see on individual pages. However, you can easily change the number of photos that appear on each page as you work. In Book mode, just select the page, and then use the Page Design pop-up menu to choose the number of photos that you want to appear on each page, as shown in Figure 18-3.

Figure 18-3: Use the Page Design pop-up menu to choose the number of photos that you want displayed on the book page.

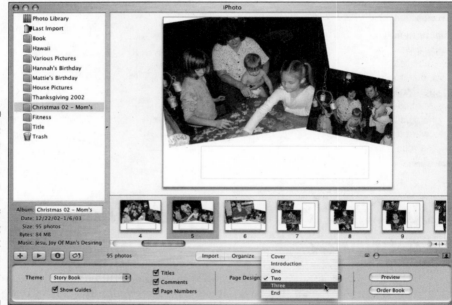

 As you are working on your book, make sure that you work on the pages in a left-to-right fashion. A change on one page affects the layout on all other pages — in other words, photos are moved around on each page after the page you changed in order to accommodate your changes. Make sure that you work in a left-to-right order so as to not affect pages that you have already changed.

How Can I Reduce a Photo's File Size to E-Mail It?

No problem, iPhoto can do it for you. Just select the photo that you want to e-mail in the Photo Library or an album, and then click Email from the Organize pane. You see the Mail Photo window, as shown in Figure 18-4. Choose Small (240 x 320) from the Size drop-down menu, and you see the estimated file size for the photo. (In Figure 18-4, the estimated file size is 63 KB.) Click Compose, and iPhoto scales the photo for you and puts it in JPEG format; then you can attach the photo to an e-mail message — all in one click!

Figure 18-4:
Use the Mail Photo window to adjust the size of the photo you want to e-mail.

How Can I E-Mail a Slide Show to a Friend?

You can easily watch your slide shows from within iPhoto. However, if you want to e-mail a slide show to someone or even burn it on a CD for sharing purposes, you'll need to export the slide show as a QuickTime movie. Select the desired album, and then choose File⇨Export. Click the QuickTime tab and make your selections for the size of the photos, the display time, the background for the show and whether you want to include music, and then click Export. See Chapter 11 to find out more about slide shows.

Index

• D •

film rolls
  clearing, 71, 318
  exporting, 72
  illustration, 59–60
  naming, 72, 308
  titles, 85
  viewing by date, 71
  viewing by name, 72
  viewing by number, 71
  viewing contents of, 70
filters (Adobe Photoshop Elements)
  Despeckle filter, 132
  Dust & Scratches filter, 132–134
  Sharpen Edges filter, 129
  Sharpen filter, 129
  Sharpen More filter, 130
  Unsharp Mask filter, 130
finding
  iDVD, 272
  photos, 91–92
  plug-ins, 295–296
FireWire drivers, 243
FireWire port, 46, 241
FlashPix picture file format, 54
floppy disks, importing photos from, 47–48
folders
  Albums folder, 66
  Data folders, 66
  film roll icons, 59–60
  iDVD, 281
  iPhoto Library folder, 63–70
  Originals folders, 66
  Picture folders, 66
  Thumbs folders, 66
Fotki online print ordering service, 166
Fott, Galen, *Photoshop Elements 2 For Dummies,* 146
4:3 aspect ratio, 199
Free space meter (iMovie 3), 240

• G •

GIF picture file format, 54
GoLive (Adobe), 190

greeting cards, 161
grid alignment of photos, 92–93
group photos, 27–28
guides (iPhoto book), 207

• H–I •

hard disk space requirements, 32
hot corners (screen effects), 294
iDisk
  accessing, 184
  opening, 186
  password protecting, 184
  read-only access, 184
  read-write access, 184
  storage space, 183
  uploading photos, 185
iDVD
  burning DVDs, 272–273, 287
  button limit per screen, 275
  cost, 272
  DVD-R discs, 272
  finding, 272
  folders, 281
  iMovie 3 movies, 269
  importing movies or slide shows, 274–276
  interface, 273
  Motion icon, 283
  movies, 274
  music, 274
  photos, 274
  slide shows, 276–280
  system requirements, 271
  themes, 282–285
  title page, 281–285
  TV-safe area, 285–287
  uses, 271
IEEE 1394 port, 241
iLife CD, 238
i.Link port, 241
ImageCapture
  preferences, 52
  quitting, 52

• *W–X–Y–Z* •

FOR DUMMIES

The easy way to get more done and have more fun

PERSONAL FINANCE & BUSINESS

Investing
0-7645-2431-3

Home Buying
0-7645-5331-3

Grant Writing
0-7645-5307-0

Also available:

Accounting For Dummies
(0-7645-5314-3)

Business Plans Kit For Dummies
(0-7645-5365-8)

Managing For Dummies
(1-5688-4858-7)

Mutual Funds For Dummies
(0-7645-5329-1)

QuickBooks All-in-One Desk Reference For Dummies
(0-7645-1963-8)

Resumes For Dummies
(0-7645-5471-9)

Small Business Kit For Dummies
(0-7645-5093-4)

Starting an eBay Business For Dummies
(0-7645-1547-0)

Taxes For Dummies 2003
(0-7645-5475-1)

HOME, GARDEN, FOOD & WINE

Feng Shui
0-7645-5295-3

Gardening
0-7645-5130-2

Cooking
0-7645-5250-3

Also available:

Bartending For Dummies
(0-7645-5051-9)

Christmas Cooking For Dummies
(0-7645-5407-7)

Cookies For Dummies
(0-7645-5390-9)

Diabetes Cookbook For Dummies
(0-7645-5230-9)

Grilling For Dummies
(0-7645-5076-4)

Home Maintenance For Dummies
(0-7645-5215-5)

Slow Cookers For Dummies
(0-7645-5240-6)

Wine For Dummies
(0-7645-5114-0)

FITNESS, SPORTS, HOBBIES & PETS

Fitness
0-7645-5167-1

Golf
0-7645-5146-9

Guitar
0-7645-5106-X

Also available:

Cats For Dummies
(0-7645-5275-9)

Chess For Dummies
(0-7645-5003-9)

Dog Training For Dummies
(0-7645-5286-4)

Labrador Retrievers For Dummies
(0-7645-5281-3)

Martial Arts For Dummies
(0-7645-5358-5)

Piano For Dummies
(0-7645-5105-1)

Pilates For Dummies
(0-7645-5397-6)

Power Yoga For Dummies
(0-7645-5342-9)

Puppies For Dummies
(0-7645-5255-4)

Quilting For Dummies
(0-7645-5118-3)

Rock Guitar For Dummies
(0-7645-5356-9)

Weight Training For Dummies
(0-7645-5168-X)

Available wherever books are sold.
Go to www.dummies.com or call 1-877-762-2974 to order direct

WILEY

FOR DUMMIES®

A world of resources to help you grow

TRAVEL

0-7645-5453-0

0-7645-5438-7

0-7645-5444-1

Also available:

America's National Parks For Dummies
(0-7645-6204-5)
Caribbean For Dummies
(0-7645-5445-X)
Cruise Vacations For Dummies 2003
(0-7645-5459-X)
Europe For Dummies
(0-7645-5456-5)
Ireland For Dummies
(0-7645-6199-5)

France For Dummies
(0-7645-6292-4)
Las Vegas For Dummies
(0-7645-5448-4)
London For Dummies
(0-7645-5416-6)
Mexico's Beach Resorts For Dummies
(0-7645-6262-2)
Paris For Dummies
(0-7645-5494-8)
RV Vacations For Dummies
(0-7645-5443-3)

EDUCATION & TEST PREPARATION

0-7645-5194-9

0-7645-5325-9

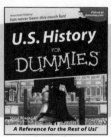

0-7645-5249-X

Also available:

The ACT For Dummies
(0-7645-5210-4)
Chemistry For Dummies
(0-7645-5430-1)
English Grammar For Dummies
(0-7645-5322-4)
French For Dummies
(0-7645-5193-0)
GMAT For Dummies
(0-7645-5251-1)
Inglés Para Dummies
(0-7645-5427-1)

Italian For Dummies
(0-7645-5196-5)
Research Papers For Dummies
(0-7645-5426-3)
SAT I For Dummies
(0-7645-5472-7)
U.S. History For Dummies
(0-7645-5249-X)
World History For Dummies
(0-7645-5242-2)

HEALTH, SELF-HELP & SPIRITUALITY

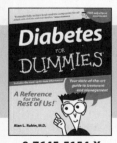

0-7645-5154-X

0-7645-5302-X

0-7645-5418-2

Also available:

The Bible For Dummies
(0-7645-5296-1)
Controlling Cholesterol For Dummies
(0-7645-5440-9)
Dating For Dummies
(0-7645-5072-1)
Dieting For Dummies
(0-7645-5126-4)
High Blood Pressure For Dummies
(0-7645-5424-7)
Judaism For Dummies
(0-7645-5299-6)

Menopause For Dummies
(0-7645-5458-1)
Nutrition For Dummies
(0-7645-5180-9)
Potty Training For Dummies
(0-7645-5417-4)
Pregnancy For Dummies
(0-7645-5074-8)
Rekindling Romance For Dummies
(0-7645-5303-8)
Religion For Dummies
(0-7645-5264-3)

Available wherever books are sold. Go to www.dummies.com or call 1-877-762-2974 to order direct

FOR DUMMIES

Plain-English solutions for everyday challenges

HOME & BUSINESS COMPUTER BASICS

0-7645-0838-5

0-7645-1663-9

0-7645-1548-9

Also available:

Excel 2002 All-in-One Desk
Reference For Dummies
(0-7645-1794-5)

Office XP 9-in-1 Desk
Reference For Dummies
(0-7645-0819-9)

PCs All-in-One Desk
Reference For Dummies
(0-7645-0791-5)

Troubleshooting Your PC
For Dummies
(0-7645-1669-8)

Upgrading & Fixing PCs For
Dummies
(0-7645-1665-5)

Windows XP For Dummies
(0-7645-0893-8)

Windows XP For Dummies
Quick Reference
(0-7645-0897-0)

Word 2002 For Dummies
(0-7645-0839-3)

INTERNET & DIGITAL MEDIA

0-7645-0894-6

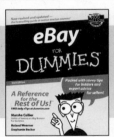

0-7645-1642-6

0-7645-1664-7

Also available:

CD and DVD Recording
For Dummies
(0-7645-1627-2)

Digital Photography
All-in-One Desk Reference
For Dummies
(0-7645-1800-3)

eBay For Dummies
(0-7645-1642-6)

Genealogy Online For
Dummies
(0-7645-0807-5)

Internet All-in-One Desk
Reference For Dummies
(0-7645-1659-0)

Internet For Dummies
Quick Reference
(0-7645-1645-0)

Internet Privacy For Dummies
(0-7645-0846-6)

Paint Shop Pro For Dummies
(0-7645-2440-2)

Photo Retouching &
Restoration For Dummies
(0-7645-1662-0)

Photoshop Elements For
Dummies
(0-7645-1675-2)

Scanners For Dummies
(0-7645-0783-4)